AMERICAN DEBATES ON CENTRAL EUROPEAN UNION, 1942-1944

Documents of the American State Department

P.I.E.-Peter Lang
Bruxelles · Bern · Berlin · Frankfurt/M · New York · Oxford · Wien

EUROCLIO is a scientific and editorial project, a network of research institutions and researchers, and an ideas forum. EUROCLIO as an editorial project consists of two aspects: the first concerns studies and documents, the second concerns tools. Both are aimed at making the results of research more accessible, and also at opening up paths through the history of European construction/integration/unification.

The EUROCLIO series meets a dual objective:
- to provide reference tools for research,
- to provide a platform for this research in terms of the publication of results.

The series thus consists of two sub-series that satisfy these requirements: the STUDIES AND DOCUMENTS series and the REFERENCES series. These two series are aimed at general libraries and/or university history departments, teachers and researchers, and in certain cases, specific professional circles.

The STUDIES AND DOCUMENTS series consists of monographs, collections of articles, conference proceedings, and collections of texts with notes for teaching purposes.

The REFERENCES series consists of bibliographies, guides and other tools. It thus contributes to the creation of a database making up a "Permanent catalogue of sources and bibliographies on European construction".

Series Editors:

Éric Bussière, Université de Paris-Sorbonne (France),
Michel Dumoulin, Université catholique de Louvain (Belgium),
et Antonio Varsori, Università degli Studi di Firenze (Italy)

AMERICAN DEBATES ON CENTRAL EUROPEAN UNION, 1942-1944

Documents of the American State Department

Józef Łaptos & Mariusz Misztal

Euroclio No. 25

No part of this book may be reproduced in any form, by print, photocopy, microfilm or any other means, without prior written permission from the publisher. All rights reserved.

© P.I.E.-Peter Lang s.a.
Presses Interuniversitaires Européennes
Brussels, 2002
E-mail: info@peterlang.com
www.peterlang.net

ISSN 0944-2294
ISBN 90-5201-976-2
D/2002/5678/10

Die Deutsche Bibliothek – CIP-Einheitsaufnahme
Łaptos, József: American debates on Central European Union, 1942-1944: documents of the American State Department / József Laptos & Mariusz Misztal. - Bruxelles ; Bern ; Berlin ; Frankfurt/M. ; New York ; Oxford ; Wien: PIE Lang, 2002
(Euroclio : Etudes et Documents ; No.25)
ISBN 90-5201-976-2

*CIP available from the British Library, GB
and the Library of Congress, USA.*
ISBN   0-8204-4685-8

Contents

Introduction 11

PART I. REVIVAL OF AN IDEA: MID-EUROPEAN UNION

Chapter 1. The Weight and Lessons of History 15

The Interwar Experience 15
Another Lesson of History. Visions of European Integration
from the Perspective of the Second World War 18

**Chapter 2. "Unite in order to Exist". Resistance
and Expatriate Views of Central European Federation** 23

Concepts of the Postwar Organization of Europe Presented
by West European Politicians and Journalists 23
The Opinion on European Integration of the Political
Emigrants from the Former Neutral Countries 26
The Federation as the *sine qua non* Condition of Freedom
and Independence for the Central European Countries 28
Main Projects for the Federal Organization of Central and
Eastern Europe 29
Britain's Attitude to the Idea of Organizing Central
Eastern Europe 40

**Chapter 3. Towards a More Concrete Realization of the Idea
of a Mid-European Federation** 43

"A Germ of a Constructive Plan": The Greek-Yugoslav
Agreement and the Polish-Czechoslovak Declaration 43
The Federation of Central Europe as a Starting Point
for a Debate on Unification 45

**Chapter 4. The Debate on Projects for a Central European
Union in the Framework of the Changing International
Situation (1942-1944)** 53

The Task and the Personnel of the Advisory Committee 53
The Committee's Work and Official American Policy
Towards Central Eastern Europe 56

Chapter 5. Consequences for Small Nations of the Growing Empathy of the Powers Towards their Soviet Ally 59
"To Keep the Russians in Good Humor" 59
Moscow Publicly Expresses its Disdain for Federative Projects 63
Reaction of the Small States to the Russian Attitude 66

PART II. DOCUMENTS

1. [Danubian Federation] 71
2. [Desirability of a Single Union for Region] 85
3. [East European Union as a Regional Approach to World Organization] 96
4. [The Council for the Economic Development of the Union] 105
5. [An East European Union as Considered to June 19, 1942] 110
6. [Northern East European Group and [or] Balkan Group] 115
7. Tentative Economic Organization of the East European Federation 134
8. [Structure of the East European Federation] 146
9. [Survey of the Suggested East European Union] 154
10. An East European Union (as Considered to October 10, 1942) 171
11. Memorandum on Russia and East European Federation 176
12. British Opinion on Postwar Arrangements in Eastern Europe 182
13. The Feasibility of an East European Union 187
14. Soviet and British Attitudes Towards East European Union 196
15. Interlocking Confederations in East-Central Europe 203
16. British Policy Concerning Regionalism 208
17. The South Slav Peoples: Political Reorganization 211
18. [Some Implications of the South Slav Confederation] 215
19. Effects of a European Union upon American Political Interests 223
20. [Legitimacy of the Soviet Desire for Control over the East European Region] 227
21. Regional Policy of the Soviet Union 231

22. [Considerations for Judging Regional Associations in Europe] 235
23. Review of Subcommittee's work 243

Introduction

Literature on the history of European integration is dominated by a well-justified belief that the United States, both before and during the war, were hostile to the idea of a European Union. Such a position mainly boiled down to fears fostered by Richard Coudenhove-Kalergi himself, who in his idea of pan-Europe saw a necessity to confront the economic expansion of the United States. As is increasingly maintained by writers on the subject, an approval for European integration came rather late at the end of the war,[1] manifesting itself in full only, if one may anticipate, in policies associated with the Marshall Plan and the containment of communism.

Roosevelt's well-known concept of "Four Policemen" – the United States, Great Britain, the Soviet Union and China – who would, as the President described it, impose order on the rest of the postwar world, bombing anyone who would not comply,[2] was incompatible with the action of small European states hoping to defend their security within regional federations. A Polish reader with some knowledge of his country's history remembers well how difficult it was for Sikorski to achieve, in his three visits during the war, any favorable reaction from Roosevelt to proposals for a Central Eastern European federation – which reaction never went beyond the oft-quoted "Fine idea!".[3]

In spite of this unfortunate attitude to the integration of Europe, we find, in the United States National Archives in Washington, a series of surprising documents that we present here. These are mainly minutes of debates of Advisory Committees of the State Department which analyze and summarize the development of certain processes, in an attempt to make forecasts. The sheer number of the meetings, the participants'

---

[1] Cf. Melandri, P., *Les Etats-Unis face à l'unification de l'Europe 1945-1954*, Paris 1980, p. 31.

[2] Papers Relating Foreign Relations to The United States (FRUS) – 1942, Vol. III, pp. 568-569, *Memorandum on Roosevelt-Molotov conversation*, 29 May 1942; See also FRUS 1943 Cairo and Teheran, pp. 530-32, *Note on Roosevelt – Stalin conversation*.

[3] Lipski, J. & Raczyński, E. & Stroński, S., *Trzy podróże gen. Sikorskiego do Ameryki*, London 1946. For Sikorski's reports about his second visit to the U.S. see Zgórniak, M. & Rojek, W. & Suchcic, A., *Protokoły posiedzeń Rady Ministrów Rzeczypospolitej Polskiej*, Vol. IV, Doc. 115. Cracow 1998.

knowledge of the subject and the choice of participants itself, show that much thinking was done at the State Department on an idea otherwise publicly ignored, rejected by, or even absent in, official American diplomacy during the war. The very existence of the documents is of interest, not to mention the arguments used in the debates, many of which have become familiar over the years.

The texts raise numerous questions. What explains the interest in this federation of Central Europe? Wherein lies the real significance of this material? Why has it been ignored by the literature of European integration? Why did a group of advisors give more consideration to a Central Eastern European Union than to a vision of a unified Western Europe?

We hope that the reader will find his or her own answer to all these questions. We think, however, that to assess the value and extraordinary character of the documents contained in this book fully, one must briefly recall the history of the Central Eastern European federation itself. It can be safely assumed that one of the principal reasons for the Advisory Committee's discussion of those problems was to consider plans, proposals, myths and hopes expressed by resistance and *émigré* authorities and to find a positive echo in the public opinion of their countries.

Part I

Revival of an Idea: Mid-European Union

CHAPTER 1

The Weight and Lessons of History

The Interwar Experience

Organizations attempting a political unification of Europe emerged quite late, in fact at the end of World War I, though the idea itself dates back to at least the 17th century. The horror and the carnage of the Great War must have had their influence on plans and ideas that would lead to the end of all destructive antagonisms. Hopes that lessons drawn from the Great War (as it had been called until its "greatness" was eclipsed by the second world conflict) might help build a new world order, resulted in the idea of a worldwide organization based on the principle of collective security. The organization in question, the League of Nations, proved, however, to be a mere palliative of the problem. Handicapped at its very outset by the withdrawal of its initiator, the United States, undermined *ex definitione* as an organization of the victors and by its inadequacy in solving ethnic conflicts, its significance waned year by year. At the same time, it served as an inspiration for those building on its heritage. To create, within a world organization, regional organizations that would group federated and confederated states of closer interests, cultural ties, geographical or, finally, economic integration, seemed a harmonizing factor in an intermediate or introductory phase of the emergence of the worldwide body. This mainly concerned Europe, which, seen as a region within the world organization, consisted of sub-regional associations helping to overcome national passions. Similar though greatly simplified ideas can be found in Coudenhove-Kalergi's Paneuropa, in the forgotten conception of Alfred Nossig, or, last but not least, in Aristide Briand's vision of the United States of Europe. In fact, pacifists of all sorts, weary with the last war, produced a wealth of ideas for a better world. All these are well publicized and described, more or less successfully, in all handbooks of European integration.

Less known were ideas concerning Central and Eastern Europe, the integration of which – to use an ironic phrase – had been the business of its powerful neighbors. After World War I, these nations were liberated from the German, Austro-Hungarian and Russian yokes, but not from old traumas and nationalist ambitions. Freedom, foretold in Wilson's Fourteen Points and realized in new circumstances, was not accompanied by guarantees of political and economic security. The League of Nations having failed, Western states underestimated the region's strategic importance for preserving peace. Of the dreams contemplated before occupation, few had any relevance to the real world. Few only remembered the ideas of the Hungarian revolutionary Louis Kossuth, who fought against the Habsburgs in 1848-49 and who after his defeat concluded that it had been caused by rivalries among the nations of the Danubian Basin. Kossuth himself, while a dominating influence in Hungary, failed to uphold the demands of Serbs, Croats and Transylvanian Rumanians. The consciousness of his error strengthened his conviction that success could only be found in a close cooperation of Danubian nations. During that same "Springtime of Nations", other representatives of the region, Czechs and Poles, were led to dream of federation. The idea of a federation that would follow independence from the Habsburgs was present in a number of nations struggling against Austria and Austria-Hungary. In the early 20th century, the idea of a transformation of the dual monarchy spread to Austrian liberals and socialists. Karl Renner and Otto Bauer preached autonomy of nations within the monarchy. The conception of the United States of Great Austria, including fifteen countries enjoying a broad autonomy, was promoted by the Transylvanian writer Aurel Popovici in his book of that title in 1906. However, most politicians were deeply convinced that this could only be realized after the fall of the Habsburgs. The course of World War I, bringing some hope of realizing those dreams, inspired Tomas Masaryk, then an *émigré* in the U.S. much influenced by Jefferson, to contemplate a regional, Central European federation of free nations, from Finland in the north to the Adriatic. He discussed the idea with Columbia University scholar James Shotwell and obtained the support of many leaders of Central European *émigrés*. Their concept was expressed in a declaration of the common aims of those nations issued in Philadelphia in 1918, manifesting the belief that a free federation of small nations and states would be a realization of this hope securing the final organization of the whole of mankind.[1]

To the despair of the supporters of the federation, the regained independence of the nations involved did not help to realize their dream. Calls for reforming the monarchy into a federation in the Empire's last days coincided with the emerging idea of a Danubian federation,

---

[1] For the full text of the so-called Philadelphia Manifesto, see Gross, F., *Crossroads of two Continents. A Democratic Federation of East-Central Europe*, New York 1945, p. 89.

supported by the French, in what was, in fact, a cynical maneuver for securing the signature of the imposed treaties of Trianon and Sevres.[1] Edward Beneš' dream of a Little Entente of Czechoslovakia, Rumania and Yugoslavia was equally distant. Partially directed at its onset against Poland, then struggling in a war against Bolshevist Russia, it was primarily a pact against Hungarian revisionism.[2] On Paris' assumption of control, it became a significant element of the French system of Eastern alliances, also including Poland in a separate treaty. There was an abyss between the unsteady alliance, the megalomaniac proposal and the dream of Masaryk, at that time already President of Czechoslovakia – an abyss filled with repeated border conflicts and national rivalries. Piłsudski's idea of a confederation of Poland, Lithuania, Belarus, the Ukraine and, in the future, other countries between the two seas, expired with the victorious counter-offensive of the Bolsheviks.

This failure triggered the emergence of new projects. These included one by Take Ionescu, an able Rumanian diplomat, who wanted Poland and Greece to join the countries of the Little Entente.

Various attempts to unify the Baltic States had been made in the interwar period. Poland was one of the leaders of plans for a Greater Baltic Union between 1919 and 1925. The first Baltic Conference was held at Helsinki in January 1920 and was attended by Finland, Estonia, Latvia, Lithuania and Poland.

The conflict between Poland and Lithuania and, in general, the fear of Polish domination resulted in the collapse of the plans, which shared the fate of attempts furthered by Helsinki and Stockholm. On the other hand, the cooperation of the three Baltic States: Latvia, Estonia and Lithuania, was becoming closer in the thirties. The conclusion of a German-Polish agreement in January 1934 led to a further strengthening of relations between the Baltic States, finding its expression in the Treaty of Defensive Alliance of 29 February 1934, known as the Baltic Entente.[3]

---

[1] Droz, J., *L'Europe Centrale. Evolution historique de l'idée de "Mitteleuropa"*, Paris, 1960; Laptos, J., "Kształtowanie się francuskiej koncepcji konfederacji naddunajskiej w latach 1918-1920", *Studia polono-danubiana et balcanica*, Vol. IV, Iogellonian University, Cracow 1991, pp. 56-79.

[2] Essen, A., *Polska a Mała Ententa 1920-1934*, Warsaw 1992; Iordache, N., *La Petite Entente et l'Europe*, Geneva 1977; Ádám, M., *The Little Entente and Europe (1920-1929)*, Budapest 1993.

[3] Cf. Łossowski, P., "Ententa Bałtycka 1934-1940", *Studia z Dziejów ZSRR i Europy Środkowej*, Vol. XVI; Laptos, J., "Od bezpieczeństwa zbiorowego do zbrojnej neutralności. Szkic z dziejów Ententy Bałtyckiej (1934-1940)" in A. Kastory & A. Essen (eds.), *Bałtowie. Przeszłość i teraźniejszość*, Cracow 1993.

The idea of regional cooperation had a long pre-war tradition in the Balkan countries. A system of close collaboration was drafted in a treaty between the Greeks, Rumanians, Yugoslavs and Turks. Signed in Athens on 9 February, it became known as "the Balkan Pact".

Though directed against Bulgaria, it did not preclude that country's future access. The Pact had then all the chances of transformation from an anti-revisionist alliance into a force for integration in that part of the continent.[1] The emergence of the Balkan Entente also strengthened the French influence in the region between the seas, already a target in an earlier plan for the cooperation of Danubian states known as the Tardieu Plan.[2] The latter, however, was but a short-lived measure in view of the appeasement policy of the late thirties and the change in Yugoslav policy, re-orienting itself towards cooperation with Bulgaria and Italy in 1937. Even before the outbreak of the war, the failure of integrative attempts were greeted by the public opinion with some regret and a keen feeling of lost opportunity. The reasons for this state of affairs were mostly seen – as viewed by another Advisory Committee member as early as in the 1920s[3] – in re-emergent nationalism. It was also considered difficult to establish peace in one region while anarchy prevailed in the rest of Europe.

Another Lesson of History. Visions of European Integration from the Perspective of the Second World War

In fact, the idea of European unification was very much alive during the war. Cynically used by Nazi propaganda in the conquest of country after country, it was complemented, after the German attack on the Soviet Union, with the slogan of "a pan-European struggle against Bolshevism" and, after 1943, with federalist terms. It was generally feared that this might compromise, or even defeat, any movement for integration.

This, however, was not the case. Public opinion both in German satellites as well as German-occupied countries soon realized that the Nazi version of a unified Europe was nothing less than a synonym for the Old German Reich aiming at colonizing Latin nations into mere

---

[1] A still-valid study co-authored by an Advisory Committee member: Kerner, R. J. & Howard, H. N., *The Balkan Conferences and the Balkan Entente 1930-1935. A Study in the recent History of the Balkan and Near Eastern Peoples*, Berkeley 1936; see also Campous, E., *Little Entente and Balkan Alliance*, Bucharest 1978.

[2] See Bariéty, J., "Der Tardieu-Plan zur Sanierung des Donauraums (Februar-Mai 1932)" in J. Becker & K. Hildebrand, *Internationale Beziehungen in der Weltwirtschaftskrise 1929-1933*, Munich 1980.

[3] Pasvolsky, L., *Economic Nationalism of the Danubian States*, New York 1928.

provinces and, according to racist theory, at exploiting and gradually exterminating the Slavs. The Holocaust, experienced by the Jews in full view of the entire world, heralded a "final solution" for other nationalities of the continent.

Thus, despite Hitler's abuse of the European idea, or perhaps indeed as a reaction to it, the concept was miraculously reborn from the ashes of war. It appeared in resistance programs and particularly in various activities of *émigré* governments and committees in the pure, idealistic form of a perspective of a free, equal and fraternal Europe with total respect for human rights.

The dreams, the hope, the psychological need for belief in the rationality of human actions, and a seemingly evangelical faith in the salutary value of pain, all gave rise to various federalist and unionist visions.

Refugees from the European continent, defeated, enslaved or subdued by Nazi Germany, working for their *émigré* governments, in London, in national committees and associations across the Atlantic, in the French and, later, the British army, showed themselves to be willing and able to reflect on their previous policy and diplomacy. Those who took part in this great discussion – politicians and publicists, soldiers and scholars – argued heatedly over the reasons for their defeat, analyzed the politics of their countries and, at the same time, exhibited a remarkable openness to a broader perspective. Economic, philosophical and even religious debates produced arguments against nationalism, totalitarianism, barbarism and paganism as opposed to patriotism, freedom, international cooperation and the defense of human dignity.

"The present war differs from all other wars in its character of a general revolution", wrote with conviction the Belgian envoy to the Polish government in London. "This is a war of nations, races, of philosophical and social systems, which leads inevitably to the emergence of a new order based on the greatest human values."[1]

Plans and visions originating from such premises filled the columns of the English press and appeared in *émigré* periodicals and in underground bulletins, competing with dreams dreamt in government offices as well as in cafés and rented rooms. They appeared in papers published

---

[1] *Archives du Ministère des Affaires étrangères* (Belgium), henceforth AMAE (B), Vol. 11 582, Rap. No. 249/53, London, 19 June 1941, *B. De Bitche to P.-H. Spaak*. Even Churchill, famous for his realism, was not immune to this sort of fantasism. In an interview with Dagens Nyheter in April 1943 on the United States of Europe, he said: "Humanity, after all it has gone through, should learn to choose good and reject evil, to continue on the road to power and welfare and to avoid the abyss of infamy and ruin". *Ibid.*, Vol. 11 440, French translation.

with great difficulty by the Resistance in occupied countries. Global and regional solutions disturbed public opinion in the first two years of the war. Paradoxically, they carried the greatest optimism at a time when the signs of an Allied victory were few.

From the perspective of London or New York, in the awareness of the humiliation and the pain experienced by one's fellow countrymen in the occupied countries on the Continent, in the constant anxiety for the fate of one's loved ones, it was easier to reflect on the inevitability of change. The Churchill/Reynaud initiative to proclaim, on the eve of the French defeat, "a declaration of indissoluble French-British union", was more than a gesture for *émigrés*.[1] It opened a general discussion, becoming "a milestone offered to the French and presumably open, *mutatis mutandis* to our other allies"[2] – to quote journalists of the time – and, at the same, an indirect confession of past sins.

The guilty were not hard to find. At the top of his own list, John B. Orr placed political leaders, who "mobilize a spurious patriotism and a distorted national history to rouse the people for the defense and extension of the sovereign power of the state. The present war is due to an acute exacerbation of this aspect of nationalism in Germany."[3]

Representatives of small countries situated between Germany and Russia (Poles, Lithuanians, Latvians and Estonians), whose historical experience of Nazism was appended by a lesson of Stalinist-style totalitarianism, had a deepened awareness of the inevitability of change in internal and external policy. Their aim in the war was not only to defeat Germany, but, more importantly, to liberate themselves from their former roles as buffer zones, bargain tokens, spheres of influence, ramparts, cordons – from all those metaphors which were a source of the region's misfortune for centuries. Some politicians were also unable to eschew a keen sense of responsibility for the short-sighted policies of the interwar period.

This *crise de conscience*, expressed and stylized in a number of ways, was best expressed by Josef Hanč:

> It was a tragic mistake of postwar statesmanship in Eastern Europe to limit collective responsibility to small risks close to home, instead of uniting forces for seemingly remote but, in reality, greater and far more dangerous

---

[1] Declared on 16 June 1940 mainly to encourage further French war effort, it enjoyed a positive response from the public and returned in discussions on the Western bloc in 1944.

[2] N.N., "The Fate of France", *The Economist*, 22 June 1940. From Walter Lipgens (ed.), *Documents on the History of European Integration*, Berlin 1986, Vol. 2, p. 188.

[3] Orr, J.B., "Federalism and Science" in Chaning-Pearce (ed.), *Federal Union*, London 1940, p. 103.

threats farther afield. The ruins of the Baltic, the Little and the Balkan Ententes serve as mute testimonials to diplomatic folly. There is no more pathetic picture than that of Lithuanians recovering Vilno but losing Lithuania, of Poles acquiring Teschen but losing Poland, of Hungarians receiving Transylvania but losing Hungary, or of Bulgarians obtaining Dubrudja and losing Bulgaria.[1]

He was echoed by Kaarel R. Pusta, Estonia's former Foreign Minister, who maintained that the notion of national sovereignty must undergo a profound change: "The sovereignty of a people must hamper the economic cooperation of the other peoples no more. It must also avoid hampering a better organization of peace defense."[2]

There was no shortage of faith and optimism as to the ability to forget petty frontier disputes which obscured higher goals. Jan Papanek, Czech diplomat, surprised by the war while living in New York, greeted the first Czechoslovak-Polish Declaration on confederation of 11 November 1940 (see below) by writing:

> The Czech and Polish nations have learned a lesson from history. Their governments in London were able to shake hands and first agreed that from now on, their cooperation will only be based on common interests and that bygones will be bygones. (...) A study of the past will be left to historians. Politicians and statesmen of both countries must concentrate on the future. The steps taken by the two governments in London are in agreement with the position and the sentiment of the two countries' societies.[3]

The same was stated by Anatol Muhlstein, former Polish diplomat:

> The agreement of November 11, 1940, shows that the terrible lesson of the war has been understood by both parties. And yet, what has not been said of this famous Czecho-Polish conflict! Only a few years ago Poles and Czechoslovaks were regarded as enemies. One spoke of an incompatibility of temper between two nations. (...) Of all this nothing remains. How is such a thing possible? The answer is simple. It is that, in reality, there never has

---

[1] Hanč, J., "From Polish-Czechoslovak Collaboration to Eastern Organization", *New Europe*, 1 June 1941, p. 175. A few months previously, J. Papanek voiced the same idea: "The Baltic, the Little and the Balkan Ententes went to pieces, as had the English-French Entente Cordiale. (...) They were doomed from the start, for it was obvious that they were not supported by their members' uniform and strong determination. They lacked concord and union in their defense against a common threat." "The Significance of the Czechoslovak-Polish Declaration", *New Europe*, 1 December 1940, p. 10.

[2] Pusta, K.A., "Federation for Eastern Europe", *New Europe*, April 1941, p. 157.

[3] Papanek, J., "The significance of the Czechoslovak-Polish Declaration", *New Europe*, 1 December 1940, p. 10.

been any veritable conflict between the two nations. There have been disputes, which were carefully cultivated by politicians...[1]

Vojta Beneš, the Czechoslovak President's brother, wrote on the same occasion of a profound spiritual transformation that had occurred in the two nations and of the will to establish friendly relations not only between them, but in the whole region as well. "We Czechoslovaks and Poles too, are now experiencing a profound spiritual change. We know that the new Europe must become a home of cooperation, mutual toleration, understanding and aid."[2]

In order to avoid simply compiling an anthology of interesting but diverse texts, let us review the main postulates of this discussion: a rejection of centralism for federalism, an opposition to the anonymous power of the capital, an emphasis on local and self-government, the foundation of an international authority for safeguarding peace, a strengthening of democratic institutions, an introduction of warranties against totalitarian regimes, tolerance.[3] Publications of the time also seem to suggest a belief that totalitarianism is an ally of imperialism and that the idea of democracy being a buttress of federalism was becoming ubiguitous. Maraget S. Jameson was straightforward in her statement that the dilemma facing Europe and the world is that of the choice between anarchy and federation.[4]

---

[1] Muhlstein, A., "The United States of Central Europe", *New Europe*, February 1941, p. 60. This extensive article, published in three consecutive editions, later appeared (New York 1942) as a separate brochure, a noteworthy indication of the range of its impact.
[2] Beneš, V., *The Mission of Small Nations*, Chicago 1941, p. 96.
[3] Cf. Michel, H., *Les courants de pensée de la Résistance*, Paris 1962, pp. 357-406.
[4] Jameson, M.P., *The New Europe Fortnightly Review*, January 1940, from W. Lipgens (ed.) *Documents on the History of European Integration*, Berlin 1986, Vol. 2, Doc. 65.

CHAPTER 2

"Unite in order to Exist". Resistance and Expatriate Views of Central European Federation

Concepts of the Postwar Organization of Europe Presented by West European Politicians and Journalists

In Britain, so important for shaping the opinion of "free Europe", as represented by the above-mentioned wave of emigration and governments-in-exile, the tone was set by two organizations. The Federal Union, founded in the summer of 1939 by a handful of young men, easily secured the cooperation of eminent figures and support in the Federal Union Research Institute, founded by an Oxford professor, Sir William Beveridge in March 1940.[1] A separate study would be needed to analyze their accomplishments. We shall limit ourselves here to those ideas which could have influenced *émigré milieux* of interest. Initially, the activities of the Federal Union were largely theoretical: a criticism of unrestrained sovereignty and nationalism. There was less interest in notions of organizing peace; a vague formula of a federation of democratic states was adopted. The first plans for specific proposals for postwar Europe emerged in the spring of 1940. Possibly the first of these was I. Jennings' *A Federation of Western Europe*. Focusing on drawing up a constitution of such a union, the general outline of which he submitted in an appendix, Jennings chose as his point of departure – an obvious one for him – a limitation of the Federation to the part of Europe emphasized in his title and including a democratized Germany. Such a Federation would constitute "the greatest power of the world". Based on the democratic system, not willing to expand its territory, it would be a tool not of war but of peace, which it would pursue in a close cooperation with the League of Nations. The development of democracy

---

[1] They included Sir Richard Acland, W. B. Curry, Ivor Jennings, C. E. M. Joad, Richard Law, Patrick Ransome, Alan Sainsnbury, Wickham Steed, Henri Usborne, Barbara Wootton and Konni Zilliacus, whose authority gave the published analyses a greater significance than could be gathered by the number of printed copies alone.

and of the cultural potential of other European nations would gradually pave the way for their access to the Federation.[1]

Limiting of such a discussion to Western Europe, a characteristic of most publications sponsored by the Federal Union, was not so much due to the impact of Jennings' work as to the deeply rooted view of Eastern and Southern Europe, already visible during discussions on the treaties of Versailles or of Locarno. C. Joad explained this paradigm, popular among his countrymen, by the preservation, in the Western part of the continent, of the basic foundations of European civilization as opposed to its Eastern and Southern parts, allegedly experiencing "an obliteration of a structure of rules inherited from Greece and Christianity".[2] Another consideration here was, even then, the possibility of Eastern Europe becoming part of the sphere of influence of a militarily reinforced Soviet Union.[3]

Due to protests by representatives of Central Europe against such a one-sided view, the Federal Union Research Institute organized, in mid-January 1941, a public debate on two versions of a federation: Western and Danubian. The debate showed that the former would be constructed around a union of France and Britain with its adherents: Finland, Scandinavia, Holland, Belgium and Switzerland. The participants were divided as to the question of Germany. The authors of the idea, backed by the English taking part in the discussion, opted for the inclusion of Germany. The French were against this, insisting on a long quarantine which would allow the Germans some time for a civic and moral reeducation. The arguments of the English were associated with the Russian issue. Although all agreed that Russia could not be part of the federation for civilizational reasons, some feared that leaving Germany out in the cold might push them under the domination of the victorious

---

[1] Jennings, I., *A Federation of Western Europe*, Cambridge 1940, p. 11-12. Mackay, R., (*Federal Europe*, London 1940), who did not preclude the access of Eastern European countries to the federation, maintained that the problem of the federation would only be solved when it was possible to "reconcile the conflicting ambitions, demands and fears of the three Great Powers, Great Britain, France and Germany". Discussing the extension of the federation to the East, the author considered Poland and Czechoslovakia, who could thus forego their armament thanks to the military protection of the Federation in the first phase. (p. 30).

[2] Joad, C., *The Philosophy of Federal Union*, London 1941, p. 26. from Lipgens, W., *op. cit.*, Vol. 2, Doc.18.

[3] "We cannot anticipate what will be the position of the Soviet Union at the end of the present war. It is possible that it will be much stronger than in present. Its sphere of influence may extend over much of Eastern Europe." Jennings, I., *op. cit.*, p. 28. R. Mackay starts from a different premise – a difficulty in adopting Russia into the Federation and states that "It is surely wiser for Russia to build up her Federation in her own way, and for Europe to build up hers". *Op. cit.*, Doc. 25.

Russians and, worse, under the influence of "aggressive Communism", as stated by Sir Beveridge. Eminent British figures reiterated in the debate, as related by Belgian diplomat Marcel Henri Jaspar, that a Western federation would become in the future a defensive alliance against Russia.[1]

The idea of a Danubian federation was considered only superficially, mainly as a return to the ties of the former Austro-Hungarian monarchy. Eastern European participants in the debate found little understanding for their notions of a gradual federation of their continent that would then pave the way for a full, pan-European federation. They could only protest against the British integrative ideas that seemed to favor Germans. They heard in reply that such proposals should particularly satisfy Poles and Czechs: Germany, as part of a federation, would not conduct its own foreign policy and, as a consequence, it would not favor rapprochement to Russia.[2]

In some projects developed outside the sphere of the Federal Union, there emerged a vision of regional ties linking other territories than Western Europe alone. William Temple, Archbishop of York, known from his earlier ecumenical proposals discussing postwar Europe for *Fortnightly Review*, observed many common elements of tradition and religion which could serve as a basis for grouping the particular countries into voluntary federal unions: a) Danubian countries, b) German states (on the condition of eliminating Prussian influence), c) Czechs, Slovaks and Poles, d) Scandinavia, e) Great Britain and France with a possible participation of Belgium, Holland and Luxembourg. These small federations would then pave the way for a more extensive and long-lasting union.[3]

Taking into account only economic considerations and the possibilities of central planning and administration, the Labour Party's chief intellectual, George D. H. Cole, in his study hastily written after the German attack on Russia, saw three groups of countries that could enter federal unions: the Soviet Union, "occupying a greater part of the continent than at present" (*sic*), Central Europe, the Balkans and Western Europe (including Switzerland and Scandinavia).[4] A somewhat different reasoning, based on common civilizational features as a historical

---

[1] From: AMAE (B) 11587, London 20 January 1941, *Jaspar to Spaak*.
[2] *Ibid*. A similar reasoning served as a basis for promoting German accession to the League of Nations in the 1920s.
[3] Temple, W., "Principles of Reconstruction", *Fortnightly Review*, May 1940, p. 453, from DHEI, Vol. 2, p. 186.
[4] Cole, G. D. H., *Europe, Russia and the Future*, London 1941, pp. 127-130, from DHEI, Vol. 2, p. 197.

foundation for federation was represented by David Davies. He observed close ties between countries of most of Western Europe from Portugal to Scandinavia (excluding Germany); he saw another group in the Balkans with Czechoslovakia, Hungary, Austria, Rumania, Yugoslavia, Greece, Bulgaria and Turkey. Poland was placed alongside the Baltic states and Finland, with a strange aside echoing a well-known stereotype: "There is no clear reason for these countries, after releasing them from Russian and German domination, to be excluded from their common civilization".[1]

Obviously, it is difficult to state the extent to which the above ideas, originating in non-government organizations, could inspire and/or affect the policies of the governments of the smaller nations, or influence the position of the great coalition. Existing documents suggest that all plans for new rules of postwar politics were generated in an atmosphere of the great powers' consent, or in the belief that such a support could be possible. This reasoning was based on the above-mentioned premise of the British proposal to France for such a union after the German attack, the proposal described in wartime London as "new internationalism".[2]

The Opinion on European Integration of the Political Emigrants from the Former Neutral Countries

Yet, although federation seemed, for Central European governments, a natural consequence of the war, countries seeking security in neutrality in between the two wars found themselves in a different situation. Almost all saw neutrality as a mistake and rejected it hastily for the future, voicing various arguments: the obvious belief that neutrality gives no guarantee whatsoever; the understanding that a nation is unable to single-handedly secure its defense; the change in war strategy etc. Here, their opinions did not diverge from those of Central European politicians. The difference consisted in their conclusions. These went in two directions: towards the need to create broader federal unions and to strengthen the role of international organizations or securing the support of the great Allied powers – with the emphasis on the former idea. This was shared by the *émigré* Belgian government's Committee for Postwar Problems Study, pointing to the importance of sea routes for itself and Holland. "In economic, and even cultural issues, seas unite rather than divide", stated one of the Committee's reports.[3] A similar reasoning was

---

[1] Davies, D., *A Federated Europe*, London 1940, p. 85, from DHEI, Vol. 2, p. 184.
[2] Vrij Nederland, September 1940. The author of an article "A new internationalism" saw a significant symptom in Churchill's proposal to the United States for the latter to establish military bases in the Bermudas and Newfoundland. DHEI, Vol. 2, p. 456
[3] Commission d'Etudes des problèmes d'après-guerre, July 1994, DHEI, Doc. 162.

Revival of an Idea: Mid-European Union

represented by Flemish politician F. van Cauwelaert. The distance between Antwerp and New York or Buenos Aires is relatively shorter, he argued, than that between the Belgian port and Sofia or Belgrade.[1]

This position was shared by representatives of the Nordic states, who were drawing sad conclusions on the insufficiency of their previous policy from the Soviet-Finnish war, observed from behind a shameful screen of the then still respected neutrality. They were also the ones who saw more clearly than anyone else the weakness of the League of Nations. Discussing the future of the region, Swedish publicist Halvar Khennet came to the conclusion that even a military alliance of Scandinavian countries would not work when confronted with an aggression, as such alliances are based on the traditional respect for its members' independence and sovereignty. This means, he argued, that the countries retained a freedom of decision in defense issues as well as in foreign policy and may thus place their own interests over the security of the group of countries.[2] Khennet's reasoning led inevitably to a pre-determined assumption of basing security on close ties with a great power. Politicians did not differ in their judgments from publicists here. Norwegian government-in-exile's Foreign Minister Trygve Lie, the future UN Secretary, wrote at the time in *The Inter-Allied Review*: "As an Atlantic nation, we desire first of all a strong and organized collaboration between the two Atlantic powers, the British Empire and the United States. This is our main care and the most important condition for our participation in an international order in Europe."[3]

Such views were thus dissonant with the popularity of federation among the "little Europe" in London. With some goodwill, they may be seen as instances of realism and foresight, going beyond the stage of a European Union as proposed before the war by Briand or Coudenhove-Kalergi. A close examination of the policy of the great powers did nothing to promote a strong belief in a complete change of international relations and gave no grounds for much optimism as to the great powers resigning their leadership aspirations. The above-mentioned Cauwelaert did not conceal his suspicion that a European federation could not emerge without the participation or domination of a "master". In his opinion, a federation without the participation and domination of the

---

[1] van Cauweleart, F., "Dangers of European Federation", Belgium, 2 April 1942, DHEI, Vol. 2, Doc. 164.

[2] Khennet, H., "The Future of the Nordic Countries", Naordens Framtid, February 1941, from W. Lipgens, *op. cit.*, Vol. 1, Doc. 226. Similar ideas were voiced by former Foreign Minister R. Sandler.

[3] Quoted by F. van Cauwelaert, *ibid.*

British or the Americans would lead to the emergence of hegemony – inevitably, that of Germany.

Summing up, it should be stressed that, paradoxically, at least in the official history of European integration,[1] it is the representatives of Central European nations who were the staunchest supporters of a union of postwar Europe on a federal basis. Internal democracy and its consequences in international affairs in the form of an equal association of a number of states appeared to them as the only optimistic possibility.[2] Political *émigrés* from France, Belgium, or Scandinavia – not unlike British politicians, the leaders of warring Europe – had better reasons to revert to the *status quo ante*, with some adjustments.[3] Their deeply ingrained realism made them sceptical of ideas promoted by the enthusiasts of the utopia – as they saw it – of a unified Europe.

The Federation as the *sine qua non* Condition of Freedom and Independence for the Central European Countries

For the numerous Central European refugees, a return to the pre-war international policy and international situation was unthinkable. Even the most nationalist politicians carefully concealed their hopes, conscious of the changes taking place in their countries' societies. Unlike the above-mentioned small Western or North European states, Central European nations, deprived of the choice of the protection of a great power, had no alternative to a federal union other than a hegemony of one or both neighboring powers. This is why, with deeply wishful thinking, they opted for a close cooperation of the countries of the region, which alone could guarantee them significant status in international relations. British and American powers were only expected to support such plans and to pressure the gruesome empires of Germany and Russia, weakened by the war.

Under changed conditions, what seemed a utopia or at least a conjecture before 1939 acquired the status of the only rational – and highly hopeful – solution. *Émigré* and resistance groups from the Central European states under German and/or Soviet occupation had a growing conviction, built on both foresight and hindsight, that there was only one alternative: "federation or death". Even in countries such as Slovakia or Croatia, achieving great satisfaction from their "geographic

---

[1] A common practice in most monographs of European unification, not to mention propaganda publications. See also Ellwood, D.W., *Rebuilding Europe. Western Europe, America and Reconstruction*, London and New York 1992, p. 29.
[2] Lipgens, W., *op. cit.*, Vol. 1, p. 612.
[3] Jordan, P., *Central Europe Union*, New York 1944, pp. 42-43.

novelty", there appeared a disappointment with their participation in the German "new order" and visions of a sovereign existence within a democratic European federation. Rumanian *émigrés*, justifying their collaboration with the Nazi camp by German pressures and unreasonable Russian policy, often referred to prewar plans of a Danubian federation.[1] Ernest Jackh, reporting his talks with the ambassador of a neutral state visiting Sofia "well-known for his skepticism", discovered that wartime greatly encouraged "a birth of Balkan solidarity".[2]

Much of this was quite spontaneous. Milan Hodža cites the common declaration by Polish and Czech refugees in the late spring of 1940, issued in Bucharest while still on their way to Britain.[3] More or less around that time, a group of *émigrés* from Austria, Poland and Czechoslovakia living in the United States founded the American Committee on European Reconstruction, promoting a common front against totalitarianism. It was on their initiative, with the support of some American sponsors, that the monthly journal came into existence – *New Europe*,[4] an independent tribune for Eastern European visionaries and realists.

Main Projects for the Federal Organization of Central and Eastern Europe

Of the numerous plans for the transformation of Central and Eastern Europe, the initiative for a Central European federation presented by Polish Prime Minister, Władysław Sikorski, was by far the best known. Polish and to a point Czech, historiography devoted quite some space to this problem, but treated it only as marginal when dealing with the

---

[1] Tilea, V. V., "An Unused War Weapon: Federalisation", Reprint of *The Contemporary Review*, November 1942, p. 1.

[2] Jackh, E., "Balkan Regionalism", *New Europe*, March 1941, p. 95.

[3] Hodža, M., "Central European Federation", *The Contemporary Review*, October 1941, p. 237. Włodzimierz Stępniewski's "List of organizational Slavic studies and political Slavic publications between 1939 and 1943", in AMSZ, Vol. 6/202/14, confirms the creation of a West Slavic Committee (Bucharest, 15 April 1940) under his leadership and contains the text of a proposal for a Federation of Western Slavs, which, according to its author, was to be discussed by both sides during the later Polish-Czechoslovak negotiations.

[4] Barrel, L. L., "Poland and East European Union, 1939-1945", *The Polish Review*, Vol. 3, Nos. 1-2/1975, p. 89. Research by Iwona Drąg, MA, for her Ph.D. thesis on the propaganda of the Polish government in the U.S. during the war seem to suggest a Polish initiative in this issue.

Czechoslovak-Polish confederation, which, in turn, was discussed mainly from the point of view of diplomacy.[1]

It is then worthwhile, in the present discussion, to restore it to its rightful place in the history of European integration and to devote some space to a vision that, as will be seen below, was to have a significant impact on the position of the whole emigration and, in general, enlivened federalist thought during the war.

The plan for a new shape for Central Europe was presented quite early on. General Władysław Sikorski referred to it in his government's first declaration of 16 November 1939. A month later, his next speech on the aims of the Polish government-in-exile in foreign policy at Angers on 18 December, included the following statement: "The new political organization of Central and Eastern Europe must have as one of its main bases a united association of Slavic nations. The new organization of that part of Europe should create a cohesive and concordant cooperation of states between the Baltic, the Black Sea and the Adriatic that would arrest the German drive to the East and separate Germany from Russia."[2]

This statement was reinforced by talks conducted at the time with Edvard Beneš, the head of the Czechoslovak National Committee and Milan Hodža, in charge of the National Slovak Committee, on stronger ties between the two countries.

The reference to the Black Sea in conjunction with the Baltic, the Adriatic and the Slavic states caused no reaction among the then addressees of the declaration – though it should have done. Until then, such statements appeared in megalomaniac visions of a three-seas-based Poland of RNR, the National-Radical Movement[3] or in ideas of post-Piłsudski Prometheanist federalists,[4] whom the Prime Minister had explicitly condemned several weeks previously after his inspection of the Polish embassy in London, shocked at "the arrogance and the

---

[1] Wandycz, P. S., "Czechoslovak-Polish Confederation and the Great Powers 1940-1943", Indiana University Publications, 1956; Kisielewski, T., *Federacja środkowoeuropejska. Pertraktacje polsko-czechosłowackie 1939-1943*, Warsaw 1991.

[2] From Kisielewski, T., *op. cit.*, p. 37; Wandycz, P. S., *op. cit.*, p. 34.

[3] In 1937, RNR, the ideological inheritor of ONR, drafted a program which promoted, from the defeat of Germany and the U.S.S.R., an organization of Slavic nations around a center: a great, Catholic Polish Nation state, extending to three seas, which would lead the nations of Central Europe against Communism and pan-Germanism. For more details, see Majchrowski, J. M., *Geneza politycznych ugrupowań katolickich. Stronnictwo Pracy, grupa "Dziś i Jutro"*, Paris 1984, pp. 103-104.

[4] See (notwithstanding ideological padding) Mikulicz, P., *Prometeizm w polityce II Rzeczypospolitej*, Warsaw 1971; Lewandowski, J., *Imperializm słabości*, Warsaw 1967, p. 67.

jingoism" of a propaganda campaign conducted under the influence of "the *ancien régime*".[1]

It seems that Sikorski did succumb to visions he officially condemned. His aide could see that very well and dismissed them with a sarcastic "Ah, those Jagiellonian ideas of Sikorski's!"[2] Exactly how strong was the charm of such ideas and what was the essence of Sikorski's plan? His close collaborators are quite taciturn on the subject. Józef Retinger, Sikorski's personal secretary, an intriguing personality, the best Polish student at the European school, is disappointing here, saying that it is due to him that the general became "a committed federalist". Others add –another surprise – that Sikorski supported a union which would include, apart from Poland and Czechoslovakia, the Baltic states, Hungary and possibly Austria and Rumania[3] All Edward Raczyński says in his memoirs is that Sikorski was an "enthusiastic" supporter of the Central European idea.[4]

The problems one encounters when attempting to define Sikorski's plan in more detail drive one to the conclusion that, for quite a long time, it was pretty vague,[5] perhaps out of necessity,[6] or maybe as a result of a certain opportunism in relation to his own collaborators as well as future partners. A certain haziness of the future federation's external contours also served to pacify Polish opposition in exile, remaining in the blessed conviction that their ideas are still likely to be realized. This lack of precision in the notion of a Central European federation is especially visible in the context of Sikorski's first visit to the United States. As can be gathered from his report, the Prime Minister presented

---

[1] See "Report from a visit to England of 23 November 1939", Zgórniak, M. & Rojek, W. & Suchcic, A. (ed.), *Protokoły z posiedzeń Rady Ministrów Rzeczypospolitej*, Vol. 1, October 1939-June 1940, Cracow 1994, p. 99.

[2] Mitkiewicz, L., *Z generałem Sikorskim na obczyźnie*, Paris 1968, p. 143, note of 21 April 1941 from Sikorski's statements at a Polonia banquet in Chicago.

[3] Pomian, J., *Józef Retinger. Życie i pamiętniki pioniera Jedności Europejskiej*, Warsaw 1994, p. 99. English edition, Pomian, J. (ed.), *Memoirs of an Eminence Grise*, London 1972. See also Grosbois, T., "L'action de Józef Retinger en faveur de l'idée européenne 1940-46", *European Review of History*, Vol. 6, No. 1, 1999, pp. 59-82.

[4] Raczyński, E., *W sojuszniczym Londynie*, London 1960, p. 11.

[5] A paper by T. Łoś-Nowakowa brings little new information, despite its promising title "Władysław Sikorski and plans for federation", in K. Fiedor (ed.), *Europejskie doktryny, porozumienia i współpracy gospodarczej w XX w.*, Vol.1, AUW, Nos. 863, Wrocław 1987 pp. 67-90). The author follows the thread of previous researchers and concentrates on the Polish-Czechoslovak confederation.

[6] Prażmowska, A. J., *Britain and Poland 1939-1943. The Betrayed Ally*, 2nd ed. Cambridge 1997, p. 132 remarks that Churchill was against publicizing Sikorski's plan.

his plan to Roosevelt in very general terms. The President was, in fact, not interested enough to query its details and satisfied himself with a curt "Fine idea" – understood by the general as an expression of support.[1]

Thus, disregarding scattered statements by various Polish figures in the press, it is easy to see that Sikorski's concept of *Międzymorze* ("in-between-the-seas") was long understood as the need for a rapprochement of Central European states, which were either already democratic or to be democratized in the future. Apart from future federal ties, the binding element was the need, seen from past experience and visible also for external observers, for consent to hand over certain sovereign rights to common organizations, as well as the need to work towards an economic – and, if necessary, military – counterbalance against Germany and Russia. The union's internal structure would be not unlike the Swiss model, highly valued by enthusiasts of European federalism of the time. The question of frontiers, seen as a secondary issue, was to be resolved after the war by democratically elected governments.[2]

The development of Sikorski's idea or, rather of the idea of Central European federation, was undoubtedly much influenced by negotiations between Poland and Czechoslovakia. As claimed by L. Barrel,[3] it took all his determination, courage, sincerity and shrewdness and a profound belief in the need to take up history's challenge for the region's security to obtain the support of Beneš, a difficult partner. This determination had a constructive effect in shaping of a vision of the future union in Czechoslovak policy.

Undoubtedly of some importance – though less than is often suggested – was the fact that Sikorski's support was needed by Beneš for Allied recognition of his Committee as a government-in-exile, which was secured finally in July 1940. Thereafter, Beneš supported neither a Central nor a pan-European federation.

It is still a mystery what influenced Beneš' position. Was it a profound revision of his policy, an attempt to defend it by using the confederation as a bridge to the Little Entente, or his disillusionment with the position of the great powers during the Munich Conference?

---

[1] Wandycz, P. S., *op. cit.*, p. 49. Kisielewski T., *op. cit.*, p. 130, See also *Sprawa polska w czasie II wojny światowej na arenie międzynarodowej. Zbiór dokumentów*, Warsaw 1965, p. 205.

[2] AMAE(b), Vol. 11582 bis. London, 16 July 1941, Rap. No. 249/53, Bitche to P.-H. Spaak, "Le nouvel ordre allemand et le nouvel ordre europeen d'après le général Sikorski".

[3] L. L. Barell's characterization of Beneš in his interesting study: "Poland and East European Union 1939-1945", *The Polish Review*, Vol. 3, Nos. 1-2/1975, p. 98.

For the present discussion, it is relevant that Beneš saw himself as a realist and was indeed one. Like the politicians of small Scandinavian countries mentioned earlier, he was convinced that grouping small states into broader associations was only possible with the backing of the great powers. Czechoslovakia's situation and its then recent experiences only made him less critical towards Russia. His – highly qualified – access to the federalist idea for Eastern Europe proved, *ipso facto*, at least for a time, that he saw it as a realistic move.

It should be stated here at once that despite the rueful tone of Polish historical literature, Beneš was not a supporter of a Central European federation. Yet Beneš had also learned his lesson from the Munich conference and the fall of Czechoslovakia, and, for a time, sincerely contemplated an economic cooperation with a Polish-Czechoslovakian leadership among Central European countries. He realized that victory would be followed by a division of Europe into two blocs and that the countries between Russia and Germany "will have to, or at least should try to, create a fairly powerful bloc". As they would not be able to count on France, the traditional yet highly unreliable ally, they would be forced to rely on sole British support and secure, *sine qua non*, the acceptance of Russia.[1] He saw this as important clearly fearing, based on his experience from the previous war, that a defeated Germany might be exposed to Communist influence. Neutralizing it would not be possible, he maintained, "without agreeing on a *modus vivendi* with Russia that would prevent our territories from being entered by Russian armies in a probable cooperation with a Communist Germany".

Due to the possible strength of those external factors, Beneš preferred not to commit himself to any form of Czechoslovak-Polish or Central European union. He stated this quite clearly – though in vague terms such as "a *suis generis* confederation", "not going too far", "special machinery". His qualifiers, "flexible", "prone to change", "particularly special", "exceptional",[2] were more than a mere display of rhetoric.

In a broader way, Beneš' idea of the (con)federation was presented at a meeting with students in Liverpool. It consisted of the liberation of all small countries and the creation of federal associations all over the continent; a new security system allowing the easing of the arms race;

---

[1] Štovíček, I., Valenta, J. (eds.), *Československo-polská jednání o vytvoření konfederace 1939-1944, Československé diplomatické dokument*, (henceforth ČDD), Prague 1994, Vol. I, Doc. 28, London, 1 November 1940, Beneš' memo to Sikorski. Similarly, instruction to J. Masaryk in Washington, 15 November 1940, *Ibid*. Doc. 30 "Celá tato akce nesmí býti v ničem protiruská".

[2] *Ibid*.

and rules for the economic cooperation of democracies aiming, among other things, at preventing the existence of an autarchic economy, a basis for all totalitarian economies.[1] As evidenced by his correspondence with Sikorski, it was to be founded on the member states' assent to limiting their sovereignty, first in the economy and finance (a customs and monetary union), then in foreign affairs and defense. Its agreement in diplomacy would be assured by the cooperation of foreign ministers, in politics by defense ministers and, eventually, of Joint Chiefs of Staff. It would be administered by three councils: Federal, Economic and Special, supported by a "delegation of parliaments" of sorts.[2]

In early 1942, Beneš still relying on the possibility of Russia's acceptance of an Eastern European federation, kept some of his, maybe ingrained, optimism. His vision of the future of Central Europe was clear: the region's reorganization would be based on a Polish-Czechoslovak confederation which should be joined by such countries as Austria, Hungary and even Rumania. Hungary's access would depend on their giving up all gains acquired with German help.

This bloc should exist alongside another, that of Yugoslavia, Greece, Albania and, possibly, Rumania (which would be free to choose its bloc). Turkey, should it so aspire, could also find its place in the Balkan federation. Beneš cautioned, however – a fact often forgotten by the literature on Polish-Czechoslovak confederation – that such associations would only make sense if they constituted "a logical step towards a consolidation of the whole Europe, a type of a worldwide commonwealth".[3]

His lack of trust in the Western powers and his realism lead him to believe that the organization of such a commonwealth should be done with the participation of the Soviet Union. Beneš was also careful to promote his image as "the only eminent politician in London who did not lose faith in the power of U.S.S.R. and its final victory over the Third Reich"[4] and supplemented his earlier arguments with a new one – that an isolated Russia would be likely to seek an agreement with Germany. Moscow's acceptance of a federal union, in exchange for its

---

[1] Howard, H. H., "British and Allied. War and Peace Aims", *New Europe* No. 5, April 1941, p. 111.
[2] *Ibid.*
[3] *Ibid.*, p. 262: "there may be no regional confederation without such a broad structure".
[4] Sherwood, R. E., *Roosevelt and Hopkins. An Intimate History*, New York 1950, p. 319.

dominant influence in the confederation, would lead, he claimed, to achieving a balance of powers on the continent.[1]

In this respect, the divergence of his views from those of Sikorski was wide. The Polish Prime Minister believed that arresting Russia's postwar expansion was possible not through a manifestation of "meekness" but through a demonstration of the power of the proposed union.[2] The changing international situation further accentuated this difference.

It should also be added that Beneš' motivation, contrary to that of Sikorski, was highly influenced by pan-Slavic tendencies. His resentment towards the Western Allies after 1938 pushed the Czechoslovak politician to taking a "revenge of sorts for Munich". Beneš was still waiting for the political situation to settle. He had been greatly influenced by his experience of the Little Entente and never got over it psychologically. Criticism of his policy change by Polish historians does not matter here much, for his concepts were treated seriously not only by the public, but also – especially important here – by the members of the Advisory Committee of the American Department of State.

Its more convinced supporters included Beneš' close collaborator, his Foreign Minister, Hubert Ripka. An analysis of his proposals, especially those presented in the Czech press, leaves one under a strong impression of his attempts at reconciling Beneš with the idea by making it more precise on issues that could trigger the latter's fears. Among other things, he stressed strongly that resistance to German expansion required "a constructive program for a reorganization of Central Europe" and supported an equal number of representatives in a future common administration to preclude a Polish domination, one of Beneš' main fears. He also agreed to loosen the federation's ties by the rule that all decisions by federal authorities would be ratified by governments or other responsible institutions of the individual countries. His qualms, already deeply rooted during talks on broadening the Little Entente, to prevent a possible Polish domination, were also visible in the two variants of the association. The first assumed the coexistence of three federations: Polish-Baltic, Danubian (including Austria, Hungary and Rumania) and Balkan (with Yugoslavia, Turkey, Greece and Albania). These three formations would be strengthened by the links between Poland and Czechoslovakia and Rumania and Yugoslavia. The other variant would be based on a cooperation between two groups of confederated states. The first would be a broader union including Poland and the Danubian countries, the second, Southern Europe. They would

---

[1] Beneš, E., "The Organization of Postwar Europe", *Foreign Affairs*, Vol. 20., 2 January 1942, pp. 229-230.

[2] Cf. Szkodlarski, J., *Epilog układu Sikorski-Beneš*, Łódź 1988, pp. 17-18.

pivot around a Polish-Czechoslovak federation and a Turkish-Yugoslav treaty. The end result would also be influenced by an analysis of the international situation.[1] In his desire to protect the future association from domination by any one of its members, he promoted a strict prohibition on the access of any neighboring great power. This was a thinly disguised opposition to Beneš, who was not opposed to closer ties between the confederation and the Soviet Union. However, he understood the need for not antagonizing Russia, seeing in its collaboration with the West a guarantee of the federation's very existence and of its rejection of a rapprochement with Germany.[2] Ripka agreed with Beneš in his idea of the federation's access to a broader pan-European union.

Beneš' ideas were made more reliable in America by his brother Vojta, head of the National Czechoslovak Council. Basing his ideas on the Polish-Czechoslovak declaration, he saw a Central European confederation of a clearly defensive character. His was a strongly nostalgic vision of the federation as, "a union for the protection of the language, the culture and the spiritual values carefully safeguarded in our beautiful fatherlands. The federation would never endanger any justified interests of its neighbors and would live with them in peace and friendship as long as their rules of coexistence be moral, behavior humanitarian, aims noble."[3]

Equally different were the ideas of Milan Hodža, head of the Czechoslovak Committee at the beginning of the war and rival to Beneš. He presented them in a memorandum of 28 November 1939 to Allied politicians, including Poles.[4] He recommended the creation, in Central Europe, of a more compact system, consisting, apart from the Polish-Czechoslovak union, of Austria, Hungary, Yugoslavia, Rumania and Bulgaria, an obvious echo of the so-called, "Danubian project" of 1936. He expanded on this in a study published three years later, suggesting a creation of a commonwealth of nations bound by federal ties with a common president, chancellor and federal government, the latter with wide prerogatives in foreign affairs, treasury, defense, foreign trade, mail and transport. Accepting Polish overtures towards Beneš, he saw a better future in an equal, tripartite Czech-Slovak-Polish union, a basis for a broader federation of eight countries – half of them Slavic, which

---

[1] Kisielewski, T., pp. 126-129 and ČDD Doc. 104, 108, 145.
[2] Ripka, H., "Is a Federation in the Baltic-Aegean Area Possible?" *Free Europe* (London) 29 November 1940, reprinted in *New Europe* (New York) February 1941. Cf. Čechoslovák of 23 May 1941 discussed by Kisielewski, T., *op. cit.*, pp. 127-129.
[3] Beneš, V., *The Mission of Small Nations*, Chicago 1941, p. 95.
[4] IPSM A. XII, 34/2 *Memorandum on Collective Security in Central Europe*, Coll. of General. K. Sosnkowski.

would allow the preservation of a balance in "all possible racial and power aspirations" as its contribution to the future New Europe.[1]

Hodža himself, the main advocate of a Central Eastern European in America according to documents accumulated by OSS, a predecessor of CIA, cited Col. Koc and A. Zaleski as those whose opinions he shared in full.[2]

It was also in London that a group of Czechs and Slovaks, including Karol Locher, Peter Prídavok,[3] and Josef Malík, gathered around *Ruch zachodnio-słowiański – Zapadoslovensky Ruch* (The West-Slavic Movement), a periodical of a non-government Polish organization. They were strongly in opposition to Beneš and supported the projects of a federal union of Poles, Czechs, Slovaks, Bulgarians, Yugoslavs, which, in case of a total capitulation of Germany, could also include Serbs. Headed by Lev Prchala, they congregated at London's Central European Club.

Influential opponents of federal ideas and plans included Zdenek Fierlinger, MP and, later, Czechoslovak ambassador to the Soviet Union. He also opposed the Polish-Czechoslovak alliance, as exemplified by his counteraction at Russia's Foreign Commissariat.[4]

Unlike many other studies of this topic, we wish to stress the role of Sikorski in the process. What is usually forgotten is that Sikorski did not limit himself to talks with Beneš on Polish-Czechoslovak federation, but he was active in an attempt to secure for his ideas the support of smaller European countries. Using the reputation he enjoyed with London's "little Europe", he initiated regular meetings of the foreign ministers of Belgium, Holland, Luxembourg and Norway, joined since mid-1941 by Yugoslavia and Greece. All postwar issues were discussed, dominated by that of the reconstruction or, more properly, the construction of Europe. Such meetings were interspersed with recurrent conferences of prime ministers in the form of working dinners. These were often attended by representatives of the great powers: Anthony Eden, then

---

[1] Hodža, M., *Federation in Central Europe - Reflections and Reminiscences*, London-New York, 1942, pp. 171-178. In an interview for *Picture Post* of 28 June 1941, he offered a vision of two federations: a Western one with Great Britain and a Central Eastern one with the Balkans. He saw Russia as a third, individual element of the European order. From T. Kisielewski, p. 139

[2] OSS INT-9 CZ-21, note from a conversation between Wiley and Hodža of 20 December 1941. *Ibid.*, INT-9, CZ 44. "Czech ex-Premier sees Central Europe Union", 7 May 1942.

[3] P. Pridavok initially cooperated with Hodža. They parted during the war. Pridavok saw Hodža as "Beneš' agent", see OSS report of 12 January 1943, NA INT-9 CZ-308

[4] Fierlinger, Z., *Paměti. Ve službách ČSR*, t. I, Prague 1951, p. 56; Wandycz P.S., *op. cit.*, p. 98, that he warned Beneš quite early on (in February 1942), that the work on the federation was doomed to fail.

Secretary of State at the British Foreign Office; Anthony Drexel Biddle, American ambassador to most of those countries' governments; and John Foster Dulles, then in England on an unofficial mission to study European problems.[1] Sikorski used such contacts in his attempt to set up a mechanism for small countries' cooperation during the war and to organize a common front for the future, inevitably dominated by the great powers. It was also an excellent forum for promoting the idea of regional ties.[2] The effects of this cooperation were by no means insignificant and resonated well beyond London. As Sikorski reminisced in his report from his first trip to the United States: "During the visit, Czechoslovaks, Yugoslavs, Greeks, even Belgians and Dutch grouped with Poles. From now on, the *émigrés* of those countries should present a unified front in matters world politics on the American continent."[3] As a result, on 12 June 1941, almost immediately after the installation of their new governments-in-exile, Czechs and Poles persuaded their leaders to publish a common declaration of a future economic and social cooperation.[4] There is considerable evidence that the idea of a Greek-Yugoslav treaty is descended from these conferences.

The very fact of advanced negotiations on a North Slavic confederation had an impact on the imagination of the new exiles. They soon found a new sphere to manifest their common aspirations and beliefs in a session of the International Labor Organization in New York of November 1941. Answering to its call for a discussion on the organization of the postwar world, delegates of four Central European countries presented an idea of fostering their closer collaboration that would take into account the particularities of the region. Paragraph 6 stated that,

> We hope that the end of this war, which was forced upon us, will save a hundred million inhabitants of Central Europe and of the Balkans from their present state of wretchedness by assuring them a possibility of stable employment guaranteed by reconstruction and by the development of their industries, agriculture and merchant marine and that those peoples will be included within the sphere of international exchanges of goods and services.[5]

---

[1] Pomian, J., *op. cit.*, p. 104.

[2] P.-H. Spaak is of the opinion in his memoirs that these ideas were authored by J. Retinger, a close collaborator of Sikorski. (*Combats inachevés*, Vol. 1, Paris 1968, p. 155).

[3] Sikorski's speech at the 4 June 1941, session of the Polish Government's National Council. In *Sprawy polskie...*, *op. cit.*, p. 206.

[4] *Ibid.*, p. 91.

[5] For the text of the declaration, see Gross, F., *op. cit.*, Doc. X, pp. 107-109. Its signatories included: J. Masaryk, J. Necas, R. Moravec and J. Kosina for the

Revival of an Idea: Mid-European Union

The wide resonance of the declaration among *émigré* masses[1] led the Eastern European participants of the conference to found a research center, which, as the Central and Eastern Europe Planning Board, functioned until 1944 and published a number of economic analyses.[2]

South Slavic politicians were equally active. Their declarations included increasingly frequent references to the idea of a Balkan Federation. It was hailed on 6 September 1941 by King Peter in a speech broadcast by American radio stations. He was supported by weighty arguments from Prime Minister Dušan Simović,[3] who pointed to the need to transcend merely bilateral ties. Once again, as in the above-mentioned plans, the lesson of history seemed unequivocal. It was expressed in the preamble to the negotiated agreement, which saw it as an introduction to a broad Balkan federation. In a rationale for the Balkan Union, to which the Greek-Yugoslav association was to serve as a forerunner, it is stated that it is born from "experience and more particularly recent experiences, which have demonstrated that a lack of close understanding between the Balkan peoples has caused them to be exploited by the powers of aggression and domination of the peninsula".[4]

Greek democratic *émigrés* also favored the idea of a confederation. Their public statements emphasized the need for such a body as well for offsetting its Slavic component. "Greeks, Albanians, Rumanians, Hungarians and Turks are the forces that will counterbalance the Slavic elements in the Federation and will create the confidence which is indispensable for the materialization of such an idea", wrote Basil J. Vlavianos, the leader of Greek liberals.[5]

Czechoslovak delegation; A. Dimitratos, G. Logothetis, D. Papas for the Greeks, J. Stańczyk, A. Falter, and F. Gross for the Poles; S. N. Kosanović, B. Bonats, and C. Milos for the Yugoslavs. For more on the organization, see Gross, F., "Planning and Federation at the International Labor Organization Conference", *New Europe*, No. 1, December 1941, p. 11.

[1] See among others Masaryk, J., "A Lasting Brotherhood of Free Peoples", *New Europe*, Vol. 2, December 1941; Kosanović, S. N., "Common Aspirations of the Nations of Eastern Europe", *ibid*.

[2] An interested reader should consult Cracow's Jagiellonian Library, the only library in Poland to boast a complete set of the documents.

[3] Herzog, M., "Yougoslavia and Federalism", *New Europe*, No. 12, October 1941, p. 323. Hodža also saw Simović as a true supporter of the federation. See OSS INT-9 CZ-21, memo of 20 December 1941.

[4] Gross, F., *Crossroads of two Continents. A Democratic Federation of East-Central Europe*, New York 1945. Appendix, Doc. 9, p. 104.

[5] *Ibid.*, p. 21.

Britain's Attitude to the Idea of Organizing Central Eastern Europe

Plans for Central Eastern European integration were received favorably by English politicians. Churchill, in contrast to his predecessors, seemed to be more convinced of the key significance of countries between Germany and Russia for stability in Europe. His attitude reflected a lingering nostalgia for the role of the Austro-Hungarian monarchy and a hope for reducing the Russians' appetite in the region. From an ideological and political point of view, it could be expected that a federation of democratic (or democratized) countries would be easier for Communist Russia to accept than the primitive notion of the *cordon sanitaire*. The then Minister of Labor, Ernest Bevin, was also interested in federation. On 3 July 1941, *i.e.* not even a fortnight after the German attack on the Soviet Union, he spoke to Sikorski in the presence of the Foreign Secretary Eden, an official of the Foreign Office, William Strang and J. Retinger, Sikorski's assistant.

Strang and Retinger report that both politicians supported the existence of a significant economic and political bloc on Russia's western border – despite the obvious need for cooperation with Stalin.[1] Retinger seems to suggest that support for a Central Eastern European federation was part of a far-reaching political idea disclosed by Bevin, to give up splendid isolation from European matters and assume leadership over regional associations.[2]

The reported meeting is also significant to Sikorski's Central European plan. Apart from the above vague statements, there is no known mention by Sikorski of including Belarus, the Ukraine and the Baltic states in one or another form of federation – with the sole and significant exception of Lithuania. Its inclusion in the Central European federation, or even into the early stage negotiated at that time with the Czechs, was possibly the final echo of Sikorski's Jagiellonian dream. Until now, work on the Polish-Czech federation did not cover this issue, as Beneš refused to discuss the status of the Baltic states.[3] It is known, however, that there were numerous attempts at gaining the support of

---

[1] Coutovidis, J. & Reynolds, J., *Poland 1939-1947*, New York 1987, pp. 62-63.
[2] Pomian, J., *op. cit.*, p. 105: "The isolation of Great Britain began in the times of Queen Elizabeth, with negative consequences both for Britain and for the Continent. Now we must bury even the memory itself of that Elizabethan policy and strive, as best as we can, to participate in European matters, even if we desist from aspiring to European leadership".
[3] ČDD, Doc. 82, 20 November 1941, Ripka's note from a conversation with Raczyński. Ripka explained his opposition to the access of Lithuania to the confederation by Czech fears of a Polish domination.

Lithuanian *émigrés*, with the foundation of Polish-Lithuanian committee in Chicago immediately after Sikorski's American trip as a first step in that direction.[1]

Thus when Churchill postulated a federation of Central European countries in his negotiations with Stalin,[2] he saw it as a union of Lithuania, Poland and Czechoslovakia, with a possible access of Hungary, Rumania and, at a later date, of the Balkan states, especially Yugoslavia and Greece. This form was pursued by the Polish government for a number of later months, reinforced by the illusion of Stalin's acceptance.

---

[1] 4 June 1941, W. Sikorski's speech at a session of the Polish National Council, *Sprawy polskie... Doc. cit.*

[2] The memo presented to the Russians in July 1941 was clear: "His Majesty's Government sees the need for creating larger territorial organizations to strengthen the smaller countries of Europe. This would enable them to successfully oppose the economic and strategic pressures by Germany. His Majesty's Government thus approves the negotiations undertaken by the governments of the Czechoslovak Republic and the Republic of Poland on the issue of confederation. His Majesty's Government hopes that this federal system will then be extended to include other States of Central Europe", From *Documents on Polish-Soviet Relations*, Vol. 1 1939-1945, London 1961, Doc. 165, p. 591.

CHAPTER 3

Towards a More Concrete Realization of the Idea of a Mid-European Federation

"A Germ of a Constructive Plan": The Greek-Yugoslav Agreement and the Polish-Czechoslovak Declaration

London's "Little Europe" greeted 1942 with much optimism and hope. Final preparations for the long-negotiated Polish-Czechoslovak declaration were underway. Representatives of Greece and Yugoslavia were tying up the loose ends of a similar agreement at a great pace, to the surprise of the public. The background of these negotiations remains unknown to this day. It is known that the above-mentioned meeting of representatives of small nations, inspired by General Sikorski, played a part here. On 15 January 1942, the governments-in-exile of Yugoslavia and Greece made public their agreement on the future of the association of their countries. Its full name is worth mentioning: "The Agreement between the Kingdom of Greece and the Kingdom of Yugoslavia on the Creation of the Balkan Union". It was signed in London by Emanuel Tsouderos, Prime Minister and Foreign Minister, much respected among Greek *émigrés*[1] and his Foreign Undersecretary of State for Greece and by Prof. Slobodan Jovanovic, Prime Minister and Minister of Internal Affairs with Momčilo Nončić, his Foreign Minister, for Yugoslavia. The agreement provided for the creation of several central bodies of the Union, as can be gathered from the definition of its jurisdiction, which had the character of a confederation. The most formally important of these, the Political Office, composed of Foreign Ministers, periodically meeting at well-defined intervals, was to coordinate the foreign policy of all the states in order to present a unified front to the international

---

[1] E. J. Tsouderos, lawyer by education, performed many political functions before the war and was a close collaborator of Venizelos. In the Greek government-in-exile, formed on 20 April 1941, he was first Minister of Foreign Affairs and of Finance, later to become its Prime Minister. His policy and individuality was highly esteemed in a report of American intelligence of 21 June 1942. NA OSS INT GR-337.

community. Its role was also to supervise a number of committees arranging arbitration, intellectual cooperation, influencing public opinion. The Economic and Financial Office, consisting of two Secretaries of State from each country of the Union dealing with economic matters was granted extensive authority in foreign trade, customs duties, economic planning and its relations with individual states. It was also empowered to create new committees on monetary union, improving transport and communication between the member states and the development of tourism.

The authors of the treaty attached much importance to defense, as evidenced by the formation of a Permanent Military Office, composed of state leaders or their deputies, working in close collaboration with the Joint Chiefs of Staff, consisting, in turn, of individual countries' staff members. Divided into two separate bureaus, that of the Army and the Air Force and that of the Navy it was to define a common defense plan and work for a unification of armaments. The function of the armed forces it supervised was to defend "the European borders of the member states". A Permanent Bureau, divided into three sections, was to play the part of a Secretariat. The agreement was still to be ratified and would become binding at the end of the war.[1]

Eight days later, on 23 January 1942, another Czechoslovak-Polish declaration was signed. In the opinion of London's Little Europe, it was a conformation of the will to create a Mid-European Federation and, in the intention of its authors, it was to constitute a basis, a paradigm, of that federation. In fact, the signatories of the declaration, described by Polish historians as the "treaty on the rules of the future confederation",[2] were hard set on highlighting such an impression. In a communiqué of the same day, both governments expressed their belief that "a confederation of Central European countries will cooperate with the Balkan Union proposed by the governments of Greece and Yugoslavia", and that "only the cooperation between the two regional organizations can ensure the security and the welfare of the extensive area between the Baltic and the Aegean".[3] Sadly, this attractive perspective of cooperation, optimisti-

---

[1] Text: Gross, F., *Crossroads of two Continents. A Democratic Federation of East-Central Europe*, op. cit., Doc. 9, pp. 104-106. Sikorski spoke in the same spirit at the time at a meeting with small states' representatives attended, among others, by De Gaulle: "I have always seen the defeat and the total overthrow of Germany as the necessary condition for a stable and just peace, based, among others, on a European federation, to which the Polish-Czechoslovak and the Yugoslav-Greek agreements should be an introduction." From Pobóg-Malinowski, W., *Najnowsza historia Polski 1864-1945*, Vol. 3, London 1960, Vol 1., p. 164.

[2] Kisielewski, T., *op. cit.*, p. 174, Doc. 4, pp. 268-269.

[3] From Kisielewski, T., *op. cit.*, p. 175.

cally received by the "little Europe",[1] found no confirmation in the actual content of the documents, which introduced this cooperation on a very limited scale. Both governments expressed a desire for the Polish-Czechoslovak confederation to extend to other European states whose basic interests were tied to those of Poland and Czechoslovakia, but neither named those countries nor mentioned any dates. The aims of the cooperation were modest: a common policy in foreign affairs, social matters, transport, mail and telegraph. The future confederation was to have a joint Chief of Staff and, in case of war, a joint military command. A further six clauses proposed a coordination of foreign trade, customs duties, monetary policy, transport, education and culture. Article twelve listed civil rights and freedoms that should be guaranteed by the constitutions of the individual countries. Final clauses stressed the will and the need to create "the confederation's joint offices".[2] Seen from the perspective of the long-lasting negotiations and projects previously announced, this was hardly a great success. Neither did the two agreements introduce any vital changes. In both cases, the structure and the sovereignty of the member states was practically preserved in full. Federal bodies mentioned by the two documents did not go beyond the formula of a permanent secretariat and fairly unsystematic meetings. One may wonder, as the State Department's Advisory Committee did, if the Polish-Czechoslovak declaration introduced any new elements in comparison to the earlier document of 1940; if the Greek-Yugoslav treaty went further than the Balkan Entente of 1934; and if both addressed the gist of the problem.[3] There is no doubt, however, that it would have been an interesting record of matters that needed to be solved in the region in terms of foreign policy, foreign trade, customs, currency policy, cultural cooperation, transport and communication.

The Federation of Central Europe as a Starting Point for a Debate on Unification

We tend to be of the opinion that a more profound analysis of the two documents is not only unnecessary but, in fact, unwelcome, for understanding the importance of the event. The truth is that even the members of this London Diaspora of small countries did not inquire too much into the content of the declarations. What really mattered for them was the spirit of the negotiations. It was sought and found in the

---

[1] Seen by M. Turlejska as evidence for the pressure of Britain, seeking to expand its influence into the region. *Spór o Polskę*, Warsaw 1981, p. 140.
[2] Text: Kisielewski, T., *op. cit.*, pp. 268-269.
[3] NA RG 59, Notter's Papers, Vol. 83, R.-6,1 T-356, 27 July 1943, *The Greek-Yugoslav Project for Balkan Union*.

political maturity of Central European politicians, in their will to limit their own sovereignty for the sake of security and peace. The content was important inasmuch as it indicated, as stated by the Greek Prime Minister, "one of the fundamental pillars of future peace"[1] and expressed, as stressed by the enthusiastic author of a Belgian memo, "a move from initial discussion to final studies" as "a germ of a constructive plan".[2]

The author in question, F. de Vanlangenhove, Secretary General of the Foreign Ministry, impressed with the two projects and, possibly, with earlier conversations with Sikorski, tried to convince Paul-Henri Spaak to instigate a similar plan for Western Europe and "to create, in a more or less spectacular way, a study committee which would at least express the will of a good neighbor policy".[3] While one had to wait for a time for Spaak's reaction, one of his colleagues, Paul Van Zeeland, the future founder of the Economic League for European Cooperation, reacted with a plan for an "Economic Union" that was to include the British and the French Empires, Belgium, Holland, Switzerland, Scandinavia and, possibly, Poland and Italy, with a beneficial cooperation with the United States but would exclude Germany. Van Zeeland based his ideas on reforms of trade and finance that would reduce the significance of currency as a tool of national interest. The project, based on more liberal economic contacts and on an elimination of gold from the currency system, was to rapidly improve the economy of the member states and thus help do away with supposed German domination in Europe.[4]

Another representative of free Belgium, the leader of the Flemish Catholics, F. van Cauwelaert, although seeing the idea of an all-European federation as anachronistic or premature, greeted the two treaties with enthusiasm. He was of the opinion that Belgium and Holland should also learn from experience and follow the same route "even should this require a great wisdom and a serious effort of good will".[5] Holland was less enthusiastic about the general idea; its representatives preferred a return to the *status quo ante*. Dutch Prime Minister, P. S. Gebrandy, possibly in a hope of preserving the colonies,

---

[1] NA OSS INT-GR... Report of 5 May 1943.
[2] AMAE (b), Vol. 11775, London 31 January 1942. de Vanlangenhove, F., *Les Fédérations régionales*.
[3] *Ibid.*, cf. Grosbois, T., *op. cit.*, pp. 67-72.
[4] *The Christian Science Monitor*, 11 July and 10 October 1942.
[5] van Cauwelaert, F., "Dangers of European Federation", *Belgium* No. 2, 2 April 1942, p. 47. "There is, in Europe, a number of ties that are a result both of its very nature and of history. Let us begin with these". Belgian socialists, in a memo of 26 August 1942, saw the need for a federation of Belgium, France, Luxembourg, and Holland.

Revival of an Idea: Mid-European Union

stated to the press that his country had extensive trade contacts and interests outside Europe and that a purely European grouping of nations was not its aim. He also reiterated the view that Holland has more in common with the United States and Britain than with other European states.[1]

The further north the continent, the cooler the reactions to the suggestion of a federalization of Europe contained in the two discussed treaties. Trygve Lie maintained in his position of a few months before of a certain cooperation between Scandinavian states but "he saw friendly relations between Britain, the United States, the Soviet Union and China and an abandonment of liberalism in economy as the most important basis for an extended international cooperation". Norwegian Prime Minister Johan Nygaardsvold shared his minister's views when he stated the need for a planned economy at a regional and international level.[2] A regional association was received with little enthusiasm in Sweden. The American mission in Stockholm, following the reactions of the local press, informed the State Department that even the idea of a Northern Union encountered some resistance there. This was for fear of Finland's inability to live in peace with the Soviet Union and of Norway's expected refusal to forego any of its sovereignty, as evidenced by history.[3]

Ideas found in the two projects under discussion met with a warm welcome among exiles from countries remaining within the German orbit. It was at that time that a project was born, later known as the "Plan of Eckhard-Pélenyi", and caused quite a stir among Hungarian *émigrés*. It proposed the existence of three closely associated federal units. These were Polish-Baltic, Danubian and Balkan, concentrated around Poland, Hungary and Yugoslavia. Their special role was determined by their numerical superiority and historical distinction.[4] Discussed by all the various factions of Hungarian exiles,[5] it was particularly supported by the Democrats of Mikhail Károlyi. The

---

[1] *Sunday Times*, London 19 January 1942.
[2] Both statements for the *Sunday Times*, 8 February 1942.
[3] AN RG 95, Notter's Papers, Vol. 84. Press reports of 16, 20, 21 and 22 July 1942.
[4] Eckhard, T., "The Problem of the Middle Danubian Basin", *Hungarian Quarterly*, Spring 1944, pp. 8-12. For a discussion of this text, see Schlesinger, R., *Federalism in Central and Eastern Europe*, London 1945, pp. 432-433.
[5] For a study of Hungarian exiles during the war, see Porter, P., "Hungarian *Émigrés* in Wartime Britain", in J. Morison, *Eastern Europe and the West. Selected Papers from the 4th World Congress for Soviet and east European Studies*, New York 1992, pp. 80-97.

Advisory Committee was also interested in the plan.[1] The idea of a Danubian federation was also promoted by Archduke Otto von Habsburg, whose vision, conditioned by the perspective of the fallen monarchy, included Austria, Hungary, Bohemia, Slovakia, Transylvania and, possibly, Croatia.[2] Some hopes were also attached to a plan of grouping Danubian states around the economic significance of the river, modeled on the American project of the Tennessee Valley Authority.[3] This was also attractive to the imagination of Americans.

Carlo Sforza, former ambassador and well-known antifascist, who found a safe haven in the United States, reacted early to the first declaration of the Polish-Czechoslovak confederation and proposed his own idea of a Central European federation. He feared that constructing such a union around Poland and Czechoslovakia might lead to their dominating the region, as it had once been dominated by Austria-Hungary. In his opinion, the confederation's *raison d'être* was civilizational rather than military. Confronted with Nazi paganism and Stalinist determinism, the inhabitants of the region were more or less consciously persuaded that they could preserve for Europe its Christian values in terms of respecting the tradition of Christian philosophy, which was vital in the area, with a stronger sense of individual rights than that in the industrialized countries of the West. Similar or analogous thinking led him to the idea of a Latin Europe. "Why should not the same state that Central Europe aspired to be also the right choice for Italy, France and Spain?" A bloc of democratic Latin countries would be peaceful *ex definitione*.[4] Meanwhile, for a syndicalist Italian monthly published in the U.S., proposals for federations was the pretext to attack ideas of partial unions appearing among the exiles and reminiscent of "neo-Guelphism" by supporters of a pan-European federation based on a modified concept of the state and a socialization of the crucial parts of the economy. Otherwise, it was argued, both a smaller, Central European federation, or a broader one, would only lead to a tyranny of financiers and of heavy industry and to more wars fought for economic reasons.[5] Documents of the U.S. State Department even include a declaration by a Basque politician, Joe Antonio de Aguire,

---

[1] Romsics, I. (ed.), *Wartime American Plans for a New Hungary. Documents from the U.S. Department of State, 1942-1944*, New York 1992.
[2] *Ibid.* pp. 8-11. Cf. Kühl, J., *Föderationspläne im Donauraum und in Ostmittel-Europa*, Munich 1958.
[3] N.N., "Danube Valley Authority", *The Times*, 8 June 1942.
[4] Sforza, C., "The Future: Federation in Central Europe" in *The Totalitarian War and After*, Chicago 1941, Quoted from W. Lipgens, *op. cit.*, Vol. 2, p. 509.
[5] "Gli Stati Uniti d'Europa", *Il Proletario*, New York, No. 1, 1942, from W. Lipgens, *op. cit.*, Vol. 2, pp. 516-517.

convinced, at the time, that the future Europe should be organized into a number of federations; Iberian problems would find their resolution in a confederation of Catalonia, the Land of the Basques and Portugal.[1]

Paradoxically, in the context of these statements, it was the authors of the Polish-Czechoslovak declaration that exhibited a more constrained optimism. Although E. Beneš published an extensive article in *Foreign Affairs* suggesting that both confederations were almost a *fait accompli* and a significant step towards a consolidation of the whole of Europe,[2] this did little to change the mood of the negotiators. The end result of their several months work was a veritable mouse brought forth by a mountain. In fact, in the light of the later revelations by Raczyński, signing the declaration in its known form was a success merely on paper. As he argued to the audience of radio Free Europe – the confederation that had already began to dwindle a few months previously, breathed its last breath in early 1942. Ripka, eager to salvage as much as he could from the effort of the coordinating committee, proposed to "commit to memory" the idea itself in special talks.[3] In the context of worsening Polish-Soviet relations overshadowed by the issue of Poland's eastern border, Beneš' pro-Russian stance was an inevitable bone of contention. Formally, his position should not have caused that much of a controversy. The Czech leader's reasoning was akin to that of the Scandinavian politicians mentioned above. The federation could not come to life without the support of the great powers. Disillusioned with Western states and free from the Poles' experience, he had no qualms about seeking Russian support.

Greek and Yugoslav politicians who had signed the declaration where somewhat taken aback by their own courage and seemed to treat the declaration as a memo presented publicly to Britain and, in a way, at that great power's bidding.[4] It is now known that during talks on broadening the confederation Ninčić confided in the British ambassador his fears as to the Russian reaction to the news of the confederation. Tsouderos, informing Eden of talks with Sikorski, spoke of the latter's pushing "to create a bloc of Balkan and Central Eastern European states that would serve to counterbalance Russia" and complained that

---

[1] AN RG 59 box 84 report cited.
[2] Beneš, E., "The Organization of Postwar Europe", *Foreign Affairs*, January 1942, Vol. 20, p. 238.
[3] Raczyński, E. & Żenczykowski, T., *Od Genewy do Jałty. Rozmowy radiowe*, Warszawa,Oficyna Wyd. "Pokolenie", 1988, p. 43. Corroborated by Raczyński's report of 19 January 1942, quoted in Polish in ČDD Doc. 85.
[4] As confirmed by data of American intelligence; even these, however, are quite scant as to the course of the negotiations. OSS Foreign Nationalities Branch, INT-14 GR, report of 3 February 1942.

Sikorski "depreciated" all arguments relating to Moscow's position.[1] This harmonized with Ripka's speech broadcast by the Czech section of the BBC on 22 January, in which, praising the signed treaties, he supported Beneš' thesis of the significant role of the Soviet Union in solving Central European problems.

Sikorski's faith was undoubtedly greater. The Polish Prime Minister, convinced of British and American support, did not forsake illusions as to the possibility of Stalin's approval and believed in securing the full backing of Britain and America for a project with a significant role to be played by Lithuania as well as Czechoslovakia. As stated above, the participation of Lithuania was, for Sikorski, a matter of prestige. The realization of this postulate could be a compromise aimed at bringing the increasing pressure for a redrawing of Poland's eastern border. Talks with the Lithuanians seemed to be bringing some results. As announced by the declaration of 23 January 1942, Lithuanian exiles were ready to revert to the ancient union of the two nations.[2]

In his talk with Klimecki of 5 March 1942, Sikorski went as far as to express a hope that Lithuania's access to the federation could be presented to Russia as a condition for an agreement with the whole Central European federation. The federation could propose an alliance directed against Germany and, to guarantee Russia's demand for "friendly states at its eastern border", promise to perform adequate changes in its internal and external policy, within the democratic system.[3] The Prime Minister was kept in his good mood by Rettinger, who said that his "friend", Stanford Cripps, had reiterated support for Poland's association with Lithuania or, even, with a part of Latvia as far as the Dzwina river.[4] It was probably on this premise that the National Council proclaimed Lithuania's sovereignty on 17 March. The lack of Russia's official reaction was an optimistic sign for Sikorski as he embarked on his difficult trip to the United States.

The Polish Prime Minister's optimism was also a result of the progress he seemed to achieve on another issue, *i.e.* on preparing a treaty of cooperation between eight small occupied states, including the four bound by the declarations of federation as well as Belgium, Norway,

---

[1] See Prażmowska, A.J., *op. cit.*, pp. 140-141.
[2] Raczyński, E., *W sojuszniczym Londynie*, London 1960, pp. 132-133.
[3] Mitkiewicz, L., *op. cit.*, p. 221. The belief in Russia's acceptance was also based on the implicit postulate of limiting the access of the confederation to Lithuania, in an understanding of the Soviet need to reach to the Baltic through Latvia and Estonia.
[4] Mitkiewicz, L., note of 9 March 1941, p. 223. Morawski discussed the idea of extending the federation in Lithuania, Rumania, Hungary, and possibly Greece and Turkey, with Bogomolov on 2 March 1942. See *Documents on Polish-Soviet Relations, op. cit.*, p. 285.

Holland and Luxembourg. On 3 February, Sikorski disclosed the even earlier project to Beneš as an extension of the two confederations and, at the same time, as an attempt by the small states to secure some influence on the postwar organization of Europe. He invited the Czechoslovak leader to collaborate on a draft of a future declaration. To overcome his interlocutor's opposition, Sikorski stressed the anti-German character of the move, arguing, as related by Beneš, who loved to insert French words in his statements, that "Churchill was not exactly *enthusiasmé*, but he didn't protest; that the U.S. reaction would most certainly be favorable; and that the Soviet Union would be informed in due time".[1] Beneš must have decided that, as far as the Czech side was concerned, the "due time" had arrived and on the same day he informed Bogomolov of Sikorski's idea, expecting the former's disapproval. He was not disappointed; Bogomolov, faithful to his instructions, advised caution in undertaking bloc-like agreements and stressed that it was too early for initiatives on postwar organization of Europe.[2] Sikorski could not have known that as early on as 7 March, President Roosevelt had indicated his disapproval of Sikorski's declaration on the postwar cooperation of small countries. "I think", he wrote in his instruction to the State Department, "Sikorski should be definitely discouraged on his proposition. This is no time to talk about the postwar position of small nations and it would mean serious trouble with Russia."[3] Neither did he know that, as a consequence, the Chief of the Division of European Affairs wrote to Sumner Welles in a memo that Sikorski's

> efforts to lay at this particular moment the ground-work for a European confederation free from Soviet influence are obviously doomed to failure since the leaders of other governments in exile do not dare to take any action which might displease the Soviet Union at a time when one of the major objectives of the British Government is to keep Stalin in good humor.[4]

As we remember, the Polish premier counted much on the support of the American administration despite the meager results of his first American trip. Relying on his assumption that even if Russia should emerge victorious from the war, it would be much weakened and

---

[1] ČDD, Doc. 93, London 3 February 1942. *Beneš' note from his conversation with Sikorski*. For a Polish report of the same, see PIMS PRM 64/3 and discussion in Kisielewski, T., *op. cit.*, pp. 178-181.

[2] ČDD, Doc. 94, London 3 February 1942. *Beneš' note from his conversation with Bogomolov*. Several weeks later, in a conversation with Ripka, Bogomolov was more severe and cautioned against adhering to blocs oriented against Russia (ČDD, Doc. 96, note of 3 February 1942).

[3] FRUS 1942, Vol. III, p. 113, note 34.

[4] FRUS 1942, Vol. III. *Memorandum by acting Chief of the Division of European Affairs Atherton to the Undersecretary of State (Welles)*.

constrained to accept British-American domination, he counted on the support of President Roosevelt for Polish postulates on the Riga border treaty and a European federation or, at least, on public pressure in this respect. The Prime Minister presented his idea once again to President Roosevelt and Sumner Welles. Their reaction was very reserved. They limited themselves to saying that the idea was interesting but they exhibited no interest whatsoever.[1] Neither was it argued for by Ambassador Biddle, who briefed the State Department before Sikorski's visit – quite the contrary. No wonder, then, that after the visit, Welles thanked the Ambassador for his help in "shelving" the plans for a postwar confederation. "Now is not the time to launch movements for postwar settlements which might be offensive to the Russians", Welles assured him, who, nevertheless, allowed himself a *boutade* in the latter part of his message of 4 April 1942: "On the other hand, we are not inclined to take the position that in order to keep the Russians in a good humor we should agree at this time to all of their various projects for a postwar Europe".[2]

We thus maintain that this point of view, seen in the context of the arguments above, could have played an important part in the appearance of the documents presented.

---

[1] FRUS 1942, Vol. III, p. 130. *Memorandum of the conversation*, 25 March 1942. This is how Sumner Welles reported on his conversation: "General Sikorski then said that the Polish government believed that the peace of Europe would be best assured in the postwar period with the creation of a federation of the Eastern European States laying between the Baltic and the Aegean Seas. I said I heard of this conception which was most interesting."

[2] FRUS 1942, Vol. III, p. 137, *S. Welles to A. J. D. Biddle*.

CHAPTER 4

The Debate on Projects for a Central European Union in the Framework of the Changing International Situation (1942-1944)

The Task and the Personnel of the Advisory Committee

The State Department's attempts at understanding Soviet policy – for such was its perspective on Central Eastern Europe – consisted in intelligence and events monitoring by diplomats and in collaboration with the OSS. A significant role was played by specialized teams dealing with analyses, forecasts and the observation of the processes underway. The well-equipped teams, free from the everyday chores of bureaucracy, prepared studies helping to work out a rational decision. The first foreign policy planning teams were created within the Department, using Department officials, not unlike the Inquiry dealing with preparing the peace treaty during World War I. In contrast to its predecessor, however, as early as 1941, it invited contributions from politicians, congressmen, journalists and other eminent figures, eventually transforming itself into the Advisory Committee on Postwar Foreign Policy. The other difference consisted in its being responsible to the Secretary of State rather than to the President. It was thus headed by the Undersecretary of State Sumner Welles, while immediate management was entrusted to Leo Pasvolsky (1893-1953) economist of Russian descent, one of Hull's advisers. The original staff of State Department and Council on Foreign Relations employees was complemented, by Cordell Hull, Sumner Welles and Leo Pasvolsky, as well as Norman H. Davis, Myron C. Tylor, Isaiah Bowman, Dean Acheson, Hamilton Fish Armstrong, Adolf A. Berle, Benjamin V. Cohen, Herbert Fels, Green

H. Hackwort, Harry G. Hawkins and Anne O'Hare McCormick.[1] At its first meeting on 12 February 1942, the Advisory Committee set up six subcommittees. The more significant of these included the Political Subcommittee, the Territorial Subcommittee, the Security Subcommittee and the Economic Subcommittee.

The Advisory Committee collaborated with lesser organizations dealing with foreign policy, such as: the American Committee for International Studies headed by Edward M. Earle; the American Council of Institute of Pacific Relations with Edward C. Carter; the Carnegie Endowment for International Peace spearheaded by Philipp C. Jessup and James T. Shotwell; the Commission to Study the Organization of Just and Durable Peace with John F. Dulles; and the Commission to Study the Organization of the Peace with Claire M. Richelberger, Walter Sharp and the above-mentioned James T. Shotwell.

Their work was made easier by technical help from the Division of Special Research, a section of the State Department headed by L. Pasvolsky. It performed an executive function for the Committee, preparing memos and submitting data.[2] It was initially staffed by junior employees of the Department, but during the summer of 1942, it hired about thirty young people with recent doctorates in history, political science, economy, law and cartography. At the end of 1942, the Division had 55 employees. This number rose to 97 in mid-1943 and was at 77 when it was dismantled in 1944. The team was headed by one of the youngest career diplomats, Harley Notter (1903-1950), also serving as Secretary to the Committee (hence the title of the collection of documents as recorded in the National Archive – Notter's Papers). His right-hand man and head of the research group working on territorial issues was Philip E. Mosley (1905-1972), a Harvard graduate and specialist in the history of Central Europe. Despite his youth, he had already spent three years in the Soviet Union and the Balkans. Similarly to Bearle, he exhibited a good understanding and knowledge of Balkan issues. Other Committee members dealing with Central Eastern Europe included Harry N. Howard, C. Campbelle, Cyrile E. Black and Thomas F. Power, who all expressed their interest in that region of Europe in various ways after the war.

All in all, the Advisory Committee was a well-informed resource for American diplomacy, with some influence (initially insignificant) over

---

[1] More extensively presented in Mania, A., *Studia z dziejów stosunków amerykańsko-radzieckich w okresie II wojny światowej*, ZNUJ. Prace z nauk politycznych, z. 38, Cracow 1989, p. 10.

[2] More on the same subject in Notter, H.A., *Postwar Foreign Policy Preparation 1939-1945*, Washington D.C. 1949.

President F. D. Roosevelt via the intermediary of Secretary of State Cordell Hull and his Deputy S. Welles Hull.[1]

The Political Subcommittee, whose proceedings on the idea of a Mid-European Union constitute the content of this collection, was directed by Hull or Welles. This was a body formulating opinions on foreign policy, including collective security organizations and specifically on Soviet-American relations. Another significant team, the Territorial Subcommittee, also frequently cited here, was charged with producing maps of regions and state borders, taking into account the uncertain frontiers in unstable regions of the world, especially those of Europe, torn with ethnic conflicts and border revisions. Resolving those would eliminate or decrease pre-war tension.

The Subcommittee was headed by Isaiah Bowman (1878-1950), a major figure of the Advisory Committee, former Inquiry member, who, as President of the National Geographic Society in between the wars traveled the world before settling down as Professor of Geography at Johns Hopkins University.

The Advisory Committee's other major figure, Hamilton Fish Armstrong (1893-1973), member of the two Subcommittees mentioned above, was the editor of *Foreign Affairs*, a semi-official publication of the State Department. His position gave him numerous contacts and a good knowledge of Central Eastern Europe. As military attaché in Belgrade (1918-1922), he met Józef Piłsudski, Edouard Beneš, Tomaš Masaryk, Albert Apponyi, Iuliu Maniu, Nicolae Titulescu and Nikola Pašić. The honors awarded to him by those countries suggest that he had a deep understanding of the region's problems.[2]

Active members of the Committee associated with the State Department included Sumner Welles (1892-1961), well versed in European issues and Adolph A. Berle (1895-1971), Professor of History and Law at Harvard and one of the youngest members of the 1919 peace delegation at Paris, dealing with Russia and Northern Europe. Roosevelt's advisor since 1932, he was the contact person with political *émigrés* from Central and Eastern Europe. Unlike Armstrong, who showed much understanding for the countries of the former Little Entente, Berle exhibited a certain sympathy for its opponents – the Hungarians and Austrians. There are signs of this sympathy in these

---

[1] A. Mania, an eminent expert on that period claims that the opinions of the Advisory Committee were taken into account by Roosevelt only from the end of 1943, Mania, A., *op. cit.*

[2] Armstrong, H. F., *Peace and Counter-peace. From Wilson to Hitler. Memoirs of Hamilton Fish Armstrong*, New York 1971.

documents in Berle's treatment of plans by Eckhardt, Pelenyi or Otto von Habsburg.

Among other leading figures encountered while reading the proceedings of the Advisory Committee it is worth mentioning – Anne O'Hare McCormick (1882-1954), a *New York Times* specialist in foreign affairs and the first woman journalist to win the Pulitzer Prize. Herbert Feis, then the economic consultant of the State Department, made a name for himself after the war, as a historian of World War II and the Cold War.

Changes in the organization of the State Department on 22 November 1943 maintained the Advisory Committee's supervision over three separate divisions: the *Division of Economic Studies* was to be run by L. D. Stinebowlee; the *Division of Political Studies* with H. A. Notter; and the *Committee on Special Studies*. Further transformations in January 1944 led to the creation of a *Committee on Postwar Program* under the new Undersecretary E. Stettinius Jr., with Pasvolsky as the executive head of the Committee. The Committee initiated and supervised studies in territorial (European, Far Eastern) and topical divisions, especially those in the Office of Special Political Affairs and two of its divisions, that of International Security and Organization under Notter and that of Territorial Studies with P. Mosely.

The Committee's Work and Official American Policy Towards Central Eastern Europe

The working system of these teams resulted in studies on various subjects, including border issues, Soviet government and the situation in Central Eastern Europe. These, apart from becoming the premises for executive decisions, are a testimony, a summary, of American knowledge of the war objectives of all its participants.

At the same time, there was a growing sense among the Committee members as of the usefulness of their work. It was of tremendous importance that the head of the State Department should be given accurate information – as argued by Bowman, quoting Wilson's famous remark while leaving for the Paris Peace Conference: "Tell me what's right and I'll fight for it – give me a guaranteed position".

It is not our task to analyze the presented documents in detail. We leave that pleasure to the reader. All we wish to do is to emphasize a number of interesting points.

What is striking in the work of the Committee is its great interest in Hungarian and Austrian plans, quite out of proportion to any public discussion, as these ideas did not influence those countries' policy during the war. Our own interpretation is that this was yet another manifestation of the nostalgia, visible already between the wars, for the Austro-Hungarian Empire as an economic and political order, as the only viable historical solution. Also acceptable, however, is the argument that the impact of Hungarian exiles on the American political scene was stronger than it is usually thought. The idea of Danubian Europe found its staunchest supporter in Bowman.

We are also of the opinion that, wherever it was possible to disregard the political reality of the time, Sikorski's plan was preferred as one that was less biased to the organizing country in view of the broad scope of the projected union. The more countries participated in the union, the lessen Poland's hegemony, a very real fear for the Czechs. Of all the Committee's members, Armstrong seemed to be the most faithful follower of this vision.

Another issue is the relationship between economic and political integration. The dominating feeling was that political issues were indivisible from economic ones, but the former are more difficult to find. Probably due to the experience with the League of Nations ("the dream that experience destroyed"), the Committee showed little faith in hopes for a new international organization, despite official American policy.

The preference for a broader union we observe in Armstrong's position was accompanied by the belief that the organization should be realized in the strongest way possible and be based on the economy. This reasoning was based on the idea that an extended and internally strong union would have a better chance of surviving and that it would be more difficult to control by a foreign power. "The formation of a single union would be desirable since it would prevent the smaller groups from tying up with respective great powers", was also said by Bowman himself (Doc. 2). This was also an answer to the recurring issue of American interests in postwar Europe. If we are right about the allusions to the role of Austria-Hungary; the fears of a revival of nationalism after the war; and the belief that these countries could not be expected to establish such an arrangement by themselves – this suggests the U.S. or (to a lesser extent) an international organization would be the organizer of those countries.[1] The idea was even born that the U.S. as the most powerful member of the United Nations could supersede Germany's economic position in the region – on condition that they invested enough to increase imports.

It seems, however, that the participants in the debates were fearful of the boldness of such ideas and preferred to retreat behind clichés on

---

[1] Taylor remarks in Doc. 5 that "it is assumed in various discussions that U.S. impose on the region the various political features".

sovereignty or politicians' self-realization, who "realize that their nations must unite in order to exist". They also had a tendency to persuade themselves that abandoning these countries as a concession to Russia would not necessarily mean giving them up to communism. This was concealed by statements to the effect that a chance should be given "to the individual state to seize advantages for itself". In this respect, conforming with Roosevelt's official Russian policy became, for many participants, wishful thinking. The belief that Russia would not follow the path of ideological warfare and imperialism led to the belief a Central European federation would be accepted by that power. After all, such a buffer zone would be a good market for Russian goods and a source of Soviet supplies.

From this point of view, the ideal solution would be: toleration from Russia; from Britain and the United States active and detailed supervision; and perhaps even control over the foundation of the federation and then careful nursing (Doc. 11).

On the other hand, paradoxically, this belief, combined with the knowledge that there were few American interests in the region, led to acceptance of the role of the Soviet Union as the organizer of those countries. Obviously, changes at the front and in Russia's position were not without impact on the course of the Committee. Did the recurring hesitation (manifest, for example, in the Committee's analyses of increasingly nationalist tones in Soviet propaganda) change in any way other related assumptions and if so, to what extent? And how did that impact the formulation (and the understanding) of peacetime as well as wartime goals? Hopefully an analysis of the views of Committee members will help to answer these questions. For a better insight into the two years' activity of the Committee, it is necessary to survey the fate of the idea of a Mid-European Federation in those years in a broader context.

CHAPTER 5

Consequences for Small Nations of the Growing Empathy of the Powers Towards their Soviet Ally

"To Keep the Russians in Good Humor"

Moscow's reluctance to take a clear position on the issue proved to be highly pragmatic. On the one hand, Russia allowed further work on plans and sounded out the Allies' position on the subject; on the other, it impeded the plans by hinting at possible disagreement. This led to a search for solutions acceptable to the Russians. The propaganda contained in politicians' declarations of 1942 and in the following years is highly instructive in this respect. It is easy to observe a general discrepancy. On the one hand, there was a growing empathy on the part of Russia's allies for its escalating demands, reinforced by a gentlemanly impulse to reward its endeavors in the war. Since signing its treaty with the U.S.S.R., Britain was leaning towards a public understanding of Soviet interests. As early as May 1942, Churchill proclaimed the idea of the World Council, directed by the Great Three, which left little hope for small nations' sovereign existence. The idea of a ruling body for postwar Europe with Russia as an equal partner found an echo in the British press. E. H. Carr wrote about in at length in his famous *Conditions of Peace* of 1942, proposing the creation of a European Planning Authority. Similarly, H. P. Whidden saw the need for a controlling mechanism that should be devised by the Allies and strengthened with centralist institutions that had already proved their viability in the German "New Order".[1]

At the same time, the public understood the spirit of the alliance with Russia from the very beginning, even if it did not analyze the content of the treaty. Treating the alliance as a reconstruction of the system of collective security (jointly with the Atlantic Charter, of which the treaty with Russia was to become merely a new interpretation) and loath to

---

[1] Whidden Jr., H. P., "As Britain sees the Postwar World", *Foreign Policy Reports*, 15 October 1942.

repeat the experience of the 1920s and 1930s with "their creation of a pasteboard structure of small states unable to defend themselves",[1] people saw a federation as an ideal solution but were increasingly ready to accept one that would be more realistic – one that answered Russian interests in the region.

> Taking into account the existing conflict between Germany and Russia, it is no longer possible to envisage an intermediary zone in that part of Europe. The countries of the region must choose. And there is no doubt as to the nature of the choice. If they wish to avoid a conflict with Germany, they have to remain in good relations, or even in a semi-alliance, with Russia.[2]

Also, the public, together with a number of politicians, was ready to accept even more. Assuming that the future peace must be conditioned in such a way that "Germany, irrespective of their new form of government, be forever unable to begin another war", the British rejected the traditional balance of powers, up to the summer of 1941, preferring long-term cooperation with Moscow to a strong German state serving to balance France and Russia on the Continent.[3]

In this situation, representatives of small states nourished growing fears as to their ability to govern their own fate. They observed the position of the great powers and had a growing realization that, once again, it was the great powers' own will that would decide the final shape of the postwar world. This did nothing to hamper the proliferation of integrative plans. What the two positions had in common was an escape from the real world into idealism, in a belief that the postwar order would be based on better rules than the one that had brought the cruel war. Yet as Moscow's official stance towards federation in general and a Central European one in particular, was unknown until 1943 and that of the other Allies was still not negated publicly, more non-government plans for a federal solution of the European problem kept on appearing, oscillating between hope and fear – with more of the latter. As Trygve Lie later confessed in a conversation with a Belgian Ambassador, Russia's resistance to confederation was very clear to its northern neighbors. As a consequence, the Norwegian Information Bureau declared in July 1942 that Norway had abandoned plans for a defensive bloc of Scandinavian states which had been to include, in previous arrangements, Norway, Sweden, Denmark and Finland. Norway proposed instead cooperation with the great powers and a

---

[1] Sir Bernard Pares, "The Russian Alliance", *Contemporary Review*, London, September 1942, p. 18.
[2] N.N. (Editorial), *The Baltic States, Nineteenth Century and After*, May 1942, p. 4.
[3] Viscount, S., "Britain, Russia and the World", *Contemporary Review*, London, August 1942, p. 56.

reborn, strong League of Nations. The statement contained no mention of federation – an eloquent silence, as the Belgian diplomat knew of an article that had appeared only a week previously in the Norwegian press, criticizing the work of Petander. Its author, G. Sannes, maintained that federation would be tantamount to reverting to neutrality, whose imperfection had already been amply shown in the war.[1] The Swedes also changed their tone somewhat and, as the Russians pressed forward, declared that they were willing to forsake neutrality in return for serving as an intermediary between the Atlantic powers and the Soviet Union.[2]

Some fears also appeared among exiles from the satellites of the Third Reich. V. Tilea, former Rumanian Ambassador in London, expressed these in *The Contemporary Review*, expressing his expectations of a denial of rumors spread by German propaganda that Britain and the U.S. had decided to abandon Central Europe to Russian influence.[3]

Tilea wondered if, in the changing situation, the provisions of the Atlantic Charter that its signatories "do not seek territorial expansion" and "will not agree to any territorial changes that would not correspond to freely expressed wishes of nations", referred to the situation of 1939 or of 1941, in the light of the English-Russian treaty which was a matter of crucial significance of the Finns, Poles, Balts and the Balkan nations.[4] A silent acceptance of the territorial status quo made the treaty "an ambiguous document, full of excuses and loopholes".

According to the Rumanian diplomat, if Britain and America truly wanted to take a clear position and attract the support of those countries for active participation in resistance movements, they should proclaim, after Wilson's Fourteen Points, a clear program, which would herald the realization of an idea that had been around for half a century – a Central Eastern European federation. The states of the Great Coalition should guarantee that this federation, alongside possible Atlantic and Scandina-

---

[1] AMAE(b), Vol. 11775, London, 24 July 1942, 3, No, 54/23. Confidential. *L. Nemry, Chargé d'affaires at the Norwegian Government to P.-H. Spaak.* W. M. de Morgenstierne spoke in the same vein in the U.S. a year later; Norway's Reply to Federation, Washington Post, 13 June 1943. Quoted from Van der Straten Ponthoz to P.-H. Spaak, report from Washington, 15 April 1943.

[2] *Ibid.*, 3 NI 70/21. London, 7 September 1943. Quoted from Van der Straten Ponthoz to P.-H. Spaak, report from Washington, 15 April 1943.

[3] After the German attack on the Soviet Union, *The Times* of 1 August 1941 suggested a division of the spheres of influence. A similar proposal appeared in *The Economist* of 16 August. The latter wondered if the bloc of Slavic countries between the Baltic and the Balkans should be uniform and strong. The answer was: "It certainly should from an English point of view; should it really be that from the point of view of Russia?" For *The Economist*, the absorption of Baltic states by Russia was a foregone conclusion.

[4] Tilea, V. V., op. cit., p. 4.

vian unions, would be accepted as a member of a greater, worldwide structure of postwar cooperation.[1] The acceptance of a federation could thus become a significant weapon for the Allies in the war; the Atlantic Charter extended with that aim of the war could prove itself to be a true Magna Carta of nations. Instead of the expected commitment, the supporters of the federation had to cope with unofficial statements like the *New York Times* article on the anniversary of the Atlantic Charter. The article proposed the formation of "federal groups" as an alternative to the inescapable limitation of small states' sovereignty after the war.[2]

As a side-effect of the widespread debate of the first two years of the war, discussion on the integration of Western states also became more active. In the spring of 1942, the idea of a close cooperation between Belgium, Holland and Luxembourg appeared to get limited support from Britain;[3] its lack of enthusiasm was due to the growing displeasure at all integrative ideas on the part of the Russian ally. As Moscow's position raised fears in the Western governments, they were stimulated to seek defense mechanisms. A combination of hopes and fears, including the fear of Russia, worked towards the development of integrative ideas. In a sense, Spaak was right when he said that it was Stalin who had earned the title of the father of European unity.[4] Thus 1942 marked a *caesura* in the policy of Britain and America; a *caesura* triggered by the actual and projected position of Stalin. Yet some politicians maintained the powers' unclear stance for quite a long time. On 21 October 1942, Anthony Eden, responded to G. Mander's question on whether the idea of federation or confederation did not stand in conflict with the Atlantic Charter: "His Majesty's Government greets with approval and is ready to support all initiatives of small states to group into broader, yet compatible associations".[5] He spoke in the same vein on 16 December, in answer to another question from the Polish-Czechoslovak confederation.[6] It later appeared that the Secretary of the American Embassy had learned from a high-ranking official in the Foreign Office responsible for Soviet and Eastern European matters that when Eden had been to Moscow in the winter 1942 and when Molotov had visited London in the spring of 1942 (May-June), this subject had

---

[1] Tilea, V. V., *op. cit.*, p. 7.
[2] *New York Times* 16 August 1942: We no longer believe that small nations could be sovereign. For an interesting analysis of the fates of the Atlantic Charter, see Stroński, S., *The Atlantic Charter. No territorial guarantees to aggressors. No dictatorships*, London 1944.
[3] FO 371/39323.
[4] Heather, D., *The Idea of European Union*, London 1992, p. 150.
[5] *The Times*, 22 October 1942.
[6] *House of Commons Debates*, Vol. 385, No. 16, 16 December 1942.

been broached by the British. On both occasions, the Soviet officials shied away from any discussion by saying that they feared that such a federation would be aimed not against Germany but the Soviet Union. They maintained this position, although the British wanted to know if the idea was to be encouraged or dropped.[1] This probably explains Churchill's presentation, on 21 March 1943, of the idea of a European Council, often seen in literature as the first indication of a unified Europe. (The European Council founded in 1949 clearly related to that idea). Within the Council, whose the subordinates were to include a Supreme Tribunal to settle disputes between members, he saw a place for small states grouped in confederations, which would be equal partners to the great powers. Churchill envisaged the following unions: Scandinavian, Danubian and Balkan;[2] he probably avoided mentioning a Central European one with Poland probably in order not to alienate the Russians.

Moscow Publicly Expresses its Disdain for Federative Projects

Thus, for the well-informed, the hope for Stalin's acceptance of a system of federations in Central Eastern Europe dwindled in the spring months of 1942. Other illusions lasted until 1943 and the Moscow Conference (19-30 October 1943). When Eden, following his instructions, tried to sound Russia's position on the federative idea, Molotov opposed the project with the full support of the American Secretary of State, Cordell Hull. Moscow no longer felt the need to conceal its plans towards its western neighbors. R. van de Kerchove d'Hallebast, Belgian Ambassador in the U.S.S.R., showed his perceptiveness in a telegram of 3 August, where he summarized an article from *Voyna i Rabochiy Klas*, entitled "What is behind the idea of a Central European Federation?" The semi-official organ of the Soviet government, also published in English, maintained that Poles were trying to go through with their territorial plans by interfering with the internal affairs of other states. The plan of the federation was described as an anti-Semitic attempt to prevent the return of the Jews from East and West. The author of the report found an analogy here with the Soviet demand to Finland to forego plans for a union with Sweden, which had pushed them into an alliance with Germany. The Belgian diplomat concluded: "This time the

---

[1] *Chargé d'affaires Matthews to the Secretary of State*, London, 17 February 1943. FRUS 1943, Vol. III, p. 335.
[2] Churchill, W.L.S., *The Second World War*, Vol. 4, *The Hinge of Fate*, Boston 1950, p. 217. The full text is in the *New York Times* of 22 March 1943, p. 4

veto concerns the whole of Europe".[1] Two months later, the same periodical, carefully studied in diplomatic centers in Moscow, used the pen of one K. Demidov to attack the Polish plans in a review of a study by T. Lutosławski, "Central Union", published under the name of G. Harrison and P. Jordan.[2] The idea of a union of countries between the three seas surrounding Poland presented there, a clear manifestation of the Jagiellonian idea, was easy prey indeed. Demidov saw the union as a camouflage for "a very old never-never land Poland from sea to sea, that would be realized by an annexation of Estonia, Lithuania and Latvia, to say nothing of parts of Ukraine and Belarus". Far from concealing his disgust with that "imperialist mania, the eternal disease of Polish chauvinists", he suggests that politicians suffering from it should be treated for insanity with cold showers. It is obvious that the same cold shower was to cool British politicians before their visit to Moscow for the conference.[3]

Another article in the same paper became even better known. The author of "On the Results of Moscow Conference", of 1 November 1943, as quoted by Harriman, wrote: "It is likewise clear that under the guise of federations it is proposed to revive the policy of the notorious *cordon sanitaire* directed against the Soviet Union".[4] In his later messages, the American diplomat informed that the Soviet opposition to federation in Eastern Europe was "bluntly" stated by *Izvestia*: an article in the 18 November 1943 edition, "On the Question of Federations of Small States in Europe", opposed the views presented in the *New Statesman* of 10 November and *The Economist* of 11 November. The two weeklies had drawn their own conclusions from Austria's declaration at the Moscow Conference that Russia is not adverse to all groupings of Central and Eastern European states. The Russian paper described this as "a figment of the authors' imagination", stressing that people should consider the real situation and not abstract projects. "The small states", it argued, "will have time, in the fluid period after the war, to adapt themselves to the new situation created as a result of the war".

---

[1] DDB, Vol. 1, Doc. 159. *Van de Kerchove d'Hallebast to Foreign Ministry, Kuybishev*, 2 August 1943. A summary of the same article was also sent by Roger Garreau, the representative of the Free French at Kuybishev, to the French Committee for National Liberation at Algiers.

[2] The study was published twice: in London in 1943, and then, signed by P. Jordan alone under a slightly modified title, *Central Union of Europe*, in New York in 1944. Its anti-Russian content, including ironic statements such as "a masquerade of a legal act, supported by a popular ballot under a foreign occupation", had little to do with the Polish diplomacy of the time.

[3] Demidov, K., "Polish Lords at Bedlam", *Voyna i Rabochiy Klas*, 15 September 1943, from a French translation, AMAE(b), Vol. 17775.

[4] Quoted from FRUS 1943, note 18, p. 592.

It then added that it would be premature to speak of any artificial corporations of small states and that access to a federation, which necessarily entails forsaking some of each nation's sovereignty, could only be done at the express wish of the nation as a whole.

Besides, as the Belgian Ambassador in Moscow stressed in his account of the article, it used a singular argument, one that had not been employed before: it would be unjust to treat the small satellite states of the Third Reich, who share the Nazis' responsibility for their crimes, as equals to other members of federations.[1] The *New York Times* report from the Moscow Conference contains a characteristic statement by Sulzberger that Russia is opposed to a *cordon sanitaire* which in reality meant an Eastern European Federation dominated by Poles.[2] Relatively early, too, Beneš abandoned the idea of a Central European federation. On 12 November 1943, he said at a meeting of the Czechoslovak State Council: "The idea of a federation of small states in Central Europe has been almost universally seen, from the very beginning, as a basis for peace in postwar Europe. However, the unclear international situation does not allow the Czechoslovak government to decide on the final solutions and to take the final decision before the end of the war."[3] A year later, in a conversation with Harriman in December 1943, the Czech politician, then in Moscow to sign the Czechoslovak-Soviet treaty of 12 December 1943,[4] said that he considered Stalin's aversion to the formation of confederations at that time as reasonable. He did not believe, however, that the Soviet Government would object to the subject being considered at an appropriate time, although Beneš himself thought the importance of confederations was being overemphasized. He also expressed his belief that the Russians would not foster a Communist revolution in Czechoslovakia or in any other European country.[5]

---

[1] FRUS 1943, Vol. III, pp. 600-604. Moscow, 22 October 1943, *Harriman to Secretary of State*; DDB, Vol. 1, Doc. 100. Moscow, 20 November 1943, *D.R. van de Kerchove d'Hallebast to P.-H. Spaak.*

[2] FRUS 1943, Vol. III, p. 607.

[3] Quoted from Kowalski, W.T., *Walka dyplomatyczna o miejsce Polski w Europie*, Warsaw 1979, p. 282.

[4] Beneš' statements that he tried to seek a compromise between the two treaties to save the Polish-Czechoslovak confederation are unclear. See Beneš, E., *Czechoslovak Policy for Victory and Peace*, London 1944, p. 25.

[5] FRUS 1953, *doc. cit.*

Reaction of the Small States to the Russian Attitude

The disclosure of the Soviet position on the federation of small nations did not stop the profusion of federative projects. The more interesting studies of the period include a document drafted in London in mid-1943 under the title of the Central and South Eastern European Union, as precise in its definition of the constitution of the future union as the Constitution Act of the Polish-Czechoslovak confederation. Its authors were members of the Danubian Club, selected from among the South Eastern Committee of the Fabian Society: left-wing representatives of exiles from Albania, Austria, Bulgaria, Czechoslovakia, Greece, Poland, Rumania, Hungary and Yugoslavia as well as England.[1] The plan minutely described the federative rules for the new Union and related them to the Atlantic Charter and the British-Soviet treaty, from which it inferred the need for the Union's good relations with its Eastern neighbor and democratic government for its member states. This also explains the absence of Baltic states in the project. The main office of the Union was to consist of two Houses. The first, called the Union Council, was to consist of representatives chosen in a direct election, with a quota for each member country. The second, the States' Council, was to defend the rights of the member states, much like the American Senate. Its participants would be appointed by the governments of the particular countries. The Government and its Prime Minister would be elected by the first House and accountable to both. The President of the Union would be appointed from each member state in turn. Lack of space here does not allow a detailed analysis of the project. It should be added, however, that the chapter on civil rights and freedom was overtly extended. Also noteworthy were the proposals for the Union's armed forces, as they show the deeper aims of the project's authors. The Union was to produce one common army, which could later become part of the European army, or any broader formation used to ensure collective security.[2]

Neither was the idea of confederation abandoned by the Czechs. Hubert Ripka, a key supporters of the Polish-Czechoslovak treaty was one of the faithful. At that time, in the changed situation, he saw a broader federation of small states as the solution not only in the context of a confederated Europe, but also in that of friendly cooperation with the Soviet Union. "At the same time, of course", adds the Minister of State of the Czechoslovak Government, "there must be no question of any Protectorate of the Soviet Union over these nations; such endeavors

---

[1] The Club was headed at that time by Phillips Price. Its members included Victor E. Budenau, Adam Ciołkosz, Milan Gavrilović, Jan Kuncewicz and František Littna.
[2] For the text of the project, see Gross, F., *op. cit.*, Doc. 13, pp. 117-138.

would of necessity encounter resistance not only in these nations but also in the rest of Europe and the world".[1]

Advocates of federation from New Europe backed Ripka by emphasizing the defensive character of the federation of small states. It was to be based on free access and constitute, in the words of F. Gross, "a bridge between the U.S.S.R. and the rest of Europe",[2] which guaranteed neither the will nor the power for aggression against Russia. Other publicists of New Europe wrote in much the same spirit, reminding readers that wars were started not by small states but by great powers, intent on conquest. As an example, Poland never allowed itself to be attracted by Hitler's anti-Soviet plans before the war. The same cannot be said of the Soviet Union, whose armies entered Polish territory on 17 September 1939.

The reaction of the small nations of Western Europe to Russian obstructions led to a correction of previous plans. Representatives of Belgium, Holland and Luxembourg worked on closer economic ties between their countries. Statements by Joseph Bech, Fernand Demany, P.-H. Spaak referred to Churchill's idea of a Council of Europe and attempted to base the contacts between their countries on federation and a customs union[3] and led to a Dutch-Belgian monetary treaty in October 1943, which confirmed aspirations to an even closer union. As early as May that year, it was called a model for international economic cooperation on a much broader scale.[4]

Holland's ambassador in Washington, Loudon, advanced the idea of regional groups at the expense of confederation. In his opinion, confederation with British and Russian participation ceased to be an option for Europe. Without the two great powers, confederation would be tantamount to German hegemony.[5] He proposed instead his old idea of an Atlantic Bloc, in which he was supported by the Foreign Minister, Eelco N. Van Kleffens. The idea was in turn close to that of the South

---

[1] H. Ripka. "No German Dominated Federation, News Flashes from Czechoslovakia, Czechoslovak National Council of America", Release No. 200, Chicago, August 1943. See also Ripka, H., *Small and Great Nations: The Conditions for a New International Organization. Czechoslovak Ministry of Foreign Affairs*, London 1944, p. 51.

[2] Gross, F., *op. cit.*, p. 81.

[3] See also Grosbois, T. (ed.), *L'idée européenne en temps de guerre*, Louvain-la-Neuve 1994, Docs. 12-13, 19-20, 24.

[4] *Ibid.*, London, 16 May 1944. L. Nemry, Ambassador to the Government of Holland, to P.-H. Spaak.

[5] *Ibid.*, Washington, 20 April 1943, *van der Straten Ponthoz to P.-H. Spaak*; appendix: "Address delivered before the National Defense Meeting of the Daughters of the American Revolution", Cincinnati 17 April 1943.

African Marshall Jan C. Smuts.[1] This version was to be based on a strong Anglo-American union, while the Western Bloc, including France, Belgium and Holland, aimed at preventing a reemergence of Germany. This powerful bloc, added Kleffens modestly, should have its counterpart in the strong position of Russia in Eastern Europe, where a similar measure was a necessary condition for security.[2]

The debates on the Western Bloc in the Western European press in the final period of the war, with their total rejection of any discussion on the integration of the whole of Europe or of a Central European federation, were an appendix to the diplomacy of the Great Three. Modifying their proposals at the conferences in Teheran and Yalta, the great powers were pushing towards furthering their own interests by an inescapable division of Europe. Puppet governments installed by the Russians in Soviet-liberated territories destroyed all hope for a return of democracy there. The ideas of cooperation within a Central European federation or confederation remained theoretical, preserved and developed by political *émigrés*. Thus, the date when the State Department's Advisory Committee discontinued its discussion on the subject is significant.

---

[1] *New York Times*, 29 December 1943, Dutch envisage Anglo-American Lines. Kleffens makes it conditional.

[2] FO 371, Vol. 39325. *Text of radio speech by the Minister of Foreign Affairs of Holland, Dr. E. N. Van Kleffens*, 28 December 1943.

Part II

Documents

1

DEPARTMENT OF STATE
Advisory Committee
Strictly Confidential
Minutes P – 10
May 9, 1942

Typescript, original
AN Notter File, box 55

[DANUBIAN FEDERATION[1]]

Present:
Mr. Welles, presiding
Mr. Hamilton Fish Armstrong
Mr. Ray Atherton
Mr. Isaiah Bowman
Mr. Benjamin V. Cohen
Mr. Norman H. Davis
Mrs. Anne O'Hare McCormick
Mr. Leo Pasvolsky
Mr. Paul Daniels
Mr. Paul B. Taylor, Secretary

Mr. Welles, in opening the meeting at 11:10 a.m., stated that, as agreed upon at the last meeting, the discussion would deal with a potential *Danubian federation* and with its component parts.

He then asked Mr. Pasvolsky to explain a map, prepared by the Office of the Geographer in collaboration with the Division of Special Research,[2] of the territories of the Austro-Hungarian Empire, the boundaries of the postwar Succession States being superimposed. Mr. Pasvolsky pointed out on the map the changes in political status which took place in respect of each part of the Dual Monarchy. Mr. Welles said that this explanation gave a very clear picture of the area.

He suggested that in approaching the problem of the morning, we might leave Poland out of consideration and attack the problem principally from the political point of view, with its economic aspects also considered, of the utility

---

[1] Document previously published by Romsic, I., *op. cit.*, pp. 57-71.
[2] An agency of the Advisory Committee, headed by L. Pasvolsky and active since 1 November 1941.

of a Danubian federation *per se*. We might then consider the enlargement of the arrangement to include Poland and possibly Austria.[1] He supposed that the initial problem is to determine whether there is anything of value in the conception of the reconstitution of Austria-Hungary. He then asked Mr. Armstrong for a statement of his views on this subject.

Mr. Armstrong asked whether the question referred solely to a Habsburg restoration or whether any type of government of the area might be considered. He himself did not believe in the practicability of a Habsburg restoration. He admitted that such a *régime* might be imposed, but he thought this would be going back to something which it had been necessary to destroy at the end of the last war – it would be a re-creation of a principal factor in creating the last war. He would not necessarily favor a *veto* of the restoration of a Habsburg (presumably Otto)[2] in one of his own countries, but he would point out that such a *veto* would not necessarily come from us but rather from within the countries in which the restoration was to take place. The *sine qua non* of a restoration would be social reforms in Hungary (*i.e.* land reform) and political reforms along democratic lines in both Hungary and Austria.

Mr. Welles then inquired the opinion of the other members concerning the general nature of a possible Danubian federation. Was it conceived as purely economic, or as also political in nature? Mr. Davis expressed his feeling that such a federation ought at the beginning to be purely economic. Such a union would help a broader kind of political unity to develop without its being forced. It would give time and incentive to work on the development of more complete union. Mrs. McCormick inquired whether the union should not also be political: even the possession of purely economic powers would force the federation to assume political functions. Mr. Davis agreed that if the Danubian countries were tied together economically, they would surely have to stand together politically. He thought that they might have to have some close political union, but he questioned whether one should try to go so far at first. He thought it more feasible to think of a confederation than of a federation.

Mr. Armstrong pointed out that here, as in the discussion on Germany,[3] the question arises whether any historical precedents exist for federation in which the countries devolve from unity to federation – in which a united country becomes a member of or is broken up into a federation. Here, of course, one could not speak of, (*sic*) a direct transition from a unitary state to a federation. Rather, this development would take place with a twenty-year period in between. Mr. Welles said he could think of no such precedent and asked whether Mr. Bowman had any in mind. Mr. Bowman replied that while there were a few cases chiefly in Latin America, some of these existed chiefly on paper, were of short duration and were in any case not applicable to the present

---

[1] A working discussion. None of the *emigrés'* visions of the Danubian Federation proposed both Poland and Austria as its members.

[2] Such ideas were raised by Austrian *émigrés* and Horthy's followers in Hungary. See Views of Austrian Exiles on the Future of Europe, DHEI, Vol. 2, pp. 629-653. For Otto von Habsburg's views see Romsic, I., *op. cit.*, p. 9

[3] Minutes of the Committee on Germany have been omitted.

Documents

problem. Mrs. McCormick added that there probably have been a few modern examples, but that they have been short. She pointed out, however, that strong support for a Danubian federation has existed for some time in the Danubian area itself and that a number of specific proposals for such a federation have been made. Mr. Welles suggested that the Central American Union[1] would be a case in point. The parallel was, however, not exact and he could think of none in Europe. Mr. Armstrong pointed out that most federations were agglomerations of individual states, but that here the process would be reversed: a devolution from unity to a looser organization.

Mr. Davis said that Dr. Beneš[2] was the main factor in keeping the Danubian countries from getting together at the end of the last war. Each of the Succession States followed a highly protectionist and competitive policy toward the others. Hungary, for example, succeeded in establishing an industry in competition with that of Czechoslovakia and then granted it high tariff protection. All of the leaders in that area realized that they should get together politically, but they found themselves unable to do it economically. Mr. Armstrong queried whether Mr. Davis' statement concerning Dr. Beneš applied to the period immediately after the Peace Conference.[3] He himself thought that the chief problem was that the leaders in all these countries felt themselves on the skids and were unable to act. Mr. Davis recalled that in 1930 and 1931 there was a strong feeling in the Danubian area that a union was necessary[4] and that they were even talking about having someone come in as a director. Each leader, however, was afraid to tackle it himself. Mrs. McCormick pointed out that the Little Entente was the chief factor in preventing the creation of such a union.

---

[1] What Welles possibly had in mind was the League of American Nations, which was to be founded at the instigation of Uruguay's President, B. Brumm in April 1920, when it was already known that the U.S. would not join the League of Nations. This idea was deliberated on a number of occasions, including the Fifth International American Conference, Santiago de Chile, 1923. It came to nothing due to the opposition of the U.S. A regional Organization of Central American States was founded as late as in 1951.

[2] Edvard Beneš (1884-1948), Czechoslovakian politician, Minister of Foreign Affairs (1918-1935), later President of the Republic (1935-1938) and Prime Minister of the Czech government-in-exile (1941-1945), he then returned to his country and served as President until the Communist coup of 1948.

[3] The information is imprecise. N. H. Davis probably has in mind the early idea of a Danubian Confederation, promoted by France mainly to secure Austria's and Hungary's endorsement of the peace treaties. Beneš opposed the plan. The author might be alluding to the Little Entente Beneš was organizing that had nothing in common with confederation projects. Cf. Laptos, J., "Kształtowanie się francuskiej koncepcji konfederacji naddunajskiej w latach 1918-1920" in *Studia Polono-Danubiana et Balcanica*, Vol. IV/1991, Prace Historyczne z. 97 ZNUJ.

[4] A possible reference to the reaction to Briand's proposal for a United States of Europe, promoted at the League of Nations as the so-called "constructive plan" of A. François-Poncet of 1931, followed a year later by the Tardieu Plan. Cf. Kühl, J., *op. cit.*, p. 44 and *passim*.

Mr. Atherton said that Lord Lothian[1] had been one of the strongest advocates of a federation in Central Europe and that he based his idea upon the British Empire scheme. Mr. Welles agreed and then referred to the plans of Prime Minister Sikorski[2] and of Mr. Tibor Eckhardt.[3] Sikorski's idea,[4] he said, is one of complete economic federation and of incipient political federation among the Baltic states, Poland, Czechoslovakia, Hungary, Rumania and Yugoslavia. The Eckhardt plan was similar but purely economic, as was categorically stated by Eckhardt. His plan, however, embraced two federations: the first to consist of Poland and the Baltic countries including Finland; the second group to include the Danubian states, that is, Czechoslovakia, Hungary and Rumania.

[1] Lothian H. Kerr Philipp (1882-1940), British diplomat, Ambassador to Washington, D.C.

[2] Władysław Sikorski (1881-1943), Polish politician, Prime Minister (1922-1923) and then Minister of War until 1925. In opposition since Piłsudski's May coup (1926). After the defeat of 1939, Prime Minister of the Polish government-in-exile and Commander-in-Chief of the Polish Army.

[3] Tibor Eckhardt (1888- ?), Hungarian politician, member of the Hungarian Parliament since 1922 and Leader of the Party of Small Landowners. Hungarian representative at the 1938 Assembly of League of Nations, and supporter of regent Horthy, who later, in 1941, sent him to the U.S. to seek contacts with the Allies and the democratic Hungarian opposition.
For the activities of Tibor Eckhardt, see Pastor, P., "Hungarian *Émigrés* in Wartime Britain" in J. Morison, *Eastern Europe and the West. Selected papers from the Forth World Congress for Soviet and East European Studies,* Harrogate 1990, New York 1992, pp. 81- 97, and Romsics, I., *op. cit.,* pp. 20-21. In the above documents the project is characterized in the following way: "According to Tibor Eckhardt and John Pelényi, Hungary recommends the division of Eastern Europe into three separate groups: a Polish-Baltic bloc; a Balkan group, and a Danubian Union, including Hungary, under the Habsburg Monarchy and a supreme legislature. Such a proposal, they argue, would promote economic and political stability in Eastern Europe, provide common defense against both Germany and the Soviet Union and exclude the Soviet Union from any participation in European affairs. (...) In the opinion of these spokesmen, the whole Danubian area must be considered as a single bloc for economic and strategic purposes with Hungary as the logical nucleus. They favor a virtual union of the states within this bloc: Austria, Hungary, Czechia, Slovakia and Transylvania. Croatia might also be included, in order to provide an outlet to the Adriatic, although this area is not absolutely necessary". Notter File, box 57, P Doc. - 46.

[4] See *Introduction.* In preparatory material of the period found in attachments to the activities of the Advisory Committee, Sikorski's Plan is discussed in only an enigmatic way: "Few details of this plan have been made available. The states to be included are the Baltic States, Poland, Czechoslovakia, Hungary, Rumania and Yugoslavia. The plan contemplates complete economic federation and incipient political federation of these states. The political advantage to Poland of such an organization is obvious. It would provide a supra-national structure under considerable Polish influence, which would include the Baltic states. However, the size of the federation would make complete Polish domination of it extremely difficult; insofar the plan expresses a certain self-restraint on the part of the Polish government". Notter File, box 57, P Doc. - 46.

Documents

While there might be links between these two federations, each was envisaged as an independent state.

Mrs. McCormick said that mention might also be made of the Hodža plan, which confines itself to the Danubian area. Mr. Hodža,[1] she pointed out, being a peasant, is chiefly concerned with the agricultural problem. His plan expresses the aspirations of the "Green International".[2]

Mr. Davis thought that the big powers – France, Germany and Italy – have always been an obstacle to the creation of a Danubian union. He himself had always had the feeling that a settlement of the Danubian area could be the key to peace and security. In his view, the most fatal mistake made at the end of the last war was the failure to create unity in Central Europe. While Wilson's Fourteen Points had called for the lowering of trade barriers, in actuality no practicable scheme for accomplishing this was found.[3] Mrs. McCormick agreed, pointing out in particular that if we could get a plan for the Danubian region, it would help considerably in dealing with the German problem.[4] Mr. Davis, referring to the difficulty of establishing a federation, said that it is a terrible problem to get local government into operation. He thought that a proposed plan should not interfere with local government but should work from it. He did not like the idea of setting up a broad framework first that would lead to dictation of all matters of local government.

Mr. Atherton queried whether it would not be wiser to proceed in the reverse direction. He said that in establishing a federation we would naturally interfere as little as possible with local governments. If, however, we could get a broad framework of a federation, it would then be possible for the local people to adopt policies which would contribute to it. If, however, no such framework were created, the local government bodies would exhaust themselves in the kind of rivalry and unconstructive effort which had gone on in the past.

---

[1] Milan Hodža (1878-1944), Czechoslovakian politician, Prime Minister in 1935-1938 left Beneš during the war. His plan was A Central European Federation, presented in *The Nation*, May 16 1942, and later expanded in a book: *Federation in Central Europe: Reflections and Reminiscences*, London 1942.

[2] "Green International" was the international association of the European peasant parties in the period between the two world wars. It was established in Prague, in 1921. Between 1928 and 1930, the number of participating national peasant parties was 18. In 1942, *émigré* representatives of Central Eastern European peasant parties announced a new program, also including a federation of their countries. Green International was reborn in New York in 1947, headed by G. Dimitrov and S. Mikołajczyk.

[3] Wilson's Fourteen Points were a presidential program for world peace, delivered to the United States Congress on 8 January 1918. The removal of trade barriers was covered by Point III: "The removal, so far as possible, of all economic barriers, and the establishment of an equality of trade conditions among all the nations consenting to the peace and associating themselves for its maintenance".

[4] A manifestation of the nostalgia for the Austro-Hungarian Empire, dominant in interwar historical literature, which saw the monarchy as a center that could prevent the "Balkanisation" of this part of Europe.

Mr. Cohen was asked whether he would have something to say on this question. He replied that, in his view, economic functions cannot be separated from political functions. The performance of economic functions can take place only in a political framework, but we should try to have the federal administration as small as possible so that each group will feel that the rules are being administered by the states. He thought this form would provide the best basis for later evolution. He pointed to the early American experience and observed that to have the states administer the rules tends to increase their power. This gradual process toward unity would be best adapted to the Danubian situation. Moreover, the economic functions of the modern state embrace much more than the problem of tariffs. The control of such matters must in some way be linked back to the states. Mr. Davis conceded that if an economic unit is created, it must have what amounts to political authority. He thought, however, that we should not try to force any exact form of government upon the countries concerned. Mr. Cohen agreed that he did not favor strong centralization.

Mr. Armstrong, referring to the Sikorski and Eckhardt plans, inquired whether these two men have definite ideas as to the arrangement which should be made for the rest of the territory. He pointed out that Bulgaria, Yugoslavia and Greece are not included in the Eckhardt plan. Each plan, he said, leaves Austria out temporarily for strategic reasons. He understood that a certain pressure exists in London and in other capitals for the *Anschluss* or Austria and Germany. Eckhardt, he said, is working closely with Otto,[1] who is interested in Austria and not in Hungary. The Sikorski plan, he thought, was a little less self-seeking in a nationalistic sense than that of Eckhardt. It must be remembered that Poland would be a relatively powerful state. The larger the group, the less power Poland would necessarily have. Thus, Sikorski's plan was not a mere scheme for establishing Polish hegemony. However, the motive of the Eckhardt proposals seemed to be that of trying to restore as much of Austria-Hungary (especially Hungary) as possible. Transylvania, for example, was included. Mr. Welles said that the Eckhardt plan leaves the political organization out. Its basic idea is that of two relatively self-sufficient economic units. Yugoslavia, Greece and Bulgaria are not included in it. The Balkan states, he said, see less economic possibilities in such schemes and are less interested in them than are the states further north.

Mr. Atherton raised the question whether the two groups envisaged by the Eckhardt plan were too small to compete with Russia. Mr. Davis said that there is no particular intercourse between the Baltic and Danubian groups. Mr. Atherton, referring to the northern of these two envisaged units, said that it

---

[1] Archduke Otto von Habsburg (1912-), a pretender to the Hungarian and Austrian crown, proposed the formation of a Danubian federal state with boundaries similar to those of Austria-Hungary in 1914. He believed that a large Danubian state was necessary since smaller units would be unable to defend themselves against Germany and Russia. The Members of the new Danubian state should, however, be free to set up a monarchical or republican system and to fix their own electoral system. See Habsburg, O., "Danubian Reconstruction", *Foreign Affairs* 1942, "The United States of the Danube, A Liberal Conception", *The Voice of Austria*, London, October 1942, excerpts in DHEI, Vol.2, pp.638-40.

would merely repeat the type of structure established after the last war – a unit with no outlet except through the Baltic. This (*sic*) must, he thought, be another outlet – to the south. This brings us back again to the Polish plan.

Mr. Welles then asked Mr. Bowman whether, in his view, the Eckhardt plan provides for two relatively self-sufficient economic units. Mr. Bowman doubted that it did, saying however that the practical question involved consideration of what would happen up to the time of the establishment of a federation. The time factor would have to be kept into consideration, as it actually overshadowed the question of federation. The height of power of the United Nations will be the end of the fighting. At that time the moral and military power of the United Nations could instantly rearrange the territorial situation. Later this would become increasingly difficult. It must be kept in mind that immediately after the fighting, some shifting could be done which was not based entirely upon what had existed before. These shifts, he said, could be stable insofar as they were rational and took into account practical political considerations. He pointed out, too, that the countries in this area are in general unstable, politically inexperienced and nationalistic. Economic matters are so confused with political motives that the meaning of the maneuvers of these countries is often obscure. We would also want to take Russia and Germany into account in deciding this question. Furthermore, how far can we ourselves go politically in making any arrangements stick? He quoted Oppenheim's statement that in 1920 the world had been "shocked at its own boldness". The peoples of the world and particularly the American people, had in 1920 rapidly retired from the bold conceptions of the Peace Conference period.

He asked whether we will experience that again. Is it not true that all of the suggestions which we would make rest on the assumption that we are not going later to be frightened by our own boldness? Otherwise, what we do here is purely "paper stuff". He wondered whether the political leaders will not soon have to undertake the task of mobilizing support in public opinion. In other words, we have a second assumption in addition to our first assumption of a complete victory by the United Nations: We assume that we are not going to be afraid of our shadow afterward. He would emphasize, therefore, that we should not limit ourselves to considering what has been done, but that we should consider what is possible with a rational setup.

He questioned whether economic associations that do not carry with them political associations – the type which we had been discussing – are feasible. What is it, he asked, that draws out loyalty? Nothing, he answered, only (1) "the dream that experience destroyed" (*i.e.* the League of Nations) and (2) nationalism. This latter, he said, rests on human nature, on the ties to the land, the family, the neighborhood, etc. Therefore, if we say "unite", public opinion will oppose the suggestion; but if we urge union for the common interest with a limitation of sovereignty, in which account is taken of these local ties and in which, purely on grounds of common interest, these local units join together, public opinion may accept it. In his opinion, a league of nations that will allow regional autonomy seems best. That was his feeling also in relation to the German question. He suggested that in considering the Danubian federation, we ask two questions: first, how did it work when free to do so? We can't ignore the fact that Germany has a preponderant interest in the Balkans. He referred to an article written by Mr. Armstrong in *Foreign Affairs* in 1932[1] in which the high proportion of German trade with this region and the small proportion of trade of Great Britain and France with it was stressed. On the other hand, Germany accounted for about eighteen percent of this trade, a figure which has been greatly increased since. Mr. Armstrong pointed out that 1932 was about the last year in which the situation in the area was normal. The Tardieu Danubian plan[2] of that year was really the last plan of this sort which received any consideration. He noted that this plan was strongly favored by Herbert Butler in a book which Mr. Welles had recently recommended: *The Lost Peace*[3] ask, namely that of seeing what it is that is to be changed. He suggested that much research work had been done concerning the actual economic structure and functioning of these countries and that this material would be very useful. He doubted whether Eckhardt and Sikorski, for example, had done much on this task. The question he then defined as being: What boundaries shall we put around what area?

Mr. Davis concurred in Mr. Bowman's suggestion that the economic group of the League of Nations could be very helpful in a study of this sort. He referred especially to Mr. Loveday and said that Mr. Loveday and his group had done more on these questions than anyone else. Mr. Bowman said that he had one thing more to add. His earlier statements had not implied any disbelief in economic regions. These regions must, however, be worked out very carefully and perimeters can be drawn only on the basis of close study.

Mr. Armstrong presented the view that it is of importance to organize these areas in the strongest possible way. This, he said, is a fundamental part of the establishment of peace in Europe. He pointed out that in earlier times there was a buffer state between Russia and Germany. When this was taken away during the last war, Germany tried to organize the entire area. Later on, after the war, we tried and the entities which we created were not strong enough. He pointed out that several regional groups have so far been envisaged. The aim must be to make these groups strong. He himself would hate to plump for a plan that would make any other regional plans unlikely. If were (*sic*) are to impose political sacrifices such as the loss of sovereignty and social and economic sacrifices such as the breakdown of the land-owning class in Hungary, it will be necessary for us to make these sacrifices general and not limited to some one country or class. He pointed out also that a larger grouping offers less chance for the play

---

[1] Armstrong, H. F., "Versailles Retrospect", *Foreign Affairs*, (October 1932), pp. 173-189.

[2] The Tardieu Plan proposed closer economic cooperation, in the form of reciprocal customs union, between five of the six Danubian states: Austria, Czechoslovakia, Hungary, Yugoslavia, Rumania (Bulgaria was excluded). The proposed liberalization of trade between countries producing and importing grain would be a loophole around the clause on customs privileges. The plan was named after French Prime Minister André Tardieu, who presented it on 2 March 1932. It failed to materialize because of conflicts between the concerned nations, and because of counter-measures instituted by Germany and Italy.

[3] Butler, H. B., *The Lost Peace. A Personal Impression*, New York 1942.

of political motives than does a smaller one. In the Eckhardt plan for example, one sees these old ambitions again. Summarizing his views, Mr. Armstrong said that the most hopeful course in the long run is that of making the area of the federation as large as possible; of securing it by an international organization; of forcing all concerned to accept the federation. This includes not only the Danubian countries; Germany and Italy must not ask preferential treatment and we and Great Britain must not ask for most-favored-nation treatment. In that way he would try to emphasize economic factors rather political factors, but to make an area large enough. He thought that there was a chance that if this were done, the federation would constitute a limit upon Germany and upon a resurgence of the old Slav-German struggle, which is a danger for the future.

Mr. Welles, concurring, said that a requisite of any plan is the recognition of nationality. What must be done is rather to avoid its becoming pernicious. He thought as large an area should be included as is possible from a practical standpoint. Whether the organization later becomes political or not, we can start in this way. If such an organization can be established, it would be a counterpoise to both Russia and Germany. Mrs. McCormick agreed that the federation would have to be large. Mr. Davis said that the Danubian countries have always put politics ahead of economics. If we should reverse this, creating solid economic conditions, the opportunity will be provided for a healthy political development. Mr. Armstrong pointed out that there is less chance that outside great powers will control a large unit than a small unit.

Mr. Atherton, returning to the question raised by Mr. Bowman, questioned how much interest American public opinion would have in Europe after the war. The average person is interested in little beyond local matter and cannot be counted on for a sustained interest in international affairs. Accordingly, it is likely to be our general policy to interfere as little as possible in most European situations. We may, however, lay down certain areas in which this country can be expected to have an interest.

One of these would be a dismembered Germany, another France and England and a third a general economic grouping of Eastern Europe as a counterweight to Russia and Germany. Mr. Atherton further voiced his opinion that American postwar interest will lie more in the Far East than in Europe.

Mr. Welles disagreed with this, stating that in his view the American people will demand a determining voice in the European settlement as well as in the Far East. Mr. Atherton, disagreeing, said that we will be drawn more into the Far East than into Europe. Mr. Welles, conceding that certainly we would be involved in Far Eastern affairs, did not believe that this would affect our participation in European affairs. Mr. Atherton observed that it possibly would not do more than to dissipate our strength. Mr. Davis and Mrs. McCormick agreed that the American public would certainly feel that it does not want another world war to start in Europe.

At that point Mr. Welles asked Mr. Pasvolsky for his views on the question of the morning. Mr. Pasvolsky began by saying that he was embarrassed on two scores: first, that he disagreed with much that had been said as to the value of a Danubian federation and second, that he considered the political questions involved in this more important than the economic ones. He believed he could best present his views by describing the course of thought pursued in writing his book of the Economic Nationalism of the Danubian States some years ago.[1] He had started, he said, in an effort to prove that the dismemberment of Austria Hungary was a crime. He found, however, that his studies led him to the opposite conclusion. He had started with the proposition that Austro-Hungary had been an economic unit as opposed to the fragmented postwar Danubian world, and that therefore it was necessary to get back to the Dual Monarchy. He had limited himself to the economic aspects of the question because he saw no reason to believe that even a start could be made on the political aspects. He found that Austria-Hungary before the last war consisted of two politically autonomous units – a true federation under the Crown. The two parts were united in a customs union and for certain other purposes. He discovered, however, that even with this organization, Austria and Hungary nearly broke apart whenever they had to revise the tariff. Concentration of agriculture and industry in different parts brought about disagreement. He found also that every ten years, in connection with the renewal of the Austro-Hungarian Bank, there was sharp strife. These difficulties were always reconciled but generally along the lines of Austrian desires. In his opinion, the reason for this was that political reasons governed all these actions and that Austria was the dominant factor politically.

Mr. Welles asked whether Austria was not also financially dominant. Agreeing that it was, Mr. Pasvolsky made a second observation about pre-war Austro-Hungarian economic functioning. Hungary succeeded, he said, in building a textile industry and in competing with the industry of Czechoslovakia. How was this possible? First, Hungary had enough banking resources; second, the Hungarian Government used its power to buy uniforms in order to further home industries; third, the Hungarian state railway administration imposed different freight rates and these tactics were paralleled in other fields by measures which are generally called administrative or indirect protectionism. In summary, pre-war Austria-Hungary solved its economic problem only through forced industrialization with the use of foreign capital and through the exportation of 200,000 men per year. After making this study, Mr. Pasvolsky had gone to the five Succession countries. He had pointed out that if they were to have a union, its tariff would have to be established by diplomatic negotiations as opposed to the method of majority vote in Congress in this country. Admitting, he said, that it would be possible to adjust internal differences among the states, "Who will determine the unified tariff?" It was clear that this would need to be done by negotiation. The uniform answer which he received on this, however, was, "We will think about that when we come to it". Only once, he said, had this question really been faced. That was in the project for a customs union between Austria and Germany in 1931.[2]

---

[1] Pasvolsky, L., *Economic Nationalism of the Danubian States*, New York 1928.
[2] The plan for a customs union between Germany and Austria was presented by Austria's Minister for Foreign Affairs, Johann Schober, on 20 March 1931. It fell through, due to the leading European nations' objections, primarily those of France, Great Britain and Italy.

Documents

He noted, however, that even in that proposal, they had omitted the unified tariff and had recourse instead to the mere grant of reciprocal tariff preferences between the two countries. The entire plan, he pointed out, was only a preliminary project for a customs union and not a customs union itself. Continuing, he said that a primary problem of an economic federation is its relations with the outside world. A second problem is whether the territory is really self-sufficient. He stated that in his view, the Danubian territory is not at all self-sufficient. Even if, he said, Czechoslovakia and Austria were willing to give up their agricultural tariff protection, this would afford to the other Danubian countries only a small additional market. Similarly, if the agricultural countries of that area were to give up industrial production, this step would increase by very little markets of the industrial states of the area. The result is that all of the Danubian states are forced to deal chiefly with non-Danubian states and are therefore thrown back on their need for relations with the outside world. This means, he added, political decision.

In concluding, he said that in thinking of economic matters, one must distinguish nation, region and world. The relation of a nation to the world is, he said, difficult enough. To throw in, however, a second element, the functioning of a nation in a regional group which would in turn have relations to the world, would introduce a new factor of strain in international relations. No regional area, he said, is better off by itself than in a well-functioning world. No region is really big enough to be self-sufficient. The evolution of the Danubian question was, he said, characterized by what followed the Tardieu plan the last regional plan which received serious consideration. Meeting at Stresa in 1932 in an attempt to alleviate the plight of agriculture, the representatives of Eastern European states turned away from strictly regional arrangements and embraced the idea that states outside the area concerned should grant preferential tariffs on their agricultural products. This illustrated the fact that the essential economic problems of the Danubian countries cannot be solved solely by those countries, but by arrangements which take account also of relations with outside countries.

Mr. Welles observed that this had been a very interesting analysis. Mr. Davis said that in the past Germany and France, not being really dependent upon the products of the Danubian states, had had the "drop" on them. Some South European states, however, such as Yugoslavia, were really dependent upon the Danubian area. Mr. Pasvolsky then distributed copies of some foreign trade statistics for the Danubian countries which revealed the small volume of trade between the Danubian countries themselves and, on the other hand, the large amount of trade which each Danubian country had with non-Danubian countries. Mr. Davis then asked whether, if these states constituted an economic unit, they would not be in a better position to negotiate as a unit. Rumania, Yugoslavia and Hungary, he said, are so competitive that they are not so susceptible to German power as are the other states. Mr. Pasvolsky indicated that he was particularly opposed to the Eckhardt plan on the ground that if a regional federation were to be established at all, it should be made within as self-sufficient an area as possible. He observed that gains might be made if competitive countries would get together and organize as sellers. This would be similar to certain recent pan-American arrangements. Such an arrangement would, however, presuppose an organization somewhat different from a federation. It would be an arrangement set up by treaty for dealing with other countries as buyers.

Mr. Welles then interjected that we might take the matter on that basis for the sake of argument. We might consider arrangements of this sort embracing Poland, Czechoslovakia, the Baltic countries, Hungary, Rumania, Yugoslavia and Austria. It would be assumed that these countries would agree on a unified tariff. The great bulk of this economic area would be agricultural with only a small industry, which would mean there would be no really balanced economy. Turning to Mr. Cohen, he then asked what the latter's opinions on this matter were in the light of the experience of this country.

Mr. Cohen repeated his view that politics and economics could not be separated because politics plays a part in the determination of the economic. However large and rich a country may be, he said, it cannot be self-sufficient and the attempt to make it so is not desirable. It does not follow, however, that some internal arrangements are not necessary. In this country, the large area of relatively free trade is an important factor in its prosperity. In Mr. Cohen's view, merely voluntary arrangements as to tariffs and the like by the Danubian countries would not work. It would be necessary to "institutionalize" these arrangements on some way. He was using the word "institutionalize" deliberately as he meant to leave his conception definitely flexible. He agreed with everything Mr. Pasvolsky had said except his conclusions.

In any case, proposals for regional arrangements would require very careful thought. As an additional possibility, he suggested that there be free trade as between the countries but not a unified tariff upon products from outside. Mr. Atherton pointed out that this would involve a central political organization of some sort. Mr. Cohen agreed, but thought its powers would be limited. Continuing, he raised the question whether we cannot create institutions that will assist in the construction of a stable order in the area. There would of course be a larger regional unit for restricted purposes; within that, smaller entities constituting more complete unions. He thought we might consider enlarging the geographical scope of the projected area to go as far south as Greece.

Mr. Welles said the point was well taken. Continuing, he asked whether it is not true that some sort of economic union would be the only manner of bringing about a rise in the standard of living. Mr. Pasvolsky observed that this was precisely what he questioned. He did not deny that it would bring about some rise in the standard of living, but did not appear to think that this rise would be comparatively important. He had no objection, he said, to the establishment of a Danubian union of some sort if the countries involved wished this. Mr. Welles replied that these countries cannot be expected to establish such an arrangement by themselves: They need, he thought, to be told how to do it.

Mr. Armstrong then asked whether some substitute of an international nature could not be found for the regional arrangement under discussion. Can't we, he asked, as relatively disinterested powers who will determine the peace, make that contribution? Such action, he said, would need to take place immediately at the end of the war. We should also, he thought, give economic direction to the efforts of these countries. All of their political decisions, he thought, must be centralized. If this is so difficult to organize in a region, he asked, shouldn't we find some international substitute for it? Mr. Pasvolsky observed that to create a world system that would enable these countries to trade, would lend them really substantial help. Mr. Cohen agreed, but stated that the problem is rather this: What is the best way to work toward a satisfactory long-range solution? Mr. Pasvolsky agreed, but indicated that, in his opinion, the best way would be to secure agreement by the powerful nations first. If this were done, he said, the smaller and weaker countries will be forced to accept the scheme.

Mrs. McCormick stated that we must take for granted that the great powers will reform to some extent. She pointed out that the responsibility for past conditions in the Balkans rests largely upon the great powers. Mr. Welles thought that there was always a possibility of our being misled, as Dr. Pasvolsky was being misled, into feeling that just because the great powers reform, human nature can't wreck the gains they had made. Some regional organization, he thought, may furnish a balance. By joining together, they can speed up their industrial organization and make themselves a more potent factor in Europe. Mrs. McCormick pointed out that up to now each Danubian country has been the rival of the others. If they could be brought to realize that their survival depends upon common action, they will accept the necessary arrangements. Mr. Welles thought there was a great deal in this point. Mr. Bowman said that these countries had once trusted the great powers and had been let down. Mrs. McCormick said that Prime Minister Sikorski and others realize that their nations must unite in order to exist.

Mr. Cohen then asked Mr. Pasvolsky whether, in the latter's opinion, if this country were divided into four states, we would have made more rapid progress with trade treaties than has been the case. Mr. Pasvolsky stated that less progress would have been made. Mr. Cohen, concurring, said that our experience showed that where central organization is weak, special influences are strong locally. This was, he said, an answer to Mr. Pasvolsky's question as to the proper approach to make. Mr. Pasvolsky answered that the problem would be somewhat simplified if we could have larger states. Mr. Cohen observed that we cannot create unitary states in the Danubian area. This fact does not, however, mean that an intermediate stage of organization cannot be found. Mr. Davis summed up Mr. Pasvolsky's view by saying that he believed that regional arrangements would be of some assistance provided the international organization was not neglected.

Mr. Welles then said that we must explore carefully the questions that had been raised. He thought it was time for this subcommittee to come into closer contact with the territorial subcommittee. For the next meeting we must have something much more definite to shoot at. It would, he said, be necessary to have a map which would show a potential economic federation with the territorial scope described by Mr. Cohen, including Greece and the other Balkan States, Austria, Czechoslovakia, Poland and the Baltic states, excluding Finland. Finland would be considered rather as a member of the Scandinavian group. He suggested that the committee try to see whether such a unit would be economically conceivable, as he was beginning to think it was. That would be the fundamental question. If this could be done, what national regrouping in that area would be necessary to make the arrangement work, assuming that the units will have complete autonomy and sovereignty? The aim would be to get cohesive national groups. To that end, where should the frontiers be drawn? In answer to the question whether frontier adjustments could be considered, Mr. Welles pointed out that minority problems might make this expedient.

Mrs. McCormick suggested that this might mean the establishment of smaller national areas in the groupings and asked whether, for example, Czechoslovakia would be envisaged as being restored with its pre-war frontiers. Mr. Welles said he would envisage as big a Czechoslovakia, as before with the possible exception of the Sudetenland, but that he had had the Hungarian minorities chiefly in mind.

Mr. Armstrong then asked whether the task was not big enough to postpone the consideration of frontiers until later and to think for the present of pre-war frontiers. Mr. Welles agreed. Mr. Bowman stated that the territorial subcommittee could take up this question in the afternoon.

The chairman closed the meeting at 12:45 p.m.

Paul B. Taylor, Secretary

2

DEPARTMENT OF STATE
Advisory Committee
Strictly Confidential
Minutes P - 13
May 30, 1942

Typescript, copy
AN Notter File, box 65

[DESIRABILITY OF A SINGLE UNION FOR REGION]

Present:
Mr. Welles, presiding
Mr. Hamilton Fish Armstrong
Mr. Isaiah Bowman
Mr. Norman H. Davis
Mr. Benjamin V. Cohen
Mr. Green H. Hackworth
Mrs. Anne O'Hare McCormick
Mr. Leo Pasvolsky
Mr. Myron C. Taylor
Mr. Harley Notter, Research Secretary
Mr. Paul B. Taylor, Secretary

In opening the meeting at 11 a.m., Mr. Welles said that the draft plan prepared by Mr. Cohen and Mr. Hackworth and circulated to all members would be considered. He suggested that the statement be read and discussed paragraph by paragraph. He then read the first paragraph of the statement, entitled "Desirability of Single Union for Region".

Mr. Taylor noted that Austria was included both in this plan and in the plan under consideration for the reorganization of Germany. Obviously Austria could not be in both groups. He thought it much more desirable that Austria be in the three-state German scheme. Mr. Welles said that we had undertaken, for purposes of discussion, to consider what advantages there might be in the inclusion of Austria in the Eastern European Union. It had, however, been intended to leave the actual decision of this matter in abeyance until the committee had reconsidered the German settlement. The decision as to the disposition of Austria would have to be made on the specific merits of the question, including in particular the economic aspects of the problem. Mr. Taylor said that he would merely note that consideration of Austria for the Eastern European Union does affect the German picture. Mr. Welles said that was one of the reasons he had suggested that the committee go over to the East European question before trying to decide on the German settlement.

Mr. Bowman said that in his judgment the following sentence of the paragraph was the key sentence: "The formation of a single union would be desirable since it would prevent the smaller groups from tying up with respective great powers". That was the point upon which a decision was of the greatest importance. He, himself, was coming more and more to the position taken in that sentence. He thought that smaller unions would be more likely to lead to dissension than a larger one. A further advantage of the larger system was that its existence would not depend upon the number of in the area. A few states might be left out, if necessary, without making the plan impossible. It was then not a matter of "all or nothing".

Mr. Welles agreed to this as a wise statement.

Mrs. McCormick concurred, saying that the chief question was whether or not the large union was practicable. We should try first for the largest possible grouping. If, later on, two smaller organizations were found to be necessary, we could use the same setup for them. She could see, for example, all of the northern states in one organization and all of the southern states in another one, if necessary.

Mr. Taylor noted that in this statement the Baltic states, in which the Soviet Union was greatly interested, were included in the federation. He asked Mr. Welles what arguments we could use with Russia to persuade it to let these countries join the union. He wondered if a brief statement could be made of the arguments which could be used.

Mr. Welles said that in his opinion the question would depend, in the first place, on whether the Soviet Union had definitely determined at the end of the war on whether or not it was going to embark on the policy of imperialism. In case it had decided against the imperialistic course, we would have two enormous arguments. In the first place, the proposed union would not in any case be a menace to the Soviet Union. It would in fact act as a buffer between the Soviet Union and the Western powers, which would be helpful to the Soviets in case the international organization should at some time break down. In addition to this argument concerning security, there would be the argument of the economic advantages to the Soviet Union. A sound economic unit in eastern and southern Europe would be a market for Soviet products and a source of necessary Soviet supplies.

Mr. Taylor noted that Russia's ambition to have a port on the sea, not closed in winter, would of course need to be taken into consideration. In reply to a question by Mr. Welles, he said that he had referred to a northern port. Mr. Welles said that this matter was one well worth taking into consideration. He thought that an adjustment of the matter would be by no means difficult of achievement. Mr. Armstrong asked whether there had not been a suggestion as to the internationalization of ports. Mr. Welles answered that such a suggestion had been made in regard to Narvik. He thought that it might be worthwhile to consider the same here.

Mrs. McCormick said that in her opinion one uncertain part of the union was the northern part. With the exception of Lithuania, which was almost committed to Poland, the Baltic states would probably prefer union with the Scandinavian group.

Mr. Bowman asked Mr. Welles whether those in the Department cognizant of the matter could not list in a brief memorandum the advantages for Russia that we could see in the inclusion of the Baltic states in the East European union. Mr. Welles said that that could be done. Mrs. McCormick asked if Mr. Welles could give the committee an inkling as to whether the Lend-Lease arrangement would have any bearing upon Russia's attitude on this question. Mr. Welles said that it definitely would that the economic arguments were the foundation of the others. He thought it was a desirable suggestion that the memorandum concerning the advantages to Russia of the inclusion of the Baltic states in the East European union be prepared. He asked Mr. Pasvolsky if this could be presented in two weeks. Mr. Pasvolsky said that it could.

He asked whether we could discuss Estonia and Latvia in terms of two possibilities. If a non-Communist government were to exist in Russia, these countries would join it within twenty-four hours for both political and economic reasons. Politically they would be more secure within it and economically they would enjoy the wide market which had made them prosperous in the old Russia. He thought that of the three alternative courses which would be open to these states in case Russia were not communistic – (1) union with Scandinavia, (2) with the eastern European organization and (3) with Russia – these countries would prefer Russia. Lithuania, he thought, was different.

Mrs. McCormick asked what, in Mr. Pasvolsky's opinion, the attitude of Estonia and Latvia would be in case Russia remained communist. Mr. Pasvolsky said that distinctions had to be observed between these states. Estonia was close to Finland and spoke the same language, while the Letts were close to the Lithuanians. It would be advantageous to Russia to keep these two northern states out of the union because it could manipulate their political and economic relations more easily if they were isolated. He thought the question of ports was of great importance. Russia had historically and in the present a desire for an ice-free port. The only Baltic port of importance, however, was Riga, in southern Latvia. He thought that the internationalization of Narvik, which had previously been mentioned in the committee, might possibly ease the situation.

Mrs. McCormick agreed that Latvia would be the most sympathetic to the Russians. This offered, in her opinion, the best possibility for a solution: that Latvia go to the Soviet Union, the northern states to Scandinavia and Lithuania become a member of the union. Mr. Welles said it was obvious that this was one of the portions of our recommendations that must be formulated in alternative form. All this government stood for was that the people of the region should have the right to decide for themselves. It will be up to the people of the region to decide between these alternatives. It appeared to be generally accepted in the committee that the disposition of this area was a matter which could not be decided upon at the present time.

Mrs. McCormick then asked Mr. Welles whether in the negotiations of the Lend-Lease Agreement[1] the Russians had really opened up and had given any reason for hope of an understanding. Mr. Welles answered that the negotiations were as yet only in a preliminary phase. Nothing final had been agreed upon. If, however, the Russians should be amenable, the approach under discussion would apparently be a good one. Mrs. McCormick thought that the Lend-Lease Agreement would be of basic importance in the whole approach to Russia.

There followed a short discussion concerning the general principle of self-determination. Mr. Armstrong said that in his opinion the lack of self-determination was one of the causes of the last war. He thought that during the postwar period much of the criticism of nationalism had been superficial. He thought the best approach would be that of ameliorating rather than of disregarding nationalism and of securing the agreement so far as possible of the different nations. Mr. Bowman said he would add as a footnote that in October 1918, in the last war the Germans subscribed to the principle of self-determination.[2] Mr. Welles asked whether we must not frankly recognize that there is an element of expediency involved in this question of the Baltic states. He thought that if Latvia should wish to join the Soviet Union and if the Soviets were willing, this would not jeopardize the project under discussion. Mr. Armstrong said that of course self-determination should not be pressed to a ridiculous point. There were practical necessities which limited its operation. Mr. Welles asked whether it was not actually a question of proportion. Mr. Armstrong said that in his opinion the existence of a false strain in some areas was actually the salvation of the self-determination principle. He wished to make the following point to Mr. Welles and Mr. Taylor. There was, he thought, a great danger of communism in Europe after the war. As between nationalist and international revolutions, he favored the nationalist one. In France, which was of great importance to our present policy, he hoped that we would adopt a policy of favoring the development of a national spirit in France which would oppose an international communist revolution. He was opposed to allowing, so far as within our power, revolutionary forces in France to come into existence that would collaborate with and be exploited by international communism. Hence, he thought it would be better on grounds of expediency that we favor self-determination. Mr. Taylor wondered why this oration had been addressed to him. He had not said anything in this meeting that indicated that he was trying to propagate world communism!

Mrs. McCormick said she had interpreted Mr. Armstrong to mean that the sentiment of nationalism was as potent as were economic forces. She thought that cultural differences entered into nationality differences to a large extent.

---

[1] Lend-Lease Act, the name of a bill passed by the U.S. Congress on 11 March 1941. It authorized the President of the U.S. to lend, lease and donate military equipment to parties at war against the Axis. At first it was only used by Great Britain. As for the U.S.S.R., the American administration granted it a $1 billion loan on 30 October 1941 and then (11 June 1942) signed a "master lend-lease agreement" with Russia for military equipment and services.

[2] A reference to negotiations with Germany on their acceptance of Wilson's 14 points.

Documents

The Czech-Slovak feud had resulted in part from a difference in cultures and of social development. In Hungary the existence of a feudal system had fostered nationalism, The Hungarian landowners had done much to keep nationalistic feelings alive. Mr. Taylor said that he thought that France was difficult to predict. He remembered that sometime ago M. Renault had taken him into the back door of his own factory because the communists were in control of the front door, Mr. Welles said that was additional proof that Mr. Taylor had not been advocating international communism.

Mr. Welles then summarized the thought of the committee in regard to the first paragraph of the statement by saying that we accepted this paragraph with the agreement that we would consider two alternatives in regard to Estonia and Latvia. He asked whether members of the committee had any other alternatives to suggest.

Mr. Armstrong, saying that he did not wish to lock horns again with Mr. Taylor, after having delivered an oration to him, said that he would however take issue with regard to the disposition of Austria. He thought our final attitude on this matter would have to be determined, to a large extent, by the conclusions which would be reached concerning the economic aspect of the problem. He would, accordingly, withhold his judgment until the economic studies had been completed. Tentatively, however, he favored including Austria in the East European region.

Mr. Welles said concerning the disposition of Austria that he thought all would agree that all the economic factors would be of basic importance. He thought it would be necessary to consider Austria in relation both to the German and to the East European group until data adequate for a final decision were available.

Mrs. McCormick said that in her view, the inclusive plan was most desirable, but that the alternative should be kept in mind of creating smaller groups such as the Balkan group. Mr. Cohen said he thought the committee had not at any time supposed that the creation of the larger group would preclude the existence of smaller groups which, he said, may even unite if they so chose. Mr. Armstrong asked whether thought had been given to the possibility of regional subdivisions within the union. He thought that the southern group might have to be treated as a developmental area. The creation of an economic developmental organization had been mentioned in the last meeting. Some Europeans, such as Mr. van Zeeland[1] thought that economic development organizations of this type were of general international importance. He thought there was something there which might allow for a differentiation within the region. Mr. Welles said that we had touched on this matter last week but had not elaborated the suggestion.

---

[1] Paul van Zeeland (1893-1973), Viscount, Belgian politician, liberal, Professor at Leuven University, Government Minister several times, Foreign Minister in the government-in-exile in London during the war, and Foreign Minister in 1949-1954. A supporter of European integration and member of the European League for Economic Cooperation.

Mr. Welles then said that we might pass to the consideration of the second paragraph of the statement entitled "Suggested Name". After this paragraph had been read, Mr. Bowman said he thought the authors had thought the matter out well; he had no criticism to make. It was the general sense of the committee that the word *union* was probably better[1] than *federation* or *confederation*. In particular, there was confusion in the people's minds as to the meaning of these words and neither type was thought to have succeeded very well. Mr. Hackworth explained that neither of the two words would be exactly accurate to describe the organization proposed. In a confederation no separate central operating control existed, while in a federation, the component units were not separate entities in the international sense.

Mr. Welles then read the third paragraph entitled "The Political Council". Mr. Bowman raised the question as to whether the arrangement for representation in the political council envisaged in the paragraph was desirable. He thought it should be considered in close connection with the proposed economic council. The committee had last time expressed favor for a small political council consisting, for example, of two members from each state. Such a council would give the appearance of equality that the small state found attractive and would, in general, promote agreement. He thought that if the political council were constituted in this manner, one might in the economic council take some basis of representation that related to economic forces. He thought that of all possible bases of this nature, population changed most slowly and was least susceptible to management. He thought that economic factors which were susceptible to management and to relatively rapid change were poor bases for representation. While population changes took place, these changes were slow. One would therefore approach the problem of changing representation only gradually. He would accordingly like to see the political council envisaged on a "two Senators for each state" basis and the economic council representation based not on manageable economic conditions but on population. The two bodies would then compensate each other to some extent.

Mr. Davis said he would disagree. He did not think that economies could be measured by population. Mr. Bowman replied that this had not been his idea. He had talked only about the problem of *representation*. Mr. Davis thought that representation ought to be on some basis of economic importance. Mr. Bowman said that if this were done, then the shooting would begin. Each state would try to weight highly the factors which were to its advantage. He had thought the committee had agreed that the system would necessarily be imposed by force. He felt that following this, we ought to establish the organization upon the simplest possible basis, proportionate to something. He thought the basis which would lead to the least difficulty would be that of population.

Mr. Cohen said he thought there would be danger that the smaller states felt that the large states had gained more strength in the organization through the mere fact of their larger population. Mr. Davis observed that the small political council would be composed, in effect, of foreign ministers.

---

[1] Another proof of the great impact of Sikorski's plan, which suggested a union rather than a federation or confederacy.

Documents

Mr. Welles asked whether it would not be well to read the additional paragraphs before going into discussion in detail. Mr. Taylor thought it would be unwise to try to fix the representation in the economic council until the report on the economic features of the problem had been completed. He did not himself know much about the internal economic conditions in those countries Mr. Welles said that we were, however, dealing with merely the general aspects of the problem based upon well-established facts. He did not think that all consideration of this matter should be postponed until the economic study had been completed. Mr. Armstrong said on the other hand that the specific suggestions resented in the plan had helped him considerably in his own thinking. He thought that it was necessary to think in specific terms.

Mrs. McCormick asked whether some decision could not be made regarding the political council before proceeding to the rest of the plan. Mr. Bowman replied that in his view, the two councils would have to be considered together. Mrs. McCormick said that in her opinion the suggestion of a small political council was a good one. She thought that to have what was in substance a legislative body with representation on some proportionate basis would bring trouble.

Mr. Hackworth thought that it would be necessary to consider the psychological effect of the proposal. If the political council were to function as set forth in the plan, should it not be a representative body?

If representation were to be equal, the big states would stay out. On a population basis there could be no complaint since the same thing could be said to everyone. He thought this was the only way to approach the problem unless a two-chamber body were to be created. In this case one body would be able to *veto* the other and he doubted the advantage of the two-chamber setup. Some of the work of the economic council would, under the plan, also be carried out by the political council.

Mr. Welles agreed that it would be utterly impossible to decide what the political council should be until it had been determined what the political council should do.

Mr. Welles then read the fourth paragraph of the plan entitled "Functions of Political Council".

Mr. Pasvolsky suggested that this paragraph should be read in connection with point II, "Organization of the Tentative Outline of a Central European Association", attached to this statement. Mr. Welles, after reading this passage, noted that it furnished a wide field for discussion.

He would frankly admit that in his own thought on the problem (which left open the possibility of further thought and conviction to the contrary), the political council should have, appropriately, the quality of a body composed of the representatives of equal sovereignties and provide the opportunity for their meeting for stated purposes. He thought it would be highly difficult to make a plan of the type suggested by Mr. Cohen and Mr. Hackworth work. In creating such a plan, one would have to use population as a basis for representation. The smaller states would then know that the larger states would be more powerful in the organization. We should go back to the German Confederation of 1815, rather than to the North German Confederation of 1867 in which one power had been able to establish hegemony. Judging from the past, he thought Poland would be in line to achieve this sort of thing if the proposed union were to be tried. He thought that the other basis, that of equality, would be more likely to work.

Mr. Cohen then explained that under the plan proposed, no action could take place in any case except by a majority vote of the states, as well as of the delegates. The larger states would have a greater power to prevent action than to induce it. Mr. Welles asked whether two or three larger states could not get together and dominate the union. Mr. Cohen answered that the plan provided for two kinds of majorities a majority of delegates and a majority of states. In some instances, even unanimity was envisaged. Mr. Welles said that the Balkan states, for example, might feel that they were in a less favorable position than the larger ones. Mr. Cohen answered that this would be true only as regards power to prevent action.

Mr. Welles said that one intrinsic difficulty in this plan was that in substance it envisaged federation rather than a union. Mr. Cohen answered that the problem was one of compromising the interests of large and small states. He thought there might be an advantage in creating a feeling that the council would be more than a meeting of foreign ministers.

Mr. Welles agreed. This was why he had not liked the expressions used in paragraph III "Conference of Commissioners or Envoys". He thought it would be necessary to think of actual representatives of the people from the political council. He would favor the election of these representatives by the voters of the component states rather than their appointment by the government.

Mr. Armstrong said that the first thing that the states concerned would do when they saw the plan, would be to take out their pencils and figure out combinations for voting in the body. He had taken out his pencil and noted that there would be about forty-eight delegates from twelve states, the majorities being twenty-five delegates and seven states. One possible combination consider would be that of the ex-enemy states, Hungary, Bulgaria and perhaps Rumania. These three states would have twelve delegates. Another possible grouping would be the former Little Entente. If combined with Poland, they would have a majority of the delegates but would need the support of three other states. If the Baltic states were not to be included there would be about forty-one delegates and nine states. This would make the achievement of a majority by these combinations much simpler. Mr. Cohen said that combinations would of course have to be expected and asked how the problem posed by Mr. Armstrong could be acquired without requiring unanimity in all cases. The plan had, in fact, provided for unanimity in some cases.

Mr. Hackworth said that the requirement of a majority of states in addition to the majority of delegates had been designed as a practical compromise between the two extreme solutions of this problem. If population alone were to be considered the big states would control the organization. If representation were to be equal, the small states would control. It was thought that the system devised had protected, to a fair degree, the interests of both groups.

Mr. Armstrong asked whether a beginning might not be well made by limiting our plans more or less to the economic council. He thought it would be of greater value to concentrate upon that problem at this stage. Mr. Davis disagreed.

Mr. Bowman pointed out that the proposal for a small political council gives play to nationality it would create the idea that these nationalities had power. This would be satisfying to their feelings. Mrs. McCormick opposed the weighting of votes in the political council. She thought that the representatives in it should represent states as such. Mr. Cohen replied that the proposed plan did not in his opinion give any more power to larger states than to smaller ones, except a greater power to prevent action. He agreed that psychologically and considering bargaining power, the larger states would be more powerful.

Mr. Hackworth thought the plan should include all states mentioned. He thought we were thinking too much in terms of small states. It was important to keep in mind that the larger states, such as Poland, would be unwilling to accept equality with Bulgaria or Albania. He thought that if we had a perfect, harmonious union, equal representation would be desirable, but instead we would start with an extremely difficult problem and it would be necessary to provide for a working, effective body. We should try to make the arrangement as palatable as possible to the bigger powers. He thought that in case the bigger powers agreed, the smaller ones would be forced to come in.

Mr. Welles said we appeared to have come to the point where a wide difference in philosophy had disclosed itself. The authors of the plan under consideration were thinking substantially of a federation. He, himself, on the other hand, had been thinking more of a union of sovereignties which were independent except as limited in the economic sphere and to a slight extent in regard to their internal order and security. The general scheme he had had in mind was more like the assembly of the League of Nations, modified so as to work in the economic sphere.

Mr. Cohen pointed out that in the plan under consideration a majority of each delegation was required in addition to the other requirements. He and Mr. Hackworth had tried, without creating too powerful a body, to provide a mechanism by which the states concerned could attain action if they wanted to. They had thought this point of some value. Mr. Armstrong observed that Mr. Cohen and Mr. Hackworth were trying to find a way of meeting the problem which had confronted the authors of the covenant of the League of Nations, Mr. Root and others in the past. He thought the solution was an ingenious one. Mr. Cohen said he did not wish the committee to think the plan before them represented sustained or mature thought on the part of Mr. Hackworth and himself. They had actually had only a short time in which to prepare it. Mrs. McCormick repeated her view that the legislative body would tend to create rather than to solve problems. Mr. Cohen said that the only question was whether some advantage could not be given to the larger states.

Mr. Hackworth said he was beginning to veer around to the other position. In our Congress, he said, the House of Representatives was supposed to represent the people and the Senate the states. However, the Senate was the more powerful of the two bodies. The question had sometimes been asked why, since the Senate can override the House, the House should exist. On this analogy he thought we might think purely in terms of a political council. Mrs. McCormick thought that in any case there should not be a representative body similar to Congress.

Mr. Welles said it was this analogy that had worried him. He thought that the draftsmen of this plan had gone too far and too fast. Mr. Hackworth said perhaps this was because they had had to think so fast.

Mr. Taylor noted that the plan had envisaged two voting schemes a majority and unanimity. He asked whether the authors had explored the question of some middle ground, such as two-thirds or three-fourths majority. Mr. Hackworth said that adjustments of that sort could be made.

Mr. Welles then said that it would be interesting to think of a completely new approach to this problem, one which had been suggested by one hundred fifty years of experience. This would envisage a political council in which equal sovereignties were equally represented. This council should have only one executive function the maintenance of internal security. This function would necessarily be delegated to an executive authority. The council might elect this executive by a majority vote, to carry out the delegated power, subject to removal by and special instructions from the council. The matters remaining were matters that would have to be dealt with by the sovereignties cooperating for specific purposes. He thought that if such a plan were to be taken as the point of departure, its details could be worked out.

Mr. Armstrong observed that in connection with such a council, an advantage could be seen in the inclusion of a large number of states in the organization.

Mr. Welles said he would like to add, in regard to his plan, that he had not even got to the point of considering a *veto* power of the political council over the economic. He was not sure there ought to be such a *veto* power. He was inclined to think that such a power should be exercised by the people or governments of the countries themselves. Mr. Davis observed that the problem to be dealt with by such an organization would be that of external security. Mr. Welles said that we could not admit at the beginning that an international security organization would not work.

Mr. Davis agreed that it would be a mistake to set up a legislative body. He did not think could get that far. He thought that if we wanted to create a real union we must start with equal sovereignties. The powers might, however, impose an economic union which should have the effect of encouraging the gradual formation of a political union.

Mr. Welles said one might add something more. If the committee believed as he that the approach to international organization should be through regional system, the representatives of the region in the central organization might be by this body. He did not himself see how we could get the hate-ridden units into a working federation. Mrs. McCormick thought that this would be the only way to begin. She thought that the small political council in which states were equally represented, was only a recognition to the world of the sovereignty of the individual states. She thought that the creation of a parliament would only bring dissension and strife.

Documents

Mr. Pasvolsky said he wished to raise one point in connection with the political council. A council with limited functions would necessarily be an executive body. Executive functions, however, could not be performed on the basis of majority votes. He thought there would have to be a delegation of the executive function. The political council would have to select an executive. This executive would have to act by the use of two instruments: (1) instruments of central control and (2) instruments controlled by the states. No matter how limited the powers of the political body, both kinds of instruments would need to be used. The second kind, in the use of which matters would be referred by the central body back to the states for execution by the states, the usefulness of the council might be that it would carry back the matter of execution to the states. It would not be analogous to the manner in which ministers of foreign affairs functioned in the League of Nations, in which decisions could not be made until they had been ratified by the member states. In this case the council would have the actual power to decide, but execution of its decisions would be left to the states. He would, accordingly, make the following suggestion: That there be a council with two representatives from each state; that one of these representatives for each state be the prime minister or his plenipotentiary and that the other be a representative of the national parliament. These twenty-four men (in a twelve state union) should come together and select a person to serve as the executive. In this manner they would be enabled to speak with the authority of representation and to be responsible for national action of the type listed under II. above. They should then go back to their own governments to secure enforcement. As to what instruments should be kept under the control of the international council, Mr. Pasvolsky said that in his opinion the council should control an armed force – it would be the basic instrument. This should exist in addition to whatever local police force there was. Mr. Welles observed that these suggestions were interesting and suggestive.

Mr. Welles asked that such members as had the physical time for it to put in writing their own suggestions as to the form of organization. He himself would put in writing the plan which he had outlined[1] and would make it available for circulation by Wednesday or Thursday. He thought we might have in mind that whatever we do here might be of value when we came to consider a Germanic federation. Mr. Pasvolsky suggested that it might also be of value in determining the pattern of world organization. Mr. Taylor asked whether. Mr. Pasvolsky's proposal could not also be put in writing. It was agreed that this should be done.

Paul. B Taylor, Secretary

---

[1] Not found.

3

DEPARTMENT OF STATE
Division of Special Research
Strictly Confidential
Minutes P - 14
June 6, 1942

Typescript, copy
AN Notter File, box 65

[EAST EUROPEAN UNION AS A REGIONAL APPROACH TO WORLD ORGANIZATION]

Present :
Mr. Welles, presiding
Mr. Hamilton Fish Armstrong
Mr. Adolf A. Berle
Mr. Isaiah. Bowman
Mr. Benjamin V. Cohen
Mr. Green H. Hackworth
Mr. John V. A. MacMurray
Mrs. Anne O'Hare McCormick
Mr. Leo Pasvolsky
Mr. Myron C .Taylor
Mr. Ray Atherton
Mr. Paul C. Daniels
Mr. Harley Notter, Research Secretary
Mr. Paul B. Taylor, Secretary

In opening the meeting at 10:50 a.m., Mr. Welles recalled that members of the committee had, at the last meeting, been asked to prepare statements of their views and noted that Mr. Taylor had such a statement ready. He asked Mr. Taylor to read the statement (appended). After reading, Mr. Taylor said that he could not seem to go further without taking into account first, the populations of the component states and second, assuming that the political body will represent this region in the general international organization, the question as to how that organization would be constituted.

Mr. Welles said that as usual Mr. Taylor had brought us down to brass tacks. These two problems were basic and raised the fundamental question of philosophy and principle involved in the problem. He asked whether any other members had statements to submit.

Mrs. McCormick said that she had only a few general observations. She then read her statement.

Mr. Welles then asked Mr. Armstrong for his opinion. Mr. Armstrong stated that he had not been "in cahoots" with the two other members from New York, but that his thought had gone in the main along the same lines. He then read his statement.

Mr. Welles observed that this statement had been an extraordinarily interesting one.

Mr. Atherton said he wished to ask a question. All three papers raised the question whether we were working for a new organization or whether the regional organization was to be the only one. It was his belief that the two organizations would be inter-related. If a League of Nations were in existence, the function of the regional organization would be almost purely economic.

Mr. Welles said it was entirely clear that the method of selecting the authorities of the regional union would depend on the decision as to the type of representation in the world organization that we are planning to construct. We could not formulate our ideas on this until we had determined whether the world organization was to be based on regional groupings or to be one similar to the League of Nations. He felt we might as well get to this question now.

Mrs. McCormick said that the great difficulty of the League had been the lack of power of the small nations to get consideration for their views. It had been dominated by the great powers. If this region had an organization, it could exert balanced power in the world organization. She thought this was important. Mr. Welles agreed that it was basic.

Mr. Taylor said that from the beginning of the discussions and as late as yesterday in the meeting of the economic committee – presided over by Mr. Acheson, we had constantly come back to the position of the continuing authority of the United Nations to set up the next phase of organization for maintaining international order and security. The more he had thought of the question, the more he had believed that the four great powers were the ones that should be the continuing body to maintain peace in case the international organization should fail. Mr. Welles said he agreed.

He asked, however, whether we were not talking now about ultimate idea which we wish to realize. Of course, the United Nations should, if necessary, employ force and this should continue until it was clear that the world organization was effectively functioning.

The thought which he had wished to interject was that in his individual opinion a new approach should be made from the regional standpoint. This would not necessarily be opposed to that of Mr. Armstrong's. For example, in the last fifteen years a regional group of Latin American representatives had been a cohesive bloc in the League of Nations. We wanted to give the component parts of the East European unit enough strength in the councils of the world so that they will not be divided and exploited. We wanted to build them up so that they can be potent in the new world organization. This was, he felt, in line with Mrs. McCormick's thought.

Mrs. McCormick said she wished to stress that if actual power were provided for the regional union, this would be an inducement to the region to continue and develop its organization.

Mr. Welles observed that the *de facto* Latin American regional federation in the League of Nations had had no cohesive strength other than its common national origins, a common viewpoint resulting from its geographical location and from its relatively common economic situation. It had been a purely natural cohesion. He felt our objective here should be also to build such a natural cohesion.

Mr. Armstrong asked whether this meant that representation in the world organization would be by states. Mr. Welles said that that was the question.

He wished to bring up a practical problem of expediency relating to the interests and position of this country. If we provided that the representation of Eastern Europe in the world organization would be regional rather than from each state, we should have to do this ourselves in the Western Hemisphere or else place the representation of the large powers on a different basis than that of the small powers. Speaking for himself, he would personally oppose such a differentiation. Hence, the question arose whether it was possible to create a group interest and power while, at the same time, maintaining the representation by states rather than from the region.

Mr. Bowman said he was in the same mood of uncertainty. He would, however, offer a few comments. Various schemes had, in the past, been proposed for regional groups. In the article or plan which had been circulated to the members of the committee, the solution had been found in a thorough-going amalgamation of the units. He himself could not find any such willingness to amalgamate. He was driven to a regional point of view, largely from Latin American considerations, but also because the great victors always fall apart after a war. He thought a four power combination would be only temporary. For the armistice period, of course, we must try to keep the great powers together. Nothing was, however, surer than that they will fall apart unless merged into some larger unit (an international organization). It was, he felt, very easy to dream of a world organization, but it was a terribly perilous undertaking and had little chance of success. Therefore, he would look around the world for natural associations and build up on that basis so long as the division did not oppose what might be called the democratic group.

Coming down to the East European region, he felt the author of the article or plan circulated to the members had missed the point that nothing can be secure if it is based upon a scheme over weighted with intellectualism. A plan, drawn up in too great detail, simply could not be carried out. His "final conclusion" about the political question, therefore, was that the political council should be as simple as possible with the expectation that complications enough would come in the future. He wished to emphasize the need for simplicity and would, accordingly, come back to the statement that two representatives, as had been suggested last time, one the Prime Minister or his plenipotentiary and the other a representative of the national parliament, seemed to be where we would *begin and end* so far as the political council was concerned.

Mr. Berle said he wished to underwrite what Mr. Bowman had said. There had been proposals in the past for political unions, especially that of the Baltic States in 1922-1923. This had been the result of the ambition and activity of one man who emerged in the locality. It had finally broken up because of mild opposition from the Russians. An attempt had been made in 1938-1939 to

Documents

revive the plan again on the initiative of one man. The Russians had again opposed. In each case, the result had been the same.

He felt that after the war very few of the present exiled governments would ever reach power. The governments which would come into existence would rather reflect local, racial and national groupings. He thought that a general formula for government was out of the question. The most we could do, he thought, was to shepherd them into getting together to consider their common interests. He thought we might do two things:

(1) Arrange some kind of regional representation, and
(2) Try to emphasize the freedom of the operations of individuals within the countries which would be more flexible than the governments. For example, there might be freedom of communication and transit and of finance.

He thought that we should have as our objective the simplest form of organization with normal national and racial freedom. He thought that the world group should try to get the region to work together and at the same time, should itself observe the self-denying ordinance of not exploiting them for its own purposes.

Mr. Bowman said that apparently this would mean a state and not regional representation.

Mr. Welles said we should try and formulate concrete ideas on the matter.

Mr. Taylor observed in relation to the economic side that the economic committee was dealing with the question which had been referred to it. He wished to summarize, for the benefit of the committee, the tentative conclusions of the first meeting of the economic committee. They favored an attempt at a regional economic organization and formulated three fundamental questions in relation to it:

(1) What would be the tariff and other trade relations within the area?
(2) What would be the tariff and other trade relations of the region with outside powers?
(3) What monetary and other economic machinery would be necessary?

Mr. Welles said that this summary was of interest to the committee. We should, however, get back to the political aspects and try to formulate our thoughts concretely. If we agreed on a regional approach to world organization with, at the same time, the *states* being represented on it, our objective should be first to tie in the political organization of the region with the structure of the world organization. If we should support Mrs. McCormick's idea of a *presidium* – which he definitely did – each state would have two members on the political council. Why, he asked, should not the representatives of the states in the world organization be the same as the representatives on the political council? He had made the suggestion in the last meeting that the representatives in the political council be elected to be sure that they were true representatives of the people rather than of what might be non-representatives governments. He liked better the suggestion that the representatives should speak for the government that is, that the Prime Minister and legislature be represented. Such representatives, while having public backing, could speak for the government as well.

He asked Mr. Notter to take down the points as the committee formulated them and to incorporate them into the plan as it had developed so far. *The first suggestion, then, would be that there be a political council or presidium of the East European Union composed of two delegates from each component state who shall be the representatives of these states in a world council.* [our italics – JŁ & MM]

Mr. Berle asked whether other powers would not still try, with this setup, to fragmentize the union again. Would not, therefore, the use of the same representatives in the world organization make the union tend to fly apart?

Mr. Welles thought that the result would be the exact opposite of this and that unity might in fact be increased.

Mr. Atherton suggested that even though representation in the world organization might be by states, voting in it be by regions. The representatives from the states in a region would, before each vote, need to meet together and decide how their quota of votes would be cast.

Mr. Welles said that this was a very interesting suggestion.

Mr. Atherton thought that the solution would also take care of the old British Empire question. Much question had risen in the past about the British Empire voting as a unit in the League. Under this system, the state representatives from any region would have to solve for themselves in some kind of a caucus just how their vote would be cast. Only regions and not states would have votes.

Mr. Welles observed that this came again to our own doorstep. The United States, being in the Western Hemisphere federation, would then have to go into a caucus with the other republics. Would we then have to vote according to what the majority of these republics would say?

Mr. Cohen said he was troubled by one aspect of the proposal. Would it not tend, he asked, to obscure differences within the region that might be important outside the region and which should be expressed?

Mr. Berle said the Latin American bloc had contained three general groupings. First, the United States; second, the northern tier of states; and third, a group of big states like Brazil which tended to support our positions. Practically, he said, a half dozen persons had emerged as the leadership of the old bloc. In this Hemisphere he thought we would have a somewhat different question. We have, he said, always had a kind of caucus here and have come out all right.

Mr. Welles said that he thought the American people had never had just this experience. He had referred, in his earlier remark, to what happened in the League of Nations before Mr. Berle had come into the Department. During the later years of the League of Nations, the Latin American countries had always voted together on questions of League organization and on some questions of economics and of international security but on other questions of an internal nature, such as labor, their votes had split. He would repeat that the United States had never had any experience in a setup such as had been proposed. He himself, could not see the American people agreeing that their policy could be determined by the majority of the other American Republics.

Documents

Mr. McCormick pointed out that with a regional approach to world organization, purely intra-regional questions would not come to the world organization. She thought one of the defects of the League of Nations had been that it had been concerned to such a degree with purely regional questions. Mr. Armstrong asked what she meant by regional questions. Mrs. McCormick said that these would be mostly economic and would concern also minorities. Mr. Armstrong thought that while economic questions might be settled in the region, non-economic questions, such as those concerning minorities, could not.

Mrs. McCormick answered that the solution of such problems could be helped in the world organization if the region would, by organizing, gain security and freedom from exploitation.

Mr. Armstrong observed that we then came around to the guarantee of security by the world organization.

Mr. Welles asked whether of the many questions in the region which seemed impossible of solution, except through the world organization, the majority would not be disposed of if certain Articles of Confederation which must be imposed, contained positive principles which the component states would have to adopt in their internal order. These would include religious freedom, civil rights, free elections and rights of minorities. Again it would be recalled that we were going to impose boundary settlements at the outset which would, he hoped, do away with some of the worst disputes which might arise. Such requirements as to internal conditions in the states might reduce the tendency of leaders in the region to bring up artificial disputes merely for the purpose of distracting the attention of their peoples from defects of their governments. He thought, accordingly, that such Articles of Confederation would tend to bring it about that regional boundary questions would not be brought to the world organization.

Mr. McCormick recalled also that there would be a judicial organization with the possibility of appeal to the world court.

Mr. Welles then stated a second conclusion based upon the first. It was clear that the political body would be greatly limited in its functions and would grow later. Its sole executive function would be the maintenance of intra-regional security through control, which it would be necessary to delegate to an executive, of the *gendarmerie* according to the terms of the Articles of Confederation.

Mr. Welles then said the committee would consider the composition of the economic council.

Mr. Cohen first however recurred to the question concerning the representation in the world organization by the members of the political council. He asked whether there could be some flexibility about that. He observed that, for example, if the political council should have important functions and be successful, it might be in session at the same time as the world organization.

Mr. Welles said that in approving the suggestion that one representative be from the executive and the other from the legislature of each country, he had been thinking of the matter of expediency from our own standpoint. Such an arrangement would make it easier in this Hemisphere. In particular, the approval of our Congress would be much easier to secure if Congress itself were represented.

He noted that, in his and Mr. Cohen's plan, it had been suggested that four interests be represented, making eight to twelve representatives for any one state. This would be a sizeable organization. In order to make it simpler and more manageable, he thought it would be preferable to have only two from each state.

He had some misgiving about the referring of matters back to national legislative bodies. If, for example, seven or eight should approve, while three or four did not, what should be done? Should force be applied to those who did not concur?

Mr. Welles thought that we must have some way to enforce decisions of the majority against the minority; to put majority approvals into effect in the whole region; otherwise, we will stultify the organization.

Mr. Hackworth suggested a further method that each state be allowed to send as many representatives as it wished while voting strength remained uniform. He thought, however, that if the council were to be a body of experts, there would not be much purpose in a large personnel.

Mrs. McCormick thought that the representation on the economic council would need to be larger than on the political council. Both agriculture and industry would have to be represented and this might be done on the basis of the number of persons employed in each.

Mr. Hackworth said it would be necessary to have qualified people as representatives. Mr. Bowman asked whether a distinction could be made between the representative and his staff. While the representative could not know everything, the staff could.

Mr. Welles then said he wished to call upon the "minority of one".

Mr. Pasvolsky said that he would like to report on the lines along which some governments in London are thinking. He said he had recently talked with a man who had discussed these matters with representatives of those governments. First, a definite idea had emerged that there should not be a single grouping, first, because of the opposition of Russia (although no clear reason for this had been disclosed) and secondly, because of the internal opposition previously mentioned in the committee namely, the fear of the northern group of states that the standard of living of the southern group would reduce their own. There was, accordingly, some thought of two groupings with some joint arrangements.

Yugoslavia and Greece were not getting far in their discussions of union. The Poles and Czechs, however, had made considerable progress and their discussions had some bearing on the questions under consideration in the committee. They had agreed first on Joint Boards on which the two governments were represented. The Czechs and Poles did not, however, agree on whether to include Hungary. The Poles apparently wished to include Hungary as a counterweight to the Czechs. In this connection, the question has arisen concerning a Joint Board for a joint tariff system. The free trade system assumed would include the competing Hungarian and Czechoslovak farmers. The Czechs had, however, devised a scheme for government control of agricultural produce in order to keep Hungarian products out of the Czech section of this "completely free trade area". Someone had then proposed a Joint Board for agricultural marketing for the whole area. On this point, however, little progress was being made because it involved a genuine limitation of sovereignty. At the moment it could not be decided whether the Joint Board could actually decide for itself or would refer back to governments.

The Poles and Czechs had also gone some distance in regard to monetary and credit relations. Both countries were interested, especially the Poles. If an economic union were established, a flight of capital from Poland to Czechoslovakia would take place because the Czech government would presumably be more stable. The plan had, therefore, been proposed that unlimited credit be extended by each central bank to the others so that each would have a sufficient quantity of the other country's currency. The Poles had suggested the plan that to counteract the flight of capital, the Czechs invest these amounts in Poland itself. Such suggestions, however, related only to day-to-day transactions. The real question, however, would result from the fact that debts would accumulate in course of time. How should those debts be handled when they became large? Transportation problems would also be dealt with by a Joint Board.

In connection with this entire problem, he would recall that the League of Nations had used three separate techniques for the discussion of economic problems:

(1) A full-fledged conference of plenipotentiaries who could, agree *ad referendum*;
(2) "Quasi-unofficial" representation on the Economic and Financial Committees. These Committees consisted in large part of government officials sitting as individuals to advise the League. Unfortunately, however, when these persons reached home, they again remembered that they were government officials and, in many cases, opposed the recommendations which as experts they had proposed;
(3) After the Economic Conference of 1927, a Consultative Economic Committee was established consisting of experts invited by the League of Nations with the approval of their governments, acting as advisers to the world. This Committee met twice but did not get anywhere. This was supplanted in 1930 by the Committee on Concerted Economic Action. This also failed to make progress.

He thought that a committee of experts would need to have powers of decision or act as technical representatives merely to make recommendations. In such case, the problem would be that of securing ratifications. How, for example, would customs measures be coordinated? This would, he thought, comprise three stages.

(1) The Board would fix duties;
(2) The governments would agree;
(3) These duties would be applied and enforced at each frontier.

The third function, he thought, was political. How would this third function be performed?

Mr. Welles thought it could be performed by the regional *gendarmerie*. Mr. Pasvolsky asked whether this meant a regional customs service. In this case, how would the individual countries share in the proceeds? Mr. Welles said this was a detail which would have to be worked out later.

He said that the earlier part of Mr. Pasvolsky's discussion was interesting even though it was more for the economic group than for this committee. He asked whether Mr. Pasvolsky's own view was that the economic council should be given final powers or be merely advisory. Mr. Pasvolsky thought that if there were to be an economically unified area – even if this were confined merely to customs – there would need to be some central enforcement authority.

Mr. Welles said he was not worried about the problem of enforcement. He was, however, worried about whether it would be possible to have an economic council that did not need to be *ad referendum*.

Mr. Berle observed that this would come down to an advisory committee. He thought, however, that three or four enumerated powers (concerning, for example, freedom of transit) could be delegated to the economic council and that such powers would probably give life to the council.

Mr. Welles said that this could be taken care of if the Articles of Confederation should lay down certain principles, such as, (1) free trade within the union; (2) regional control of customs with provisions for distributing the proceeds to the component states; (3) financial arrangements.

Action on these questions would then have to go back to the parliamentary bodies. Mr. Cohen said that if these matters must be referred, the best results of expert consideration would not be obtained. He thought there was much to be said for giving control over customs, etc., to the political council, leave the economic council purely advisory and have action left to the states. Mr. Welles said that this latter suggestion was an interesting one.

Mr. Taylor asked whether the sections concerning the economic council could be re-drafted by Mr. Cohen and Mr. Hackworth. Mr. Welles said that these changes should be included in the overall picture. In order that all members might have the picture as it is at present, he asked that Mr. Notter incorporate these changes in the statement of the plan which he prepared.

He asked whether the members of the committee could meet at 10:30 instead of 10:45. The committee needed more time for its work. In July it might be necessary for the committee to hold two sessions each Saturday.

Mr. Armstrong asked whether copies of the memoranda read by the members could be circulated. Mr. Welles assented.

Mrs. McCormick asked whether the members should not prepare memoranda on the economic council. Mr. Taylor said he was interested in its compulsory functions.

Mr. Pasvolsky asked whether it would be agreeable if he would prepare a memorandum on possible functions of the economic council. Mr. Welles assented.

The chairman closed the meeting at 12:50 p.m.

Paul B. Taylor, Secretary

Documents

4

Department of State
Division of Special Research
Strictly Confidential
Minutes P – 15
June 13, 1942

Typescript, copy
AN Notter File, box 54

[THE COUNCIL FOR THE ECONOMIC DEVELOPMENT OF THE UNION]

Present:
Mr. Welles, presiding
Mr. Hamilton Fish Armstrong
Mr. Adolf A. Berle
Mr. Isaiah Bowman
Mr. Benjamin V. Cohen
Mr. Green H. Hackworth
Mr. John V. A. MacMurray
Mrs. Anne O'Hare McCormick
Mr. Leo Pasvolsky
Mr. Myron C. Taylor
Mr. Ray Atherton
Mr. Paul Daniels
Mr. Harley Notter, Research Secretary
Mr. Paul B. Taylor, Secretary

(...)[1] **Economic Council: Composition**
The committee then took up the document entitled "A Central European Union as So Far Considered".[2] It was suggested that each member state have two delegates, one appointed by the Prime Minister or executive, the other elected by Parliament. In this view, stronger states could secure their aims irrespective of the basis of representation. Economic activities within a state could not be represented adequately. Their number and type would differ from state to state.

---

[1] The first part of the session, dealing with the Chart on the Armistice Period, is omitted.

[2] Though instructions on how to refer the attachment to Minutes P-14 of 6 June 1942 has not been found in the archives, the résumé below, together with the typescript of P-14 quite clearly suggests its content. See also the next document.

No adequate way to represent consumers had been found; transportation and commerce were largely international and their problems chiefly technical. Finance was international and tied in with other interests. For labor, agriculture and management to be represented would tend to accentuate their differences and it would be hard to get satisfactory representatives. In Poland, for example, there was the peasant leader Witos who could be representative, but representation of industry and finance would be difficult. Representation of labor in all cases involved the political problem of choosing between the left and right wings. Practically, governments would probably dominate all choices.

It was noted that such a body would be almost a replica of political council. A different kind of representation (even if equal) was desired. Economic representation might possibly get these countries out of vicious circle and result in representatives of a different type from those who had done so little for Eastern Europe in the past.

To designate the body as an expert economic council might also help to cause the choice of men with expert economic competence. Some definite means should, however, be found to effect this. Although the representation of interests would be artificial in some cases, the members might become increasingly representative if the system succeeded.

It was suggested that in countries which have little industry, the professional classes were important. Taken together with commerce and industry, they might be represented separately from labor and agriculture.

It was noted that in Eastern Europe the Central Banks had more to do with industry, movement of crops, etc., than anyone else. One of the states' members might be a representative of the Bank. The Central Banks had an especially broad point of view. If, however, they had this power, there was a risk that the governments might place politicians in control of them.

It was suggested that the government of each country appoint two or three experts and that we rely on this to provide representation for economic groups. Formal representation of competing interests had, (*e.g.* in the Labor Board) emphasized differences and made agreement difficult. We could not prescribe too definitely for the governments. To succeed, the plan would require their fullest cooperation. The choice should be left to them with perhaps a general indication of the purpose of the organization. In another view, a definite standard for selection should be set. If not, the economic council would be purely political.

The basic difficulty in the problem lay in the fact that the organization would have constantly to "allocate advantages" among states and affect their internal conditions. This, as reparations had done in the case of Germany, might cause acute resentment. To have the *governments* select experts cut through this difficulty – "it asked only if the expert was economic, not if he was representative". A maximum number of delegates might be fixed, corresponding roughly to the number of important economic groups; each state could select any number up to that maximum. States might see that they needed real experts. No need was seen for special representation of governments.

In summary it was accepted that each state should be represented in the economic council by not more than five experts, to be selected by the governments

Documents

– from the Central Banks, labor, industry, agriculture and the professional classes – and that the terms of reference should stress that the delegates should know what they were to consider and also be experts in these subjects.

The question was raised whether members should serve fixed terms. It was thought that even though governments changed rapidly, competent representatives would tend to be kept in office. The consensus was apparently that there should not be fixed terms.

Procedure for Passage and Approval of Recommendations

It had been previously agreed that the delegation from each state in the economic council would vote as a unit. The question was raised, by what majority the council could submit recommendations to governments. In one view a two-thirds majority should be required; in another unanimity; in a third it would not be necessary to specify precisely the procedure for making recommendations since the functions of the council were advisory; and while unanimity should in practice be sought, minority as well as majority views should be circulated to the governments.

It was thought desirable, however, to fix the recommendation procedure definitely, so that the value of and support for recommendations could be known. A requirement of unanimity was opposed as enabling one state to deprive the union of its value.

The committee had earlier discussed but had not decided the point (on page 3 of the summary of the plan) that recommendations approved by a majority of states might be placed in effect for the whole region. It was thought that a bare majority of approvals would not be satisfactory. A "double majority" of two-thirds, *i.e.* a two-thirds majority in the economic council and approval by two-thirds of the states, was suggested. Another suggestion called for a three-fourths majority. The possibilities of states combining their votes should be considered very carefully before a definite majority was fixed. In one view, if a two-thirds or three-fourths majority of approvals were provided, a simple majority should suffice for passage of a recommendation by the council. This was analogous to the procedure for amendment of the American Constitution through proposal by majorities in Congress and ratification by three-fourths of the states.

It was suggested that provision be made for the adoption by some of the states of proposals which failed to receive the stipulated majority of votes in the council. In some matters, such as the establishment of electric power grids or the fixing of hours of labor, arrangements among a minority of states might be practicable. Voluntary action of such a type pertained to the states a right. It was pointed out, however, that states could take any action not contrary to the articles of union. It was queried whether to provide arrangements for minority action might not foster divisions and hamper real unification. In many cases, it was believed that uniformity of action might be necessary. It was decided that decision of this matter should be postponed for the present.

Question was raised whether the functions of the economic council should be limited to the referral, by a stipulated vote, of recommendations on specific matters to the states or whether broad powers to recommend general economic policies might be vested in it. Such action might foster a natural development of regional economic unity. It was thought that the powers of initiation of the economic council should be as wide as possible.

It was suggested that arbitration might be provided for in some cases involving the execution of recommendations, though this would involve difficulties because of the number of states in the union. It was noted, however, that the establishment of a regional judiciary with possibility of appeal to the international court was envisaged. Such appeals would be allowed only on cases of a nature important to the union or its members. Appeals might be allowed in such cases as:

(1) disputes or differences between component states;
(2) any cases arising from an allegation that any state had not performed its duties under the Articles of Union;
(3) any allegation by an individual that the Bill of Rights had not been carried out in respect of him and that he had no redress.

Such appeals would involve recommendations of the economic council only if it were alleged that the council had exceeded its powers under the Articles of Union.

Foreign Advisers to the Economic Council

The United Nations should appoint economic advisers to represent them in the economic council as a whole. It should be definitely specified that these advisers had a voice in the Economic Council but no vote or *veto* power. Their practical *veto* power, the power to refuse economic benefits in behalf of the United Nations would, however, be very great. They would be assisted by staffs.

It was thought that the number of foreign advisers should be as small as possible. In order to secure continuity of policy their terms of office might be fixed at for example, five years. On the other hand, in order to avoid predominance by some accidental groupings it was suggested that the terms be short. Advisers might be confirmed annually by the international organization. On the other hand, a tenure of one year was thought too short for securing the kind of advisers desired. It was suggested further that the economic council might have a *veto* of appointments of advisers or that advisers be appointed by the United Nations "after consultation" with the economic council.

It was believed that for economic advisers to represent interested powers would be disadvantageous. Such arrangements had led to constant conflicts and would set a bad example for the economic council. Nor should the foreign advisers represent individual economic interests.

The thought of the committee was summarized as follows: There should be a total of three foreign advisers with overlapping terms of office – one might come up for re-appointment after one year, the second after two years and the third after three years. These advisers should not come from Europe (including Russia). The question was raised whether we would accept such an arrangement as this in our Hemisphere. As to this, it was said that no need for advisers of this type was envisaged in this Hemisphere.

It was suggested that the foreign advisers should be similar to the Economic and Financial Committees of the League, which had excellent research staffs and conducted discussions on a high plane. Such committees would be re-created in the international organization and the foreign advisers of the union would be closely linked with them. The suggestion that these committees appoint the foreign advisers commended itself but was not the subject of decision.

It was suggested that the economic council be called "The Council for the Economic Development of the Union", an this was generally approved.

5

DEPARTMENT OF STATE
Division of Special Research
Secret
P Document 24

Typescript, copy
AN Notter File, box 55

[AN EAST EUROPEAN UNION AS CONSIDERED TO JUNE 19, 1942]

Basic Assumptions

The regional organization should have the form not of a federation but of a union of independent and sovereign states, cooperating for limited objectives through common non-legislative institutions, loosely rather than tightly organized. Provisionally the union is considered as including all states of Central and Eastern Europe between Russia and Germany from and including Estonia on the North to Austria on the West and Greece on the South.[1]

The union should be imposed, if necessary, and should be guided for an indeterminate time, by the United Nations.

Its main object should be security, but economic incentives and advantages should be developed. Overall international security would be guaranteed by the United Nations and the world organization and the security organization of the union should be integrated with the world security organization within which should function.

The United Nations should promote the formation and stability of the union by making all necessary boundary adjustments in the region as rapidly as possible after the war.

Summary of Functions of Regional Organization

(1) Security relations with the outside world and with international organization;
(2) Intra-regional security and order by means of a regional constabulary or *gendarmerie*;
(3) Foreign relations of the union as such and cognizance of external relations of component states;
(4) Intra-regional economic relations; and
(5) Economic relations with the outside world.

---

[1] Such a broad confederacy would suggest a prevalence of supporters of Sikorski's plan and was a result of Armstrong's convincing arguments.

Constitution

The regional constitution, in the form of articles of union, would include written guaranties of certain individual and group rights – certain civil rights such as freedom of speech and religion, free elections and rights of ethnic minorities. The union organization would have clearly defined and limited powers at the beginning, with the possibility of growth provided.

Executive

An executive would be chosen by majority vote of the political council (or presidium) and empowered to carry out delegated duties in regard to security. He would be subject to removal by and special instructions from the political council.

Political Council

(a) Composition

The political council should consist of two members from each component state. One of the representatives from each state should be the Prime Minister or his plenipotentiary; the order should be a representative of the national parliament or his alternate.

(b) Functions

At the outset at least the functions of the political council would deliberately be limited.

Its sole executive function would be the maintenance of intraregional security, effected through control of the regional *gendarmerie*. It would establish and exact the regional quota of forces required of the component states for the maintenance of the *gendarmerie* of the union. And it would be responsible for filling the regional quota required for the police force of the international security organization. Discharge of the security function would be lodged in the executive described above.

Its political functions would include the foreign policy of the union in its relations with the rest of the world and the taking of cognizance of any national relations of component states with outside nations or groups which were in violation of the undertakings of the union. The council would seek to prevent disputes between component states or to undertake their settlement so far as possible. And it would decide the contribution of the component states for the necessary expenses of the union.

Its administrative functions would be the maintenance of a regional administration including a central secretariat. Whether this council would have responsibility for collection and apportionment of customs duties remains under discussion.

The members of the council would be responsible for the action by their individual governments to secure national approval and enforcement of decisions.

Economic Council

(a) General Nature

The economic council would be separate from the political council. It would be an advisory body except in certain contingencies not yet agreed upon. Its recommendations would be referred to the governments of the component states for approval. It would represent the region as a whole and not merely the interests of individual states; accordingly the council might be called "Council for the Economic Development of the East European Union." This council might be the medium through which international plans for economic development of the region were handled.

(b) Functions

This council would be charged with making recommendations of the governments of the component states on economic interests of concern to the region and it would have powers as broad as possible to initiate recommendations on general economic policies. Remaining under discussion are (a) whether it should be responsible for union administration of economic arrangements approved by the component states and (b) whether it should be charged with enumerated functions relating to such matters as freedom of transit, communications, etc., in the union as a whole.

(c) Composition

Each state should be represented in the economic council by not more than five experts. Each state would select any number of experts up to the maximum. Such experts would be selected by the government in each state, from the Central Bank, industry, labor, agriculture and the professional classes. The terms of reference to the governments regarding the selection of representatives should stress that the delegates should know what they were to consider and should be competent as experts in those subjects. The experts would be assisted by staffs.

(d) Tenure of office of the members

The length of terms of the members would not be fixed.

(e) Voting

The delegation from each state in the economic council would vote as unit. The question of voting in the council as recommendations remains for discussion after receipt of a report on the economic council requested from the subcommittee on economic problems; the proposed possible solutions are: (a) no percentage specified and minority views circulated with the recommendations; and (b) a fixed percentage of two-thirds or three-fourths; and possibly unanimity in certain matters. As to approval by the states of the recommendations, tentative conclusion of views is also deferred until the requested report is received; proposed possibilities are that two-thirds or three-fourths of the component states should approve measures to become effective for the entire union, but possible unanimity should be stipulated in certain matters. While a "double majority" of the same percentage – *e.g.*, two-thirds of the council and of the states – might be a satisfactory solution, it might be feasible to require only a simple (or two-thirds) majority in the council if the required number of state approvals were set at higher majority of two-thirds (or three-fourths).

Any number of states could voluntarily undertake measures they might desire provided not contrary to the articles of union.

(f) Foreign Advisers

Three economic advisers would be appointed by the United Nations to represent them in the economic council. These advisers would serve for three-year terms but initially so scaled that one might come up for appointment or reappointment after one year, the second after two years and the third after three years. No one of the three should come from Europe (including Russia).

These advisers would have a voice in the council but have no vote or *veto* power. Their practical power would reside in the denial or grant of economic benefits by the United Nations. They should advise the whole council, not the component delegations. They should be competent on economic problems in general. They would be assisted by staffs. They should have the widest possible power or initiative with respect to recommendations on economic problems of the region.

The advisers should be closely linked to appropriate world organization committees which would be established, (possibly similar to the Economic and Financial Committee of the League of Nations); these committees might appoint the advisers or they might be selected by some type of United Nations' body, perhaps set up for the purpose, representing the United Nations' authority. These matters were deferred for discussion in connection with problems of world organization.

Judicial Organization

A regional judicial system would be created, to include a regional court with provision for appeals to a court of international Justice in cases important to the union or its members. Appeals are envisaged in the following:

(1) disputes or differences between component states;
(2) any cases arising from an allegation by an individual that the Bill of Rights had not been carried out in respect of him and that he had no redress.

The Component States of the Union: Rights and Duties

Each state of the union could maintain the diplomatic relations customary to independent and sovereign states. Each state would be responsible for contributing to the international security force such quota as political council agreed each state should provide. Contributions of men from state would be in accordance with the population. The state quotas of men in the regional *gendarmerie* are neither envisaged to be situated in the states from whence they came, nor in the event of need to use union security forces to maintain peace in the union would the state quotas be used in their own states if avoidable. No state would have national military forces; municipal police forces only would be permitted in the states.

States would retain the power to approve or disapprove the recommendations from the economic council and they would be free voluntary to make economic arrangements among each other that were not in the violation of the articles of union. Remaining under discussion is the percentage of states approvals of recommendations which would be required for adoption as binding in the union.

In the event of a regional approach to international organization, the delegates of each state to the international political organization might be its two representatives in the political council of union, voting by states rather than together as a region, but this remains for consideration in connection with world organization.

Relations with the Unites Nations and International Organization; Summary of Tentative Views

(a) Gendarmerie

The United Nations would vest control of the regional *gendarmerie* in the political council after making the essential decisions concerning military forces in the region. The commanding officers would at the outset be selected by the United Nations, which would also determine the size of the force for a stated period.

(b) Security

The general security organization would require of the union the regional quota or contribution necessary for the international police force. Regional security arrangements would be integrated with the general security system.

(c) Political Relations

The union as such might be represented in the international political organization; this remains for later consideration.

(d) Economic Relations

The United Nations would give advice to the union on economic questions through three advisers.

(e) Judical Relations

Provision for appeal from the judicial organization or tribunal of the union to an international judicial organization would be made.

Documents

6

DEPARTMENT OF STATE
Division of Special Research
Political Subcommittee
Strictly Confidential
Minutes P – 17
June 27, 1942

Typescript, copy
AN Notter File, box 55

[NORTHERN EAST EUROPEAN GROUP AND [OR] BALKAN GROUP]

Present:
Mr. Welles, presiding
Mr. Hamilton Fish Armstrong
Mr. Adolf A. Berle
Mr. Isaiah Bowman
Mr. Benjamin V. Cohen
Mr. Green H. Hackworth
Mr. John V. A. MacMurray
Mrs. Anne O'Hare McCormick
Mr. Leo Pasvolsky
Mr. James T. Shotwell
Mr. Myron C. Taylor
Mr. Paul C. Daniels
Mr. Harley Notter, Research Secretary
Mr. Paul B. Taylor, Secretary

At the opening of the meeting at 10:45 a.m. and before beginning discussion of the topics for consideration, Mr. Welles said to Mr. Bowman that he had thought more and more of Mr. Bowman's memorandum of a statement by President Wilson while they were *en route* to Europe in December 1918. In it the President had called for his assistants to give him "a guaranteed position". Mr. Bowman, supplementing this, said that in the memorandum he had said, "Tell me what's right and I'll fight for it – give me a guaranteed position". In this connection, Mr. Bowman said he wished to take the opportunity to say what he had said elsewhere – that the necessary element was not memoranda but people and that the crucial discussions at the making of the peace can only go part way – what is necessary is that people be able to bring information and developed thinking actually to bear in negotiations. It was of tremendous importance that the head of the State be given accurate information.

Mr. Welles said that before beginning discussions, he wished to say that two weeks from today Senator Connally and Senator Austin would join us. In his own mind, it was very important that they should come. It was particularly important that they join us at this time and he felt that, through their membership, what the President wishes done would be advanced. He knew that these two gentlemen had this problem very much on their minds and that they were keenly anxious to advance the cause for which we were working. There was, he said, no thought of enlarging the committee further. The committee was definitely larger than had been planned at the beginning. The implications of the inclusion of Senators Connally and Austin could not be over-estimated.

In connection with the size of the committee, he said that, in his thought, there were distinct advantages in holding the meetings of the committee in this room in its more informal atmosphere: this would be more productive than to hold them in the large conference room where everyone would feel somewhat strange. He asked if the members of the committee did not feel the same way. There was general agreement.

Beginning the discussion, Mr. Welles then said that, according to our agreement of last week, we would go back to the consideration of an East European Union. He referred to a note in Mr. Notter's memorandum[1] that there seemed to be question about the nomenclature to be applied – whether the organization be called the East European Union or the Central European Union. He himself had always thought of the East European Union as more appropriate than the Central European Union[2] – to him, Central Europe meant Germany. Mr. Berle said that he agreed.

Mr. Welles then said that he would like to call on Mr. Pasvolsky concerning the report of the economic committee on the economic aspects of the East European Union which he had believed and hoped would be available. He understood that Mr. Pasvolsky had not been able to attend the economic committee, but that he was nevertheless ready to make some statement regarding it. Mr. Pasvolsky said that the economic committee had quite a job under weight. The committee yesterday had been willing to consider only a general statement on a customs union. There was, he said, now in preparation a series of studies, to be completed shortly, on the distribution of population in the region which would tend to show the effects of the removal of population; the effects on industry and agriculture in each country; the effects on communication and transportation; and the effects on imports and exports. The memorandum which had been discussed yesterday had dealt with an examination of different types of economic unification – a *régime* of preferential tariffs; a customs union alone; a customs union with monetary arrangements; and a form of more com-

---

[1] Missing in the Notter Files.
[2] This suggests a poor knowledge of the contemporary literature on the subject, where the notion of a Central European Union or Federation was already there to stay, as in "New Europe", published in the U.S., and as evidenced by the periodicals' titles: *Central European Observer, Central European Federalist*.

plete economic unification. As he had understood it, the feeling of the committee had been that some kind of economic unification, even though it would face political difficulties, would be better than none at all. The memorandum had been inadequate in that it had failed to show what inducements could be offered to the countries of the East European region for the formation of such an organization. The memorandum was being re-drafted in such form as to contain some discussion of this. There was, he said, some real difference of opinion as to whether a customs union would really work. The economic subcommittee would need to consider that question more fully, drawing on the experience of other customs unions. He assumed that, pending these studies, the memorandum – as revised – should be distributed. Mr. Welles said he felt it should be distributed.

Mr. Welles then asked Mr. Pasvolsky whether it might not be helpful to call on Mr. Taylor and Mr. Cohen, who had been present at the meeting of the economic subcommittee, for any statements that they would care to make about the meeting. Mr. Pasvolsky strongly endorsed the suggestion. Mr. Taylor said he had gained the impression from the discussion that some form of union would be generally desirable. For himself, however, he would need to know more about the particular products of particular states. He was unable to measure the assistance which should be given, or the form of the union until he had more information on this. He understood that the revised memorandum would present these facts. He felt that the memorandum, as revised, should be circulated; it had stimulated discussion. As to the internal situation in the Danubian States, which was in everybody's mind, the problem would be to improve their situation. As to the external situation, we would need to consider the effect of unification upon our own country. In some particulars, especially in regard to industrial production, our export items – such as automobiles or other products of our mechanized industries – were generally able to vault over various tariff barriers. He thought that they could probably do so in this region, particularly when one considered that our degree of industrialization and of technical development was so much higher than that of the region. He had nothing further to add on the question.

On being asked for his opinion by Mr. Welles, Mr. Cohen said he had nothing significant to add. He might mention that there was some feeling on the part of the members of the economic subcommittee that even if a full customs union could not be arrived at, we should be inclined to view favorably any reasonable preferential tariff arrangements which might be made – in general, to accord in that case as favorable treatment as we would accord in case a customs union were found to be feasible.

Mr. Taylor noted that in our various discussion here it had constantly been assumed that we were going to "impose" on the region the various political features. As to economic matters, there would be an Economic Council which would make recommendations which the states might or might not accept. This latter, he said, was different from imposing economic unification.

Mr. Welles said that, as to that point, his own thought had been that the imposition would include the basic economic features as well as the basic political features. The economic arrangements would be imposed in the same fashion as would the political. In his understanding, the recommendations of the Economic Council would be made after the initial step had been taken. He asked what the views of the other members of the committee were on this.

Mr. Cohen said that, in speaking of this matter outside of the committee, we might say that the United Nations would bring "influence" to bear to establish the arrangements desired. Outsiders might feel that the word, "impose" had undesirable connotations. Several members said they understood that these matters were not being discussed outside of the committee by committee members. Mr. Cohen said he referred merely to what had happened in the economic subcommittee. A member of that subcommittee had asked whether we intended to "impose" such an arrangement upon the East European group. Mr. Taylor and he had not, however, pursued this point. Mr. Taylor said that the word, "impose" had appeared in the minutes of this committee. Mr. Welles said that the minutes, however, were regarded as strictly confidential. He thought there was no doubt that, when the time came, we would "find a satisfactory facade" and that we might begin now to use the word "induce".

Mr. Shotwell asked whether any useful hints had been found in the German-Austrian customs union arrangements which were finally arrived at in 1918. He asked whether that matter had come up at all in the discussion. Mr. Pasvolsky said it had not been considered, but that its aim had not been the same as the one under consideration. Mr. Shotwell said that they had, however, found a formula for dealing with tariff matters. Mr. Pasvolsky pointed out that the formula had changed during the course of the negotiations. In both cases the determination of a common tariff had been left for further decision. We should consider the import of this. If tariff unification were to be left to the Economic Council which was, as he understood it, to operate *ad referendum*, this might turn out to be a long drawn-out process. In the case of the Belgium-Luxembourg customs union,[1] it had taken three years to negotiate a common tariff. In that case, moreover, the problem had been a relatively simple one, involving relations of only two small, similar countries. If we wanted to induce a tariff union, he thought we would have to get the countries *themselves* to work in the matter of tariff unification. We would not be able to work this out for them. As he understood it, neither the Polish-Czechoslovak nor the Yugoslav-Greek unions had yet seriously approached the problem of a unified tariff. It seemed to him that it would be necessary for the countries concerned to apply themselves to this question as soon as possible.

Mr. Armstrong noted that the Tardieu Plan had run up against this same difficulty in the London Conference April 6-8, 1932. Accordingly, an initial ten percent slash had been arrived at as an earnest of intention – but no further reduction had proved possible. Mr. Pasvolsky said that in this case a ten percent slash would not be of much good to anyone. The tariffs in this region were, he said, high. Especially where eight to twelve countries were involved, a mere horizontal cut would merely indicate without solving the problem. That was

---

[1] The Economic Union of Belgium and Luxembourg, a *de facto* partial customs union, signed on 25 July 1921, was seen as an encouraging experience and was a premise for the creation of the Benelux in 1944.

why he thought imposition of a solution of this would be necessary. The same thing had been done at the Ouchy Convention June 20, 1932 between Belgium, Luxembourg and the Netherlands,[1] as part of the broad program of the Oslo group.[2] Mrs. McCormick asked how far the Ouchy Convention had gone in its slash. Mr. Pasvolsky said that the cut had been ten percent; the aim was to provide a fifty percent slash by ten percent stages. Mrs. McCormick said that Colijn, the former Dutch Prime Minister, had told her that they could not get anywhere in the Oslo Group because of the opposition of the British and of the Germans, – great autarkic states (*sic*).

Mr. Welles said that Mr. Pasvolsky had mentioned two points which seemed to him to be of extreme importance. He himself could not imagine a plan of this sort having even a "ten percent chance of success" unless it were imposed from the outset. He would say again that the economic features must be imposed just as the political ones would. He had, however, hoped that the countries of the region would see positive inducements to enter into such an arrangement. The second point, he thought, was also extremely important. This was the natural question as to how the arrangement would affect our own trade interests. He had felt from the beginning that the most vital objections would come from the British Government because the plan would make it hard for British industry to get over the tariff hurdles. We were, he thought, in a better position in this regard – he thought that the plan would definitely help us! In a narrow sense, however, he thought and for the short run, it would cause trouble in England. Mr. Pasvolsky said that would depend on the height of the tariff to be arrived at. If the arrangements involved an actual reduction of tariffs, the British might benefit; but if tariffs were to be increased (which he thought might turn out, in individual instances, to be necessary in order to protect particular interests in the region), then there would be objections. He thought Mr. Taylor's point in this case might be an important one, even for us.

Mr. Welles then said that he thought it would be necessary for us to get things going. He had himself felt that we were not making enough progress. He asked whether we would not have to canalize some of our research endeavors in two ways. He thought Mrs. McCormick agreed with him in his worry as to the general nature of the plan which we were considering. He wondered whether it should not be looked at from two points of view; namely, that it consist of two unions instead of one, a Northern East European Group and a Balkan Group. If we were to conceive of an independent Austria, he thought such an Austria should have an outlet at Trieste. Questions would arise concerning the eastern frontiers of the entities. If, he thought, we were going to regard this problem from these three angles (*i.e.* of an integral union, a two-way division and a

---

[1] Ouchy Convention – a Belgian-Dutch treaty of 1932 aiming at preventing the two countries' economic isolation or their subjugation to France. It was projected as a broader sphere of free trade, with the possible access of Britain, France and Germany.

[2] Oslo Group – in the thirties, a loose intergovernmental structure of neutral Scandinavian states, plus Belgium, and Holland, aimed at coordinating their policy in view of the growing threat of war.

separated Austria), the economic subcommittee and the economic secretariat of the committee would have to work intensively on this problem. It would have to be approached not only from the angle of trade; it would be necessary to see what could be done by the United Nations for the development of the region: mineral resources, etc. The basic question would be what inducements of an economic nature could be offered to make a union attractive. He asked whether we had not got to the point where the political subcommittee should decide what the economic subcommittee would work on in this matter.

Mr. Taylor said he wished to make a statement, since Mr. Pasvolsky was present, which he might not want to make if he were absent. Mr. Pasvolsky had been unable, due to pressure of work, to attend the meeting of the economic subcommittee yesterday. The meeting had been very unsatisfactory. He felt it was utterly essential that the subcommittee have Mr. Pasvolsky's attendance and his time. This was extremely important work and Mr. Pasvolsky's position was an extremely important one. If the work were successful, it would reflect great credit on him; if it failed, the reverse would be the case. He repeated that he thought it was indispensable to have Mr. Pasvolsky's attendance and his time for this work. Mr. Welles said he wished to say that the responsibility for non-attendance was not that of Mr. Pasvolsky. He knew that in the last two weeks Mr. Pasvolsky had had a tremendous burden placed upon him by other work. He thought, however, that it would be necessary for us to get the work which we wanted from the economic subcommittee in as concise terms as possible. He thought that Mr. Berle could help us in this.

He suggested that we take the three alternatives which he had stated before as a starting point; namely, the possibility of a Northern East European Group and of a Balkan Group. The alternatives would be whether Austria was to be attached to one or the other of these economic units or to be independent, in which case, he would like to have consideration given to the inclusion of Trieste in Austria. If this were done, it would be divided up into three further portions:

1. The assistance that could be given by the United Nations, particularly the United States, in the development of the resources of the region.

At this point, Mr. Berle said he thought it was impossible to go immediately into the whole group of questions involved. Instead of trying to cover the whole territory, he thought we ought to take up two or three concrete projects. Thus, he thought we could make a study of:

(1) The principal transportation systems which ought to be connected;
(2) The development of parts of the region in terms of electric power – that is, the establishment of grids;
(3) The development of mineral resources.

He himself was not fully informed to the degree to which the Germans had exploited the mineral resources of these countries. He thought it would be possible to block out a program of solid improvement along these lines. After these three questions had been dealt with, he thought three others could be taken up:

(1) The type of industrial factories which would tend to give the best immediate service to the region. He did not know what type this would turn out to be; whether it would be textiles or other lines;

(2) Bracketed with this, the question of what imports would be needed by the region for this development. Again he did not know what the Germans had done.

Mr. Pasvolsky said one other point should be taken up; namely, agricultural development. The problem of an agricultural credit system might be dealt with; but if we should get that far, we could sketch out monetary arrangements. Mr. Berle said that he had left out the whole subject of financial structure and relationships, which should be included.

Mrs. McCormick asked about the cooperative systems which existed in the region. She wondered whether some norm could not be set up from the outside which would apply to these systems. Mr. Pasvolsky said the cooperative movement was at the moment going in the wrong direction in most of these countries.

Mr. Welles thought that the suggestions which Mr. Berle had made would be of distinct help to the economic subcommittee. He thought that if the committee was in accord, Mr. Pasvolsky might refer these proposals to the economic subcommittee. In working on this problem, he had the feeling that the work of the economic subcommittee should be "to tell us what we need in order to make our political decisions work" instead of merely telling us that our political decisions were, from the economic point of view, impracticable.

Mr. Bowman agreed. He said that we had two main jobs: to work out various concrete ways in which we could make a union attractive; the other, to get a very clear notion as to what to do, how to do it, when to do it in the event a scheme were set up and a rebellion should start against it as the protection of the United Nations spread its wing over the area. He thought it was most important to have this matter in mind. He felt, accordingly, that at one end we had the problem of attraction to the union; at the other end, what to do when dissension should come along or separation ensue. He thought that the real trouble would come in this latter area. Could we, he asked, sustain the advantages which we would offer?

Mr. Welles said he thought we had the right to assume that, in the transition period, the United Nations would have the power to prevent disruption. He thought the scheme would have to be good and, in addition, it would have to have time to prove itself to the people of the region. Mr. Bowman said that, in other words, it would depend upon the United Nations.

Mr. Armstrong noted that, at the end of the last war, the Rumanians had seized Budapest against the will of their own allies, but that nobody had been in a position to send troops to prevent it.

Mr. Bowman said he wished to make a further statement on the canalization of the research. He recognized that the second of his overall considerations could be analyzed only when the other studies had been made. He asked, however, whether it might not be desirable to have the members of the research staff, who were working on the points suggested by Mr. Berle, keep the second point which he had mentioned in mind. In other words, "What happens if it doesn't work?" In war one must have both tanks and anti-tank weapons; the same thing would hold here.

Mr. Berle asked what the practical application of this would be. Did Mr. Bowman mean that an economic structure should be worked out which would go on even though the union were to break up? Mr. Bowman said he thought that if there were to be a break-up, the theory that would be followed would be the classic theory (which one would apply, for example, in relation to electric power systems) that natural connections and associations should be worked out. Our solution would be, in some degree, artificial. If we were to follow the line of natural advantages, what would we do in case of a break-up? For example, would control of the electric power enterprise be through "paper certificates"? Who would control the certificates in case of a break-up? What would happen if the scheme did not work? He thought it might confuse the research workers if too much emphasis were laid upon the second point. It would, however, help us if in their work they considered those possibilities.

Mr. Berle said that, in other words, Mr. Bowman conceived that the work might be carried on at "two altitudes":

(1) the job on the ground;
(2) to find a means of strengthening the scheme when it does work and of making it flexible so that it could adjust to varying conditions.

Mr. Bowman said that was what he had had in mind.

Mrs. McCormick thought that the nearer we came to natural solutions, the better the chance that those solutions would work.

Mr. Welles said that his mind went back to the type of determination which took place in the Peace Conference of 1919, when boundaries were determined not by where they should be located, but by such factors as the location of railways. Mr. Bowman said that, for example, in determining the boundaries of Czechoslovakia, the railways had been of decisive importance. Mr. Armstrong asked why those railways had been built. They had, he said, been built to make a coordinated system of defense for Austria-Hungary. They were not, in other words, a "natural" situation. Mr. Welles said that that was exactly the point he had intended to make. He asked whether, at least at the start, we should not be seeking for ideal solutions rather than limiting ourselves too much by railway locations and such material considerations.

Mr. Armstrong said that before the last war, every Croat prune had to be sent up to Budapest to be stamped before it could be exported. This was not, he said, a "natural" situation. Mr. Welles said that, with that clarification, the main points that Dr. Berle had set out could be taken up.

Mr. Shotwell asked whether consideration had been given to the factor of security. Railways, for example, were constructed with this in mind. He thought that the question of security tended to falsify what would be otherwise reasonable arrangements. Mr. Welles said that the committee had assumed from the beginning that a general international organization would intrinsically produce security. The committee had, therefore, deliberately omitted it from discussions of particular problems.

Mrs. McCormick said that what we should do was to follow in our solutions the natural line and then to have the world organization take care of the matter of security. As a matter of fact, to posit a world security organization made it really possible to seek natural solutions. Mr. Bowman asked what one mean by "natural". Mrs. McCormick said that was, of course, the problem – she suggested the word, "reasonable". Mr. Berle suggested that what was meant by "natural" was simply "that which would develop the region". Transportation lines would, to a certain extent, have to be controlled or determined by the United Nations.

Mrs. McCormick thought that we would have to begin with the development of the region by the Economic Council. That was, she felt, the most fruitful method of approach.

Mr. Taylor admitted that it was always good strategy to plan a possible retreat; he thought, however, that our interest was not to plan a retreat, but rather "to win the battle". He did not think there was any point in our going on any other assumption.

Mr. Bowman said that, in the amicable atmosphere of this committee, he wished to present the opposite point of view. The more we elaborated on a system, the more problems we raised and the more we tended to "act like God" and dispose of everything; and the more we gave a chance to the individual state to seize advantages for itself and hold out against the rest. He thought it was only prudence to watch out for this. We would need to identify trouble in advance and provide against it. Such a counsel was not one of defeat. Mr. Welles said that, in fact, it might be likened to a rather wise insurance policy. The redetermination of boundaries inevitably created troubles. He thought that the troubles of postwar Europe would probably be greater after this war than they had ever been before. Mrs. McCormick thought that Mr. Bowman was "burdening the victors even more than the vanquished".

Mr. Welles said that he was beginning to get concerned over the tremendous size of the problems which confronted us. After the committees had reached their decisions and the President had reached his decisions and before the war is over, this Government had got to reach agreements with the other United Nations, particularly with the countries of the British Empire, the Soviet Union and China on all the basic terms of peace. All this, he said, would take a tremendous amount of time. Time was passing. The sooner we could reach tentative conclusions, the better chance we would have. He asked whether it would not be desirable to canvass the problem under consideration from the political standpoint again.

The more he had thought over the question, particularly during the past week, the more difficult it seemed to have a complete East European Union covering the entire area we had thought of. He wondered if success would not be more likely if we were to have a Northern East European Group and a Balkan Group. Our whole objective was the inducement of peace by removing the possibility of war or exploitation by big powers, such as Germany, Russia and Great Britain, against the small states of the region; and by making the people of the region as prosperous and contented as possible. We had thought the best way to achieve this was by creating a buffer, not subservient to

Germany, the Soviet Union, or to Great Britain. The question thus arose whether a division of the area into two parts would diminish the possibility of accomplishing that objective.

Mrs. McCormick thought it would be necessary to define the boundaries of the two groups and to determine what liaison there should be between them. It would, she thought, be extremely hard to get the antagonistic peoples together at the beginning. She thought Austria offered a possibility as a sort of liaison country – a meeting ground. Turning to Mr. Welles, she said that she did not know what conversations he and other officials had had on such questions. Mr. Welles said that so far as he could determine, it would be an appallingly difficult job. The bitter feeling of Yugoslavia and Greece toward Bulgaria – the justifiably bitter feeling – was one which he, personally, had rarely seen equaled. Mrs. McCormick referred also to the bitterness between Hungary and Rumania. Mr. Welles added the hatred of Czechoslovakia and Hungary; and of Yugoslavia and Hungary. There would be question whether the danger would diminish by having all of these countries together. Mr. Pasvolsky asked whether we could draw a line between the groups which would minimize the effects of these antagonisms. Mr. Welles said that one group would be Lithuania, Poland and Czechoslovakia (and Austria?). The Balkan Group would consist of Greece, Bulgaria, Yugoslavia and Rumania.

Mr. Armstrong raised the question as to what power would try to exploit the area and under what conditions it could succeed. Mrs. McCormick thought that Russia would be likely to dominate the Northern Group while Germany would dominate the Southern. Mr. Welles said, "Or *vice versa*". Mr. Armstrong thought it would be more likely to be *vice versa*. The question would arise as to the social policy maintained by Soviet Russia after the war. This could, he pointed out, override all other considerations. He felt that the appeal of pan-Slavism was the strongest in Yugoslavia and Bulgaria. He thought there was some possibility of improvement of the relations between Bulgaria and Yugoslavia if there were very radical Bulgarian and Yugoslav régimes. This possibility had been indicated by the Stambulisky[1] régime in Bulgaria; if, however, the Bulgarian dynasty were to hold, he thought there would not be this possibility. Mr. Berle said that the Bulgarian-Greek antagonism was worse than the Bulgarian-Yugoslav. Mr. Armstrong thought, however, that even this might be better in a successful organization.

Mrs. McCormick said there had been a movement at one time toward a *rapprochement* between Venizelos[2] and a Bulgarian leader whose name she had

---

[1] Alexander Stamboliiski, Prime Minister of Bulgaria between 1919-1923. The leader of the Peasant Party, his reforms helped the farmers but aroused the anger of the urban population. He was murdered in 1923.

[2] Eleutherios Venizelos (1864-1936), Greek politician, active in securing the union of Crete with Greece of 1908, Prime Minister in 1910-1915 and again in 1928-1932. In 1933, while declaring the idea of Balkan concord, he managed to join a part of Thracia to Greece after the Balkan wars of Epirus and Macedonia. Sought a *rapprochement* with his country's neighbors in the twenties. Emigrated to France after a failed coup.

Documents

forgotten (Stambulisky?). Mr. Armstrong concurred that there had been such a movement between the two countries in 1925 and 1926. The Bulgarian dynasty had been the chief obstacle to it, while the Greek Church had been a great assistance.

Mr. Shotwell said that it had been very surprising in 1912 when the two countries had got together in an alliance.[1] They *could* do things. He thought that if they were to get rid of the nationalists, the peasants would not cherish hatreds as in the past. The Secretary to Stambulisky, who had worked for him, had been convinced that the peasants were kept from friendly relations with the Greeks by their nationalist leaders. Mr. Armstrong said that they were kept from it by being killed.

Mr. Armstrong, continuing the earlier discussion, said that half of the area would be very likely to come under Russian influence.

Mr. Bowman said that in studying this question, we would have to ask what were the minimum conditions of success. What were natural affiliations? On top of that, explorations would be made in the direction of Mr. Berle's five points. It would be necessary to investigate what natural affiliations had taken place in the past; in what directions they had been capable of extension if others had seen the need of it. He asked whether that would be a good direction in which to go. He asked whether the economic experts could not give us in a short paragraph a statement of these natural developments during the past twenty or twenty-five years.

Mr. Welles said it was clear that an association of Lithuania, Poland, Czechoslovakia and Austria would have historical background to it, provided that the "bogy" of a Habsburg restoration were removed. He would assume that in a new world situation, some old objections would be in part removed. Then we would have the problem of Hungary. From every standpoint of expediency, Hungary would have to be part of the Northern Union. If we took the historical background, Yugoslavia would form part of this group; but if we were to go further back, Yugoslavia should be a member of the Balkan Group in case there were to be two groups. So far as he was concerned, he was not "wedded to the view that just because Slovenia and Croatia had been part of Serbia in the past, they should always be".

Mr. Armstrong said he wished to refer again to Hungary – the character of the régime, to the need for changes of agricultural tenure and to the feudal set-up which existed in Hungary. These had been of extreme importance in Hungary's politics. Count Apponyi had, he recalled, made the claim to the Crown of Bohemia[2] through Archduke Otto in 1926. Mr. Welles asked whether this claim had been made at the League of Nations. Mr. Armstrong said that Count Ap-

---

[1] The reference is to the First Balkan War of 1912, when Bulgaria joined forces with the armies of Greece, Montenegro and Serbia against Turkey.

[2] This event is unknown. Armstrong was wrong; there was no confirmation of his statement. Count Albert Apponyi (1846-1933), a supporter of a federation within the Austro-Hungarian monarchy. He headed the Hungarian delegation for the Peace Conference (1919-20) and was later, in 1923-1933, Hungary's representative at the League of Nations.

ponyi always went to the League of Nations; at the same time, making such individual arrangements with states as he could. In that atmosphere it had been no use to ask Masaryk to talk about frontier adjustments in Slovakia. He thought, therefore, that the character of the régimes in Hungary, Poland and Bulgaria – these three, he thought, were the most backward socially, especially Hungary in the matter of land tenure – was a factor of great importance.

Mr. Berle said it appeared that there were really only two possibilities as to the division between the North and South Groups. The question concerned only whether Austria and Hungary were to go with the Northern Group or with the Southern Group. He wished to suggest, as a new possibility for consideration, that we turn them south. The east-west line might be at the southern Czechoslovak boundary, running from there to the northern part of the Black Sea.

Mr. Welles asked Mr. Berle whether he meant that the Northern Group would consist of Lithuania, Poland and Czechoslovakia. Mr. Berle said that that was what he had meant. Mr. Cohen said unless one did that, there would not be a cohesive force to hold the Balkan Group together. Mr. Berle said that had been the reason for his suggestion.

Mr. Cohen said one reason that had induced us before, to limit the functions of the union was that of making possible the inclusion of all the states of the region. He wondered, accordingly, whether if we were envisaging smaller unions, more powers might not be given to such unions. Moreover, the territorial division suggested by Mr. Berle enabled us to use the Northern Group to help hold the Southern Group together while leaving also the possibility that Austria and Hungary could go either way.

Mr. Welles thought that, from the standpoint of our objectives, it was clear that the larger group was the better of the solutions. However, having in mind the point which Dr. Bowman had made as to insurance against difficulties, he was puzzled as to whether the disruptive forces of such a union would not be so great as to defeat our purposes.

Mr. Shotwell said that at the last Peace Conference maps like those presented to the committee,[1] representing a possible East European Federation, had been prepared and presented by Masaryk. It had turned out, however, that Masaryk could not even overcome the nationalism in his own country. It had been a great tragedy. He thought there was a danger of our deluding ourselves as to the realities. The intellectual leaders of the area in the nineteenth century had become the nationalist leaders of the twentieth. Until recently there had been few political contacts and only limited social ones. The peasants were not, he thought, nationalists, but their intellectual leaders had adhered to the disruptive forces. This was the most difficult problem of federation. There was no place where people understood the American principle of federation. For example, the fact that Count Apponyi's estates had been in Slovakia had dominated his thinking. He did not think we could place our hopes too high unless the movement were not to be dominated by the intellectuals of the past generation.

---

[1] Missing from the Notter Files.

Documents

He thought something could be done along these economic lines. He was glad that Mr. Berle had mentioned communications first. He could remember the time when it took three days to travel from Skopje to Monastir. That time had later been cut from breakfast to tea. He wished that he knew more about what the Germans had done to smash these old ideas. He thought, however, that the strongest pull which there could be toward union would be something outside the region – some international influence or activity.

Mr. Welles asked Mr. MacMurray for his opinions. Mr. MacMurray said he was completely puzzled. He had to contend with the idea that the easiest way would be the largest organization. However, this would involve so many disparities and irreconcilables that he was afraid that we were proposing something too big to be put together. Accordingly, not on any definite grounds, but merely on an instinctive feeling, he thought that there should be at least two of these groups. In this case, he thought that Turkey should be included in the Southern Group. It had, in recent years, been a most useful factor in the Balkan meetings. It had no territorial ambitions and had been a very useful means of communication between the other governments. Mr. Welles said that this was a very interesting suggestion.

Mrs. McCormick referred to another difficulty which had been faced in the postwar period and which was embodied by Count Apponyi. Apponyi and others had maintained a policy of grievances. Their whole feeling had been dominated by their grievances. She thought that this time we should not think too much of victors and vanquished. She recalled an experience she had had when visiting the American College at Sofia. The students had just discussed the death of John Buchan.[1] It was a very international meeting. At the end, the President of the college had asked them to sing. They had then broken immediately out into their "Dobrudja" song. There was, she said, an amazing underlying feeling for Dobrudja[2] in Bulgaria. Mr. Welles said that this was very interesting.

Mr. Armstrong said that there were two factors; first, the Bulgarian claim to Dobrudja; and second, the Apponyi attitude – "something natural plus". At one time when he was visiting[3] Count Apponyi at his home, the latter had said, "I don't need to talk to you about the Rumanian problem. You have a negro problem in your own country and so you understand it." He said that both of these things existed in different countries.

Mrs. McCormick said that the Bulgarians had always felt that the Balkan Entente was aimed against them. Mr. Shotwell said that even in their own meetings of the Bulgarian Entente, the old Macedonian question had come to

---

[1] John Buchan (1875-1940), Scottish writer, best known for his popular adventure novels such as *The Thirty-nine Steps*.

[2] The reference is to Southern Dobrudja, conceded to Bulgaria by Rumania in the treaties of San Stefano (1878) and Bucharest (1913). Dobrudja finally reverted to Bulgaria through the so-called 2nd German-Soviet Vienna arbitration.

[3] The visit took place in 1922. For details see Armstrong, H. F., *Peace and Counterpeace. Memoirs of Hamilton Fish Armstrong*, New York 1971.

the fore.[1] He thought that mediation by a present day Turkey would be very useful.

Mr. Welles agreed that this was a very interesting suggestion indeed. He wondered whether the inclusion of Turkey would not mean the very determined opposition of Russia. Mr. Armstrong asked whether Mr. Welles meant the opposition of Turkey's "own ally".

Mr. Welles: "Their ally?" He said that the position in this respect had materially changed. This would raise, moreover, the old question of the straits again.

Mr. Shotwell said that the adoption of the Stalin or Curzon Line[2] as the boundary of Poland might affect the problem. Mr. Bowman said that the territorial committee would give the committee "an earful" on the Curzon Line two weeks hence.

Mr. Welles said he wished to go back to what Mr. Bowman had suggested in regard to the terms of reference to the economic subcommittee. Taking the entire area as now indicated, where should the line be drawn? He asked whether the members agreed to Mr. Berle's suggestion that Austria and Hungary be included in the Southern Group. There was, in addition, a third possibility – that Austria remain outside. Mr. Armstrong thought there were great disadvantages of "leaving Austria hanging". It would make a sort of football out of Austria.

Mr. Bowman thought there was a partial answer to the Polish dynamite[3] which Mr. Shotwell had referred to. His own mind ran back over to what mathematicians would call an "inescapable series", the difficulties mentioned by Dr. Shotwell and further difficulties. We could then say that we saw no hope. We would then have individual states, at least eight. We could wipe the slate clean and start again. If we should do this, what combination could be indicated? What loose arrangements of states could we envisage? This empirical, *ad hoc* method was realistic, "but never had a solution in it". When he got through his own thinking, he still felt that somewhere, even in the distance, there was a goal. He was forced back to some more generalized picture of the East European problem. He would place great emphasis on the identification of mutual advantages and working arrangements of the last twenty years; what advantages had they? What could have been done? That seemed fundamentally a job for an

---

[1] The Balkan Entente was established on 9 February 1934 by Turkey, Greece, Rumania and Yugoslavia. The regional security organization was formed to maintain the status quo in the Balkans and to discourage Bulgarian revisionist attempts at the annexation of the Macedonian-inhabited territories belonging to Greece and Yugoslavia. However, it did stipulate for Bulgaria's access, depending on a number of conditions, at a later date. See Campus, A., *Little Entente and the Balkan Alliance*, Bucharest 1978.

[2] The "Curzon Line" was the demarcation line proposed during the Polish-Bolshevik war by G. N. Curzon, the United Kingdom's Foreign Secretary, as the ethnic border at which the Red Army was supposed to halt its counter-offensive of July and August 1920. Stalin referred to this proposal to justify his claims after the invasion of 17 September 1939.

[3] An unfortunate description of the significance of territorial issues for the creation of a Central European federation.

economic specialist to go into a history of the attempts which had been made. He thought we would be aided if we knew factually what the experience had been. He asked whether anyone was prepared to bring forward experience on this.

Mr. Shotwell said it should not be forgotten that Habsburg Monarchy had rested on prestige; the prestige of its army, the church and the bureaucracy. Were there some possibilities in the intellectual cooperation of the United Nations? In the League of Nations, Austria had asked that the intellectual cooperation work be centered there. This had been refused. Could there be something of this nature alongside the economic factor?

Mr. Bowman said that Dr. Shotwell's colleague, John Dewey, had written an article in the first volume of *Foreign Affairs* on "Ethics and International Relations".[1] It had dealt with the terrible problem which confronts a world in a time of territorial fragmentation and confusion in developing common bases of ethics. Each nation favored its own ethic, sought to aggrandize it and looked at everything in terms of it. The thought of the writer had run forward to the point that the greatest consideration was flexibility. His only concrete suggestion was the outlawry of war. (Mr. Shotwell noted that the outlawry of war had been taken as an example of flexibility). Continuing, Mr. Bowman said that these conclusions had left him flat. This was, he said, nearly always true of writings on international affairs. It was also true of the discussions of this committee.

Mr. Welles said he wished to go back and insist on claiming for this Government a "guaranteed position".

He was still worried (although physically and for other reasons it seemed most reasonable) about the approach to our Southern Union through the inclusion in it of Austria and Hungary. Mr. Berle said he was not sure of this himself; he had merely thought it worth consideration. Mr. Welles thought that Austria, finding herself in that position, would assume a certain prestige. This would be entirely justified, as we all knew, that from the standpoint of culture Austria would assume a leadership. Mr. Shotwell said that it would naturally assume a leadership in economic matters as well.

Mr. Welles then said we should then make our terms of reference to the economic committee *on that line*, with an alternative to include Austria (and Hungary?) in the Northern Group.

Mr. Taylor observed that our approach now seemed to be that of "dividing up the trouble" between the Northern and Southern Groups and of segregating most of the trouble in the Southern" (*sic*). He wondered whether we could handle the matter better in that way. Mr. Welles said his own feeling was that the better solution was the whole union, but he wondered whether we could still achieve our major objectives and lessen the objections if we had two groups.

The question was asked whether Mr. Welles and Mr. Berle had talked with representatives of these countries on this matter. Mr. Berle said that no one of that group had the concept of a single union. Mr. Welles said he had never found one who had the conception of one union, most favoring three unions;

---

[1] *Foreign Affairs*, March 1923, pp. 85-89.

some, two. Mr. Berle said that the Czechs were the only ones who had offered any support for a single union.[1]

Mr. Pasvolsky said that the new Russian frontier on the map[2] (pointing to Map V) was most significant. It put the Russians next to Czechoslovakia. He thought that a balance of power in the region was of great importance.

Mr. Welles asked whether Mr. Pasvolsky had meant an internal balance of power. He agreed that this was of great importance. Mr. Pasvolsky said it might be useful to have a memorandum on the political history of the region.

As to the internal balance in the union as a whole, taking the three possibilities: (1) in the north, a reduced Poland would be about equal to Czechoslovakia.[3] Czechoslovakia would have much friendlier relations with Russia. The Poles wanted to bring Hungary into the group as an offset to Czechoslovakia. Poland plus Hungary would be difficult for Czechoslovakia to handle even with Rumanian influence; (2) in the Southern Group the line of development would be in the direction of close relationship between Yugoslavia and Bulgaria. That would be the dominant factor. It was not clear what the Russian policy would be. He thought that Russia was not nearly so close to these countries as to Czechoslovakia.

Mr. Welles said that if the lines were to exist as shown on that map, there would be a fairly good balance. Russian influence would be preponderant in Czechoslovakia, Bulgaria and Yugoslavia while anti-Russian influence would be preponderant in Hungary, Poland, Austria and Rumania. He thought this would make a fairly equal balance. If the region were divided into two groups and the Northern were left intact, Poland, Lithuania and Czechoslovakia would have a balance; in the South there would also be an internal balance in sentiment regarding Russia.[4]

Someone asked whether Rumania was anti-Russian. Mr. Welles said that if anything could bring Rumania and Hungary together, it would be hatred of Russia. Mr. Armstrong thought, on the contrary, that Rumania might conceivably be on good terms with Russia. Mrs. McCormick said that Davila,[5] who was working closely with the Czechs, was certainly not on good terms with the Russians. Mr. Armstrong said that Manin had not been particularly anti-Russian. Mr. Welles said, however, that when one considered the Bessarabian massacres and a whole series of other incidents, one saw that all of these would have the effect of creating hatreds between the Russians and Rumanians.

---

[1] This surprising statement seems to be a result of the *émigré* Czechoslovakian government's skillfulness in propaganda.

[2] Missing from the Notter Files.

[3] Pasvolsky either seems to consider very significant concessions for the U.S.S.R. while returning to the pre-war Polish-German borders, or suggests an important cut in the status of Poland in the region.

[4] Purely academic discussion.

[5] Carol Davila, Rumanian diplomat, envoy to Poland and the U.S. Emigrated during the war. In 1949, he entered the *émigré* Rumanian National Committee and represented it thereafter beginning with the 1954 Assembly of Captive European Nations.

Mrs. McCormick mentioned the problem of Transylvania. Mr. Pasvolsky referred to the antagonism between Carol and Antonescu.[1]

Mr. Armstrong said that in some countries the idea of not bringing Austria and Hungary into the Southern Union would be very agreeable. Since the last war they had tried to break the old ties; for example, in trade and banking.

Mr. Welles said that he had asked the committee to take so much time for the discussion of this matter – and the discussion had confirmed him in his own judgment – because all the views tended, in case there were to be a separation, to show that there would have to be a three-way division and not a two-way. Mr. Armstrong asked what the third division would be. Mr. Welles answered that it would be Austria, either with one or two other states or alone.

Mr. Armstrong asked whether the economic subcommittee was working on projects of actual help regarding the Balkan area. Such projects would, he said, constitute the bait which we could offer. Mr. Welles said that we had crystallized just this.

Mr. Taylor said that the first problem was to discover the needs of the area and the particular economic facts; and that when this was done, we might pass on to the question of the means of assistance.

Mr. Welles said that he was clear in his own mind that if we could reach a decision as to what was politically desirable, then the economic subcommittee should see what it could do to carry out this decision – to bolster up the system envisaged.

One thing similar to what Mr. Armstrong had referred to, which we had done in this hemisphere, might be mentioned. It was the so-called development corporations. We might make the same kind of gift to the East European Group. It gave a great leverage power to us. Mrs. McCormick thought the most important thing was to try to convince the people of the area of the advantages of a union. Mr. Taylor asked whether these groups had to do with the operations of business. Mr. Welles said that the projects went on ostensibly under the guise of local operation and control; ostensibly with American consultants and advisers. Really, he said, these American advisers "run the show".

Mr. Shotwell said that another alternative would be American interest in the Balkans through the period of relief into the period of reconstruction. This raised the question whether the Department of Agriculture would help on problems of soil erosion an the like. Theoretically, we could stimulate an interest in the common peasant in this way which might override nationalism. Mr. Welles said that was really the idea he had had in mind.

Mrs. McCormick said we might consider again the problem of the three groupings. We could, she said, easily see two. The question then concerned the disposition of Austria and Hungary. The other two seemed fairly logical. Mr. Cohen said that in regard to Austria and Hungary, he felt somewhat as Mr. Armstrong had. He would rather view it as having the possibility of going

---

[1] On 6 September 1940, General Ion Antonescu, head of the Rumanian extreme right, forced King Carol II to abdicate and leave the country. He was succeeded by the 19 year-old Michael I, who abdicated in December 1947.

either north or south than as being a third group. It seemed cut off from markets. Mr. Armstrong said that Austria and Hungary cut the Northern Group off from the Southern. Mr. Berle said that we must pre-suppose that Austria would have Trieste. This would canalize the German trade in that direction and would also absorb a lot of that which went through Czechoslovakia. Mr. Armstrong said that if joined, the Czechs could use it too. Mrs. McCormick thought that Austria and Hungary should be with the Northern Group.

Mr. Welles again said that the entire union was a desirable objective. However, from the standpoint of economic arrangements, we would consider two units as a possible alternative; whether Austria and Hungary should go north or south to be determined by the economic advantages which the economic subcommittee would show us. This was, he said, the reference to the economic subcommittee. This reference would, in turn, be broken up into the six or seven points stated earlier in the meeting.

Mr. Cohen said that, in this connection, the three alternatives might be considered.

Mr. Taylor asked whether when the report on the entire group were revised, it should be distributed to the members of this committee for their consideration. Mr. Welles said we would need this as soon as available. We would, however, return in two weeks to the Germanic problem, especially as regards East Prussia and other problems affecting the Polish frontier.

Mr. Armstrong referred to certain questions connected with this problem which had been referred to the Council group. Studies of the Eastern[1] and Western industrial regions had been worked out in terms of alternatives and would be supplied to Mr. Pasvolsky before the next meeting. One study dealt with territorial problems while one dealt with financial and economic ones.

Mr. Welles said he gathered that the Council on Foreign Relations had done a considerable amount of work which would be of value to us. Mr. Armstrong said the Council had not done anything specifically on an East European union. Mr. Welles said that he had meant that they had worked on economic aspects of these problems.

Mr. Pasvolsky noted that there might also be a report from the security subcommittee on the military aspects of partition.

Mr. Welles said he wished to say one more thing before the meeting adjourned. In order to save time, it seemed to him that some helpful preliminary work could be done on a problem which would come to this committee in time – that was the problem of an international organization which had been made the last point in the chart. At the rate at which the committee was now moving, a long time would elapse before this matter could be considered. He thought it might be desirable for a subcommittee of this committee to consider this question and to draft something in concrete terms for the full committee. If agreeable, he would ask a small subcommittee to sit on that question during coming weeks. Mr. Pasvolsky said that that subcommittee might offer projects for research on this problem. Mrs. McCormick said it would be more important

---

[1] See Doc. 6 with annex.

to have ideas than research. Mr. Welles stressed that what was desired was something definite and concrete for the whole committee to work on. Mrs. McCormick said that she had constantly felt it necessary in our discussions of particular questions to have some definite ideas of the overall organization. Mr. Welles said that it was agreeable, he would ask a small subcommittee to work with him on that and perhaps to get one or two outside consultants. He said that the committee would meet again two weeks from today.

The meeting was adjourned at 12:45 p.m.

Paul B. Taylor, Secretary

7

DEPARTMENT OF STATE
Advisory Committee
Economic Subcommittee:
Memorandum to the Political Sub-Committee
Secret
P- Document 45
August 21, 1942

Typescript, copy
NA Notter File, box 54

TENTATIVE ECONOMIC ORGANIZATION OF THE EAST EUROPEAN FEDERATION

Economic Relations of the East European Federation with the United Nations Organization

It is not possible to consider the economic organization of the East European Federation without first considering the economic organization of the United Nations.

The Economic Committee is of opinion that the United Nations should have, as a part of the permanent machinery of world organization, certain economic agencies.

These agencies should be organized so that they can work together as a fairly close-knit world economic organization. But, because world economic organization is of extreme difficulty, each agency should be so organized that it can stand on its own basis, without being wrecked or crippled by the fate of any of the companion organization.

The Committee are agreed that there should be constituted:

1. A United Nations Bank

The functions of the Bank should include:
– The stabilization of exchanges. This might be done either by a division of the Bank itself, or through operation of a stabilization fund.
– The extension of long-term credit for investment credit operations.
– Some of the functions of a bank of Issue.

The foregoing are minimal; the list is not limitative.

2. A Transport and Communications Authority

The functions of the Transport Authority should be:

- To assure freedom of transit; at reasonable rates and with suitable safety standards.
- To promote and assist, in conjunction with other United Nations agencies and through local, national and regional institutions, the construction and improvement of transit facilities where desirable; and to connect non-communicating transport systems;
- If desirable, to own and operate or provide or assist in providing a pool of mobile equipment capable of being made available for international transport;
- To assist, and where necessary for orderly communications, to regulate the flow of telecommunications between countries.

3. A Raw Materials Administration whose functions shall be:

- To facilitate the production and distribution of raw materials essential to the general welfare of all nations.

4. The Economic Committee has under consideration a *Food or Agricultural Administration*, which it considers of major importance, but in respect of which it is not as yet prepared to report

The recommendations here made in respect of the economic organization of the East European Federation presuppose the existence of economic organisms of the United Nations capable of carrying out at least the foregoing functions. Tentatively, it is assumed that the economic agencies of the United Nations will be grouped under a United Nations Economic Council; but this assumption is not essential to the subsequent discussion.

It is likewise assumed that the United Nations economic agencies in their operations will require the observance of certain minimum standards laid down for all participants, especially the observance of covenants looking toward international security.

Tentative Economic Organization of the East European Federation

The Committee believe that the East European Federation should set up as a part of its constitutive arrangement the following agencies:

1. A Power and Development Authority

The territories comprised within the proposed East European Federation (whether in one part or two) represent one of the least developed areas in Europe from the point of view of industrial development and of electric power.

In considerable measure, the development of power is of necessity beyond the powers of any of the constituent states. By way of illustration, the greatest single source of power development would be the damming of the Danube at the Iron Gates. This would be comparable to the large power developments in the United States. It is now technically possible to transmit power within a radius of more than three hundred miles. This circle would include large parts of Hungary, Yugoslavia, Greece, Bulgaria and Rumania and parts of Poland,

Slovakia and Turkey. The dam itself would cross a national boundary, and would remove a major obstacle to navigation of the river.

Other important though less spectacular illustrations could be given in other areas.

Adjacent to such power developments there are available raw materials making possible the development of a number of industries, notably, aluminum, paper and chemicals. Proper handling would likewise make possible the irrigation of considerable tracts of land not presently used or irrigated in the most rudimentary fashion; and would make possible flood control.

It is to be expected that individual and local consumption of electricity would increase, both with the availability of power and with the growth of industrialization.

Functions of the Power Authority:

The Power Authority should have functions somewhat analogous to those of the Tennessee Valley Authority,[1] namely;

– The power and the mandate to construct works for the generation and transmission of power and the assisting of navigation and flood control;
– With the assent of the relevant local authority, to construct and operate manufacturing plants;
– With the assent of the local authority and on a nondiscriminatory basis, to work with cooperative societies, communities and similar enterprises.

Note: *It will be seen that the Committee drew a distinction between direct development of manufacture in any area, which the Power Authority might choose to do but which is left primarily to the local government; and the provision of electric power itself, which the Power Authority has the authority and the duty to do in the right of the entire Federation.*

2. *A Transport Authority*

The Transport Authority should be charged with the duty of assuring free and uninterrupted transit within the East European Federation by rail, truck, inland waterway and by air. It should have power to work with and coordinate existing transportation lines. Should the East European Federation so decide, it should have power to take over, unify and directly operate such lines. It should have power to construct and operate lines of its own, either separately or in conjunction with existing lines or for the purpose of fortifying existing lines. In general, it should have authority to assure that the national frontiers within the Federation shall not be or become a bar to the free transit of goods.

The Transport Authority should be charged with the duty of regulating rates and maintaining safety standards in respect to the facilities within its jurisdic-

---

[1] Tennessee Valley Authority – a program of regional development adopted in 1933 by F. D. Roosevelt as a part of New Deal; a successful measure against unemployment and the consequences of the Depression.

tion and of assuring nondiscrimination as between localities, enterprises and various elements and races within the population.

The Transport Authority should have like duties in respect to telecommunications within the area.

3. Development Corporation

Should the East European Federation so desire, it should have the power to set up a *Development Corporation* charged with the task of the continuing exploitation of the natural resources within the area, the improvement of its harbors and roads and the setting up of industrial enterprises. Such a corporation should be so organized that it could in right of the entire region initiate and operate development enterprises.

4. An East European Federation Central Bank.

The Committee is unable at present to suggest even a tentative form of organization of the Central Bank, since that organization must take into account the existence and condition of central banks which may be functioning within the region at the time of their liberation.

Were the conditions analogous to those existing prior to the German invasion, a logical method would be the operation of a single central bank, under a directorate composed of representatives of each of the central banks organized and operating within the component countries. Prior to 1939 each of those countries had a fairly well developed central bank system and use could have been made of these component elements. In such case, the central bank in each of the countries could have been constituted as a regional headquarters of the East European Central Bank and could have carried on their functions as agencies of the Central Bank.

It is presently impossible to know whether these banks or any of them will be in such shape that they can be made use of upon liberation. It is necessary to be prepared to undertake the organization of an entirely new system – or in the alternative, to assemble the former central banks as parts of the Federation system, as circumstances may develop.

The Committee is of the opinion that a single currency system, operated through the Central Bank, should prevail throughout the East European Federation. Should an interim period be desirable to dissolve historic or sentimental attachments to local currency, it should be possible, upon the assumption by the Central Bank of currency powers, to establish control over all of the component national currency systems, establish a fixed rate of exchange and gradually retire the local currencies as opportunity arises.

Subject to such agreements as it might make with the United Nations Bank, the Central Bank should have the powers normally exercised by a modern central bank of issue.

It should have supervision and responsibility for the local banks in all parts of the Federation.

5. East European Economic Council

The Economic Council of the Federation should include representatives of the regional authorities (Power, Transport, Central Bank and Development Corporation). But it should also include a representation which shall energize the various local groups having connection with the masses of the people.

The Economic Council should be charged with the duty of laying down general policies under which the Federation's economic authorities should act.

It should likewise be the channel through which the regional authorities should deal with the economic agencies of the United Nations.

It should be so constituted that it can give the sanction of the Federation to the projects and policies of the authorities, both externally in the privileges they ask or obligations they incur towards the United Nations and internally in the operations they undertake and the functions they exercise in respect of the population of the East European Federation.

6. Economic Arrangements Between the East European Federation and the United Nations

The East European Federation, of all areas given, is likely to find itself in a most depressed and chaotic state. Starvation in Greece, disorder and disease and famine in Yugoslavia, upheaval in Rumania, fruits of the terrible depression in Poland and the Baltic provinces will make a region drained of resource, without defined institutions, physically and psychologically tormented and very possibly wrecked by the passage of armies.

To expect this region to rehabilitate itself economically by automatic processes in any reasonable period of time is to ask the impossible. [our italics – JŁ &MM]

It will therefore need help, both the emergency services of relief and repatriation and also services for the intermediate period which make it possible for men once more to rebuild.

For that reason the Committee is of opinion that the United Nations should enter into an agreement with the Eastern European Federation designed to give such help.

The content of such an agreement is still under discussion by the committee, based on the assumption that there will be certain defined United Nations organisms available to give the needed assistance.[1]

Should this assumption prove unsound, it is believed that the great powers will have to render like assistance if the political settlements suggested by the Political Committee are to have a reasonable chance of success.

---

[1] A reference to the preparatory work of, among others, the State Department and the Foreign Relief and Rehabilitation Operation directed by Herbert Lehman for the United Nations Relief and Rehabilitation Administration (UNRRA), founded in Washington on 9 November 1943 to give UN aid to nations freed from occupation. See Woodbridge, G., *UNRRA: The History of the United Nations Relief and Rehabilitation Administration*, New York 1950, Vol. 1.

7. Immediate Development Projects

There is attached (Annex A) a tentative list of public or quasi-public projects which might be undertaken upon the liberation of the East European countries and their organization to a point at which they can carry out useful work.

These projects would all be of assistance in the economic integration of the region. In greater or less (*sic*) degree they look toward the industrialization of certain areas and the more effective use of resources.

It is, of course, impossible to draw a final list until conditions at the close of the war are ascertained. Nor is it possible as yet to make a quantitative analysis sufficient to indicate whether the projects here presented would without more be sufficient to give adequate stimulus to the area.

It is clear that the realization of these projects and the work contemplated by them certainly would prove of considerable assistance in creating within the area a better condition of affairs than is likely to obtain at the time of their liberation and probably offers a swifter avenue to improvement than has been available to these countries in recent economic history.

ANNEX A
Confidential
August 19, 1942

PUBLIC WORKS PROJECTS
IN THE EAST EUROPEAN REGION

The following list of public works projects which might be undertaken in the East European Region includes items compiled from several sources which reported projects under contemplation by the various national governments. Much of this material is several years old, but it indicates the extent of planning by national governments and gives an idea of approximate costs. The list also includes suggestions arising out of the work which has recently been done in the Division of Special Research. These are based upon general information rather than detailed surveys. Projects of the latter kind may be distinguished by the absence of a footnote indicating a source.

An appraisal of the merits of these various projects and suggestions would require detailed investigation, much of which would probably need to be done at the site of the project.

In connection with the economic development of the region, special attention should be given to various methods of improving agricultural production which are not included in the attached compilation because they are not public works in any strict sense of the term. These include the provision of capital at low rates of interest for agricultural credit, assistance in the creation of cooperative organizations and the dissemination of technical knowledge.

Agricultural credit has been one of the most important needs of the region and is particularly important where large estates have recently been broken up into small holdings.

Cooperative organizations, which have become of considerable importance in some parts of the region already, are useful not only in connection with purchasing and marketing, but also for utilization of such things as threshing machines and bulls, which a single peasant family could not afford to possess for its own use. Cooperatives have also, in some cases, exercised a healthy influence over the political life of the country.

As regards technical improvements, great benefits have resulted in recent years from the general introduction of such elementary forms of equipment as steel plows, seed drills and threshing machines in some of the more backward areas of the region.

LIST OF POSSIBLE PUBLIC WORKS PROJECTS FOR EAST EUROPEAN REGION

I. Transportation:

A. Airways

Airports will need to be developed throughout the region, principally close to the major cities. Such projects would employ primarily unskilled labor and could use for the most part locally produced materials. They would be urgently needed for transport of needed supplies to certain areas pending reconstruction of normal transport facilities.

B. Railways

Railway construction would employ considerable unskilled labor, use local steel, but might require considerable imports of machinery and equipment.

1. Double-track the main international routes, for example:
   a) Zagreb to the Trieste-Vienna line.
   b) Fiume, via Zagreb, to Budapest.
   c) Budapest to Belgrade via Szeged.
   d) Belgrade to Bucharest to Danube to connect with Constanza.
   e) Belgrade to Istanbul via Sofia.
   f) Belgrade to Athens via Salonika.
   g) Sofia to Bucharest to Cernauti to Lwów to Warsaw.

2. Develop the following lines:
   a) Southwestward from Belgrade to the Adriatic. This might involve either the reconstruction of the present narrow gauge line or construction of new lines.
   b) Eastward from Albania to connect with the Yugoslavian system. A relatively low pass exists in northeastern Albania, through which an old Roman road was built to the east.

Documents

c) Eastward from Albania to connect with Greece.
d) Sofia to the Aegean Sea. The greater part of this line has been in operation for some time and is now being converted to standard gauge. Only a short stretch connecting the existing Bulgarian and Greek lines would have to be entirely new.

3. Carry out the specific plans formulated by national governments prior to the war. (Some of these plans may have been completed.)

a) *Poland.* The execution of a full program of improvement, reconstruction and extensions, including rebuilding of bridges and new equipment for a ten-year period. This program would have entailed an annual expenditure of 150 million zloty ($28,500,000 at 1938 exchange rate).[1]

b) *Yugoslavia.* In 1934, Yugoslavia reported projects involving construction of 234 kilometers of narrow gauge at an estimated cost of 888 million dinar ($20,200,000 at 1938 exchange rates).[2] Other projects were a program for the construction of a railway line and of a bridge over the Danube, 50,500,000 Swiss francs ($12,400,000); and a program for the improvement of State railways, 180,000,000 Swiss francs ($40,600,000).[3] (This latter program might duplicate part of the first projects listed above.)

c) *Rumania.* Program for the construction of railways, 280 million Swiss francs ($63,250,000).

C. Highways

Except in a few areas, there are practically no modern highways in the area. Construction of highways would employ large numbers of unskilled laborers and could use locally produced materials.

1. Specific programs for road and bridge construction were reported by the following countries in 1934 and 1935:

a) *Austria.* Program for modernization of long-distance routes, 95 million Swiss francs ($21,500,000).[4]
b) *Bulgaria.* Program of road and bridge construction, 11 million Swiss francs ($2,500,000).
c) *Czechoslovakia.* Program for immediate future for non-State roads and bridges 274 million Czech crowns ($9,600,000).[5]
d) *Estonia.* Program of road and bridge construction, 8,100,000 Swiss francs ($1,803,000).
e) *Greece.* Two hundred kilometers of roads. (No cost estimates.)[1]

---

[1] *League of Nations, Organization for Communications and Transit,* National Public Works, Addendum, Geneva 1935, p. 168. (This and all the following notes in this document are by the American authors of the study).
[2] *Ibid.,* p. 264.
[3] *International Labor Office,* Public Works Policy, Geneva 1935, p. 165.
[4] *Ibid.,* p. 162.
[5] *League of Nations, Organization for Communications and Transit,* National Public Works, Geneva 1934, p. 250.

f) *Hungary*. Program for the reconstruction of national roads, 35 million Swiss francs, ($7,900,000).

g) *Latvia*. Program for construction of roads and bridges, 98,500,000 Swiss francs ($22,200,000).[2]

h) *Poland*. Program of reconstruction of the principal road system and the construction of bridges, 186 million Swiss francs ($42,000,000).[3]

i) *Yugoslavia*. Program for the improvement of the principal road system, 137,500,000 Swiss francs. ($31,000,000).[4]

D. *Waterways*

Inland waterway development would include construction of canals and the improvement of navigation on rivers. The latter type of project might also involve hydro-electric power, irrigation, flood control and drainage projects. In general, work on inland waterways could employ large numbers of unskilled workers and would require principally local materials.

1. Particular projects contemplated or planned:

   a) *Bulgaria*. Program of drainage and river correction (works at Kara-Boaze, at Messemvria and at Mandra-Yakezli), 1,300,000 Swiss francs ($294,000).[5]

   b) *Poland*. Reconstruction of the Royal Canal, 35 million Swiss francs ($6,875,000).[6] Development of Vistula from Silesia to he sea to accommodate 600-ton vessels, 300,000,000 zloty, ($57,000,000).[7] Rebuilding the Royal Prypéc-Bug Canal for 600-ton vessels, 35,000,000 zloty ($6,650,000). (Embassy dispatches indicate that the Bug River system has been connected with the Dnieper and that these waterways were improved between 1939 and 1941, before the German-Russian hostilities. Undoubtedly there will be need for reconstruction and development of Polish waterways after the war.)

   c) *Czechoslovakia*. The completion of regulation works to make the Morava, Danube, Tisa, Vah, Elbe, Vltava and Oder rivers navigable or improve present navigability over a total length of 210 kilometers will cost 800 million Czech crowns ($28,000,000) and the construction of dams, 250 million Czech crowns ($8,750,000).[8] A canal system, designed to link the Oder, the Elbe and the Danube has been begun and the estimated cost will be about 760 million Czech crowns ($26,600,000).[9] (This development would provide an important north-south waterway link between Poland and Silesia and Austria and

---

[1] *Ibid.*, p. 159.
[2] *International Labor Office, op. cit.*, p. 162.
[3] *Ibid.*, p. 164.
[4] *Ibid.*, p. 165.
[5] *Ibid.*, p. 162.
[6] *Ibid.*, p. 163.
[7] *League of Nations*, National Public Works, Addendum, p. 175.
[8] *League of Nations*, National Public Works, p. 255.
[9] Young, E.P., *Czechoslovakia*, London 1938, p. 88.

Hungary. It is reported that some Czechoslovakian interests, principally the Moravian coal operators and the railroads, have opposed this project.)

d) *Yugoslavia.* The Nazi-dominated Croat government is reported to be considering the construction of a 37-mile canal between Vucovar on the Danube and Slavonski-Samac on the Sava River.[1] The present water route between these two points is 295 miles. The cost of this project would be approximately 500,000,000 kuna ($10,000,000).

A canal linking the Adriatic with the Danube basin has also been contemplated recently.[2] If a canal could be constructed from either Trieste or Fiume to the Sava River, it would be of tremendous significance for the entire region. This project would be worth further investigation as to its engineering and financial practicability.

The development of the Iron Gate on the Danube for Hydro-electric power could provide improved navigation. At present, these rapids limit the size of vessels which can pass between the lower and upper Danube (see details under Electric Power).

II. Electric Power

The principal large-scale power projects which might be developed in the region are on international rivers, although some sites lie entirely within one country. In most cases, power development would represent only one phase of a multiple-purpose project which might also include improvement of navigation, irrigation, flood control, or water supply. Although large amounts might be expended for local labor in the construction of dams and transmission lines, hydro-electric projects would require heavy outlays for expensive machinery and equipment, much of which would have to be secured outside the region.

A. The Iron Gate Power Project[3]

The two principal rapids on the Danube between Noldova and Turnu-Severin lie at Greben and at the Iron Gate, although there are four other sections where navigation is difficult. There are two alternative schemes for the development of these cataracts. One plan calls for the construction of one high dam below the Iron Gate, with twin locks for navigation and a power house. The other calls for two smaller dams with locks and power houses, one below the Greben rapids and the other below the Iron Gate.

Engineering and geological studies, although incomplete, indicate that either project is feasible, but that the best system would be the construction of the two dams, with two locks and either one or two power houses each. The two-power-house scheme was advanced particularly so that at each dam one plant would belong to Rumania and the other to Yugoslavia. The generators at each dam

---

[1] *Foreign Commerce Weekly*, 8 August 1942, p. 18.
[2] *Zeitung des Vereins Mitteleuropäischer Eisenbahn Verwaltungen*, 2 May 1942.
[3] Unless otherwise noted, data are from League of Nations, Report on Danube Navigation. Annex V, pp. 128-32 (Submitted in 1925).

would provide 500,000 horsepower, or a total of 1,000,000 horsepower. More recent estimates indicate a total of 1,460,900 horsepower could be developed.[1] This is approximately equivalent to the present combined installed capacity of all hydro-electric stations operated by the Tennessee Valley authority. This project, operating at 50 percent of capacity, could generate 25 percent more power than the 1937 output of all steam and hydro-electric plants of Rumania, Yugoslavia, Hungary, Bulgaria, Albania and Greece. The project would also improve navigation, regulate the lower Danube and prevent flooding on areas bordering the river and provide water storage for irrigation.

The original plans called for the construction of metallurgical and chemical plants close to the sites. These industries would consume about 85 percent of the contemplated 2,900,000,000 kilowatt hours produced at the Greben dam. During the past twenty years, however, the range of economical high-tension transmission has been greatly enlarged and the present limits are close to 300 miles. This range would cover the most of Rumania, Bulgaria, Hungary and Yugoslavia and parts of Poland, Slovakia, Albania, Greece and Turkey.

In 1925, it was estimated that the entire project would cost 800,000,000 gold francs, or $155,000,000 at the old exchange rates. Recent United States hydroelectric development costs have run from $150 to $300 per kilowatt. Using this basis and a capacity of 1,460,900 horsepower (1,100,000 kilowatts), the project would cost between $170,000,000 and $330,000,000.

The League report expressed doubts concerning an industrial development sufficient to absorb the electric output. However, with the greatly increased distances of power transmission which are now possible, a more extensive consuming area could be reached. Furthermore, by building one dam at a time, the project could be developed gradually and expanded as demand increased.

B. *The Oder River in Silesia*

A project has been contemplated for harnessing the Oder close to the former German border. This project would develop hydro-electric power for Upper Silesia and improve navigation on the Oder. No estimates of either the quantity of power available at this site or the cost of this project have been found.[2]

C. *National Projects*

1. Austria

A large power development in the Tauern Mountains has been under consideration by two private firms and more recently reports indicate that development was begun by the German government, though subsequently stopped by war conditions. This power would probably be exported to Germany, although it might be diverted to Eastern Austria and Slovenia. It is claimed that the complete project could have an installed capacity of 2,100,000 horsepower which would provide over 6 billion kilowatt hours yearly, or the equivalent of

---

[1] Data from Mr. Strauss, B. E. W.
[2] Oral information received from Mr. Friedricks of B.E.W.

the power produced by four million tons of coal.[1] No estimates of costs are available.

2. Czechoslovakia

The development of the Van River in Slovakia involving construction of fourteen dams and with a total generating capacity of 292,000 kilowatts was under consideration by the government of Czechoslovakia.[2]

3. Poland

Poland had prepared a program of electrification works costing 116 million Swiss francs ($26,200,000).[3] Another plan envisaged electrification of the Warsaw suburban railway system, 25 million Swiss francs ($5,650,000).

4. Rumania and Yugoslavia

Many potential water power sites exist in the Transylvanian Alps and in the Yugoslavian mountains, but no details are available at present.

5. Estonia

The Estonian government had drawn up plans for construction of a hydro-electric station at the 26 meter falls of the Narva River. This site, located on the river which drains Lake Peipus, has been estimated to have a potential capacity of 90,000 horsepower.[4] The government places envisaged expenditure of 40 million kroon ($10,8 million at 1937 exchange rate).[5]

---

[1] These estimates seem very big, but are the only estimates available. British Department of Overseas Trade, Report on Economic Conditions in Austria, 1930, p. 44.
[2] Third World Power Conference, 1936, Transactions, Vol. II.
[3] International Labor Office, Public Works Policy, p. 164.
[4] Estonia, Central Bureau of Statistics, *Estonia – Population, Cultural and Economic Life*, 1935, p. 104.
[5] *League of Nations*, National Public Works, 1934, p. 107.

8

DEPARTMENT OF STATE
Division of Special Research
Secret
Minutes P- 23
August 22, 1942

Typescript, copy
NA Notter File, box 55

[STRUCTURE OF THE EAST EUROPEAN FEDERATION]

Present:
Mr. Welles, presiding
Mr. Hamilton Fish Armstrong
Mr. Adolf A. Berle
Mr. Benjamin V. Cohen
Mr. Norman H. Davis
Mr. Green H. Hackworth
Mrs. Anne O'Hare McCormick
Mr. John V. A. MacMurray
Mr. Myron C. Taylor
Mr. James T. Shotwell
Mr. Paul Daniels
Mr. Harley Notter
Mr. Bryce Wood

In opening the meeting at 11:05 a.m., Mr. Welles said that in accordance with the arrangement made at the last meeting the subcommittee would discuss today the economic organization of the East European Federation. Mr. Berle would be the rapporteur for the economic subcommittee.

Mr. Berle said that most of the members of the subcommittee have already had a preview of the economic subcommittee's "Memorandum to the Political Subcommittee, Subject: Tentative Economic Organization of the East European Federation" (appended as P Document 45). This memorandum represented a report of the agreement reached in the economic subcommittee in the time at its disposal. He had already given the general drift of the memorandum to the territorial subcommittee. The economic subcommittee thought *that the situation in this area would be so chaotic that no political arrangement could endure without immediate and continuing economic assistance from outside* [our italics – JŁ & MM]. This outside assistance, it was felt, would come from the United Nations and the effort was made to envisage how such assistance might be applied to the problems of the proposed East European Federation. Various assumptions were made by the economic subcommittee: First, there should be a United Nations bank which would have the functions of stabilizing the exchanges, the handling of long-term credit for investment and certain functions of a bank of issue.

Mr. Davis inquired whether the Bank for International Settlements might not be used in this connection and Mr. Berle said that a study of the BIS was now being made by an inter-departmental committee. It is a question whether to start anew or not, but the economic subcommittee felt that it should be left to the interdepartmental committee just mentioned.

Continuing, Mr. Berle said that the second assumption was that there would have to be a transport and communications authority concerning which he read the relevant sections from the appended memorandum.

He added that it was possible that demobilized army trucks might be used at the beginning to assist in moving food and other necessary articles.

The third assumption of the economic subcommittee was that there should be established a raw materials administration as provided in the memorandum; and the fourth assumption was the setting up of a food or agriculture administration. Mr. Appleby in the Department of Agriculture has some ideas on this question, but the details of any such organization have not as yet been clarified. These agencies with others might form the foundation of a United Nations Economic Council – that, however, is not essential in the thinking of the economic subcommittee.

Going back to the beginning, Mr. Berle said that the instructions were that the economic organization should support the political organization and in the memorandum there was no effort to create agencies for economic purposes since political decisions had been held to be of primary importance. However, it had been assumed that there was to be only one federation in Eastern Europe. The plans herewith presented could be split so as to make arrangements for dividing the area into two or three parts, although some adjustment will be necessary, particularly as regards public works.

General agreement had been obtained in the economic subcommittee to the effect that there should be a regional power development authority. It should have the right to develop and transmit power and the capacity without special mandate to develop manufacturing in a region where such development seemed desirable. Powers of this authority should be similar to those of the TVA.[1] For example, it should have the power to work with local government agencies, to deal with cooperative associations or cities or even national governments in the carrying out of its functions.

Mr. Davis inquired whether the authority would actually be the operating and development agency and Mr. Berle said that he thought it would have to do so in order to become a unifying force within the area. As an illustration to indicate why the plan developed as it had, Mr. Berle mentioned the possible establishment of a great power site at the Iron Gates on the Danube River.

---

[1] Technical details have been omitted.

Power from a station there could be distributed in a circle of some three hundred miles.

(...)

Economic Council

Mr. Berle said that the economic subcommittee did not undertake to define the nature of the economic council, pending the decision with regard to the political organization. If the plan is to build the political organization around the economic, then the economic subcommittee would be glad to tackle that problem. However, the political had been considered as the dominant interest and therefore no institutional decisions had been made by the economic subcommittee.

Mrs. McCormick asked if the economic council was supposed to be a council for the development of the region. Mr. Welles said that the council, it seemed to him, had rather broad powers; it could, for example, deal with tariff questions. He thought that it was imperative that questions of this type should be decided by the economic council but that details had so far not been worked out.

Mr. Taylor wondered whether in case of difficulty the economic council might appeal to the political council. He had thought that the economic council would consult with and receive the advice of the political council.

Mr. Welles said that his recollection was that the economic council would report back to the political council, but otherwise would have no contact with it. He asked Mr. Notter if he had at hand the record of the proposed plan for the East European federation.

Mr. Notter answered affirmatively, saying that there were three relevant sections and he read these as follows:

(a) *General Nature*. The economic council would be separate from the political council. It would be an advisory body except in certain contingencies not yet agreed upon. Its recommendations would be referred to the governments of the component states for approval. It would represent the region as a whole and not merely the interests of individual states; accordingly the council might be called "Council for the Economic Development of the East European Union". This council might be the medium through which international plans for economic development of the region were handled.

(b) *Functions*. This council would be charged with making recommendations of the governments of the component states on economic interests of concern to the region and it would have powers as broad as possible to initiate recommendations on general economic policies. Remaining under discussion are:

1) whether it should be responsible for union administration of economic arrangements approved by the component states and

2) whether it should be charged with enumerated functions relating to such matters as freedom of transit, communications, etc., in the union as a whole.

(c) *Composition*. Each state should be represented in the economic council by not more than five experts. Each state would select any number of experts up to the maximum. Such experts would be selected by the government in each state, from the Central Bank, industry, labor, agriculture and the professional classes. The terms of reference to the governments regarding the selection of representatives should stress that the delegates should know what they were to consider and should be competent as experts in those subjects. The experts would be assisted by staffs.

Mr. Welles said that that covered the situation very clearly. There does not seem to be any reason to modify the plan. Mr. Berle's point would be met by having the heads of these bodies named *ex officio* to serve with a voice but without a vote. He asked Mr. Taylor's opinion on this and Mr. Taylor agreed with Mr. Welles' view.

Mr. Welles said that it seemed to him that Mr. Berle's economic plan gives us just the kind of foundation that the subcommittee needs. It provided the welding material, as he had previously said, which was needed and it should be of great value in making attractive the idea of federation. We have evaded, so far, however, the final determination as to whether we should recommend one or two federations. This plan is based on the assumption of one. The conversations going on in London[1] have provided for two – one northern and one southern federation. The more he thought about it, the more he thought that the one federation for the whole region was the desirable objective and he wondered if the committee was not now in a position to form its judgment on this point.

Mrs. McCormick thought that our objective should be to form one federation. She thought that the subcommittee ought to put its sights as high as possible, so that if it were necessary to compromise, the committee would have placed the whole idea before these countries. There are problems because of different economic conditions but she thought that these could be overcome. The southern group might gather about the Iron Gates project, but it would also take in some of the northern states.

Mr. Davis had felt that the northern part was so economically separate from the southern and possessed such a different outlook that unity was hardly feasible. However, he now felt that one union should be worked for. After all, Poland and Czechoslovakia are growing closer together. Mr. Welles wished to remark, however, that serious obstacles remained between Poland and Czechoslovakia.

Mr. MacMurray said that he had been in favor of two federations because of their economic disparity and the differences in attitudes but he thought that these elements were less important than those to which Mrs. McCormick had referred. He thought that the physical desirability of a single unit was very great.

Mr. Bowman said that Mr. Davis had expressed his point of view. He had thought it necessary to break the area into two or possibly three groups but the difficulty of breaking it up is that we cannot forecast its internal politics or the

---

[1] Welles refers to the Polish-Czechoslovak and Greek-Yugoslavian declarations of early 1942; see *Introduction*.

combinations which various states might form. If Poland, Czechoslovakia and Hungary were combined, for example, the latter could play off the former two against each other. The result is that one is driven very reluctantly to the conclusion that the whole area should be joined together. He said "reluctantly" because if the Baltic States are included, that makes a round dozen countries. Mr. Berle's memo showed that to do something comprehensive economically and to make an imaginative scheme, the boundaries stand in the way. In the territorial subcommittee one principle had been generally accepted, namely, that ways and means should be found for diminishing the importance of boundaries. For that reason we see in an economic plan of this kind a great hope since it lowers the value of frontiers. He asked Mr. Berle whether questions of public health had been considered.

Mr. Berle answered negatively saying that he did not think the economic subcommittee had done more than merely to scratch the surface on this job. He thought it was necessary to get the problem into scale and to ask oneself how much work would have to be done to manufacture the United States of 1830.[1] There you have an idea of the size of the job.

Mr. Bowman said that the health section of the League of Nations had done very good work and it would be possible to take advantage of this work in making plans for the EEU, as the Rockefeller Organization[2] and the Health Section of the League of Nations have shown that the problems of sanitary engineering are international. Returning to his first point, Mr. Bowman said that the pool seemed to him to be the best solution – it has the advantage of giving full publicity to the machinations of one state.

Mrs. McCormick said that since she had discovered how hard it was to get two of these nations together to cooperate on a common scheme of any kind, she did not think that the difficulties would be any greater in getting twelve of them together.

Mr. Taylor referred to another paragraph in the "Proposed Plan for East European Federation" and requested Mr. Notter to read it as follows:

"Any number of states could voluntarily undertake common measures they might desire provided not contrary to the articles of union".

Mr. Taylor said that on this basis you might expand the idea – common measures might be made applicable to the whole area and then leave room for a group within the federation to carry out within limits, their own desires. Mr. Taylor thought Mr. Notter should also read from the section on economic advisers and Mr. Notter complied:

---

[1] This is probably an allusion to the sharp debate in Congress over the "nullification doctrine", the right of a state to nullify a federal law that "violated the sovereignty and independence of the states". The supporters of the primacy of the federal law argued that it was the people, and not the states, who created the Constitution and that if the states could defy the laws of Congress at will, the Union would be a mere "rope of sand". President Jackson, despite his sympathies to states' rights, was against nullification, realizing its danger to the future of the Union.

[2] An allusion to John D. Rockefeller's charity organization, founded in 1913.

(d) *Foreign Advisers.* "Three economic advisers would be appointed by the United Nations to represent them in the economic council. These advisers would serve for three-year terms but initially so scaled that one might come up for appointment or re-appointment after one year, the second after two years and the third after three years. No one of the three should come from Europe (including Russia)."

Mr. Shotwell said that his opinion had shifted to the one which appeared to be accepted at this meeting. He came to it by another road – namely, trying to work out how you could have a Hungary in the midst of the group. You could have it more safely in a larger group than in a smaller one. This is the most dangerous part of the situation, for the Hungarians are accustomed to rule. He was much impressed with the memorandum and thought that it provided a good starting point. He noted that agriculture was not mentioned and hoped the economic subcommittee would get around to that subject. Mr. Berle said that the subcommittee was not yet ready to talk about that, but was proceeding to study it. Mr. Shotwell thought that in agriculture there was a larger degree of unifying interest than in some of the other elements mentioned. He thought that Mr. Bowman's reference to the lessening of importance of boundaries was significant. One other point of local interest; he thought that an advantage of having one federation would be that the plan would then be easier to sell to the American people as an investment in peace. He thought that this was the most constructive method of dealing with a hot-bed of nationalism in a dangerous part of the civilized world.

Mr. Armstrong said that he agreed that it had been more usual to think in the direction of two or more groups: Balkan and Baltic groups and a Polish-Czech group. However, these ideas had not gone very far and as Mr. Welles had mentioned, there were serious difficulties facing the Polish-Czech negotiations. He had been in favor of one group from the beginning for reasons which have already been mentioned. The advantages of making individual states safer from being ganged up on by others in a larger group rather than in a small one, and the advantage of a large group's being safer from intrusion by one of the two great bordering powers are so plain that the idea could be, in his opinion, sold to the nations. He thought Mr. Shotwell's point about Hungary was an important one and he wished to mention Austria in this regard. While Hungary is hard to include because of political and racial reasons, it is also hard to include Austria almost in the same degree. He thought, however, that this was another argument in favor of the larger group, for not only Hungary but also Austria would be likely to enter it. He thought further that there would be more danger in a smaller group of there being a division which would persist between the ex-enemy states and the members of the United Nations. The ex-enemy states, with different social and political ideals, we trust, might become part of various combinations in a bigger group more readily than in a small group. These considerations merely supported the other reasons already presented and on the whole he favored a larger group.

Mr. Hackworth said that he was also in favor of the larger group. He thought that if there were common problems and interests there would be a greater tendency to amalgamate the people. On the question of power, serious questions would arise unless a union existed. When you dam rivers you tamper with rights both above and below the dam. He was reminded of the fact that the Grand Coulée Dam[1] would raise the water of the Columbia River in Canada one and a half feet above normal. Some opposition developed, therefore, in Canada but the Canadians' feelings were soothed when the United States indicated a willingness to refrain from making any objections to the building by Canada of a dam on the Pend Oreille River. In building their dam, water would be backed up within United States' territory and in this compromise fashion the two issues were amicably settled. However, if the Canadians had said that we could not raise the water in their country, we would have lost a large block of the power which Grand Coulée will now generate. Another similar case was that of the Skagit River where dams provide electricity for the city of Seattle. This river runs into Canada and there was some opposition among Canadians when it was desired to increase the height of the dams for Seattle's purposes. However, the Canadians finally agreed to the increase in the water level of the river within Canadian territory. If in this East European region you have two unions instead of one and one wishes to build a power project, the other might well raise objections to such a plan, but if all the people are in one group, you will have greater cooperation and fewer difficulties.

Mr. Welles said that this was a very practical consideration.

Mr. Cohen said that he had started out in favor of one federation but the firmness of his opinion had been somewhat shaken by some of the objections presented here and elsewhere. However, he still felt that one federation should be the objective. He thought that the economic subcommittee's program might involve a considerable increase in the power of the political council, so that it might be necessary to implement it more than we had originally thought. This had both disadvantages and advantages.

Mr. Davis wished to raise another point. He thought that it would not be impossible to persuade these nations to accept the plan, because of the fact that there is more protection for them both politically and militarily in one big union.

Mr. Shotwell asked if it was not more easy to strike the imagination of the American people with a plan for one federation than to try to explain to them the complicated reasons why two groups or more had to be established.

Mr. Welles said that from the political standpoint he fully agreed with Mr. Shotwell's observation. Mrs. McCormick noted that this union would create a large slice in preparation for a possible European federation.

Mr. Taylor said that the mention of Austria touched on the minority point of view concerning the partition of Germany. He would like to make a reservation on this point since he had not yielded any ground from his stand.

Mr. Welles said that if it were agreeable to the subcommittee, we would refer back to the economic committee the project presented this morning which

---

[1] Grand Coulée Dam on the Columbia River (Washington), completed in 1941, is the largest concrete dam and the greatest single source of water power in the United States. It is permitted to irrigate more than 200,000 ha and produces 2,000,000 kW energy.

has been enthusiastically received by this committee, with the request that it be fully elaborated in line with the suggestions of this meeting. We have reached the point, he thought, at which, for the time being, we could put the East European union project into the basket and leave it there until final revision, unless other members of the committee felt that it should be further reviewed.

Mr. Taylor said that he would like to say that while the members of the economic subcommittee had given Mr. Berle considerable assistance that this fine piece of work is largely Mr. Berle's own and that he had been indeed very industrious.

Mrs. McCormick asked whether Mr. Welles meant that further consideration of the union was precluded.

Mr. Welles said that this thought was that until the economic program is more fully worked out, we should defer discussion of the whole issue. He would like to suggest that at the next meeting the committee take up the question of the Middle East. It seemed to him that at this stage we should put one or two meetings on the Middle East. At the next meeting we should like to have Mr. MacMurray and Mr. Allen to aid the subcommittee in reviewing this area. He suggested that the subcommittee discuss this region for two meetings and then return to the most thorny issue of all – the Germanic problem. This plan received general acceptance.

Mr. Davis wished to say that in regard to the Far East the subcommittee had reached conclusions as to what to take away from Japan and what should be left to her, except with regard to the Bonin Islands, the consideration of which was deferred because of their possible strategic importance. The security subcommittee had discussed this question at its last meeting and it had been felt that the only island concerning which action might be desirable was one of the Bonins. This is a strong base now and the issue was felt to be so vital that it is being referred to the combined army and navy staffs. The security committee, however, has not yet finished its discussions and is not ready to make a report to the political subcommittee.

Mr. Welles said that this subcommittee had left this decision in abeyance until hearing from the security subcommittee.

The meeting adjourned at 12:40 p.m.

Bryce Wood, Secretary

9

DEPARTMENT OF STATE
Division of Special Research
Secret
P Minutes – 28
October 10, 1942

Typescript, copy
NA Notter File, box 55

[SURVEY OF THE SUGGESTED EAST EUROPEAN UNION]

Present:
Mr. Welles, presiding
Mr. Hamilton Fish Armstrong
Mr. Adolf A. Berle
Mr. Isaiah Bowman
Mr. Benjamin V. Cohen
Mr. Green H. Hackworth
Mrs. Anne O'Hare McCormick
Mr. John V. A. MacMurray
Mr. Leo Pasvolsky
Mr. James T. Shotwell
Mr. Ray Atherton
Mr. Maxwell M. Hamilton
Mr. Harley Notter
Mr. Bryce Wood

In opening the meeting at 10:55 a.m. Mr. Welles noted that according to the agenda it was planned to conclude the survey of the suggested East European Union and take up at the outset the two remaining points: (1) the preliminary determination of the details of the economic and political councils and (2) the relation between them and the executive body of the international organization. He asked Mr. Notter to read the relevant part of P Document 24-b,[1] "An East European Union (as considered to August 28, 1942)". Mr. Notter read the section on the political council.

Mr. Welles wished first to raise the question as to the composition of the council. Was there any objection on the part of the subcommittee to the draft

---

[1] Missing in the Notter Files. It can be surmised from the discussion and the fragments quoted that it does not differ significantly from the 24-c version of 10 October 1942 – see document 9.

proposal concerning the composition of the political council? There was apparently no objection. Mr. Welles noted that the draft provided that the functions of the council should be deliberately limited. He thought this was wise, since, as the scheme works out, the functions could be enlarged as the need might arise. He thought that the council would have to have the control of foreign policies provided in the draft, since the executive alone could not be trusted with this power.

Mr. Berle asked whether the council was to appoint the chiefs of staff of the *gendarmerie*. Mr. Welles thought that it would have to do so. Mr. Armstrong wondered whether there would be only national *gendarmeries* and Mr. Welles said that each member state should have its own local police force to maintain public order, but that there would have to be some overall *gendarmerie* which could be sent from one place to another in case the local authorities could not maintain order. The comparison might be made with the federal government in the United States, which may intervene to maintain order.

Mr. Armstrong wondered whether, in case of civil war or social disorders, the *gendarmerie* could be called in to protect a national government and so aid it to maintain itself against a revolution.

Mr. Welles said that it was clear that those particular details were not provided for. Mr. Armstrong said that the problem bristled with difficulties if this were the case. Mr. Welles said that the question was whether the council and executive should have the right, of their own volition, to determine where the *gendarmerie* should be employed, or whether they could only employ it on the request of one unit.

Mr. Berle asked whether the function of the keeping of the peace was one for the federation, or one for the international organization as a whole.

Mrs. McCormick thought that the regional *gendarmerie* would be called on to intervene only in international disputes and not to exercise control in case of internal disputes. Mr. Armstrong objected that the disturbance might be international-social trouble in Bulgaria might be Russian in origin.

Mr. Welles considered that the most expedient thing would be that the council would have the right to use the *gendarmerie* to take care of disturbances which might arise between the component parts of the union and would have the right to send them into a unit's territory upon the request of the government of that unit. He agreed with Mr. Berle's suggestion that it would have the right but not the duty to take such action.

Mrs. McCormick noted that if disturbances arose because of powers outside the union, then it would be a matter for the overall organization. Mr. Welles thought that that was perhaps the most expedient way to handle the matter. Mr. Bowman agreed, saying that one can always devise alternative ways but he did not see anything wrong with this one. He could imagine a later phase of discussion in which the circumstances of the union as reviewed by the statesmen of the different units might lead to a shift in emphasis, but it seemed to him a workable scheme, granted the overall possibility of the union.

Mr. Welles suggested that the following line be adopted: First, that the world organization take care of the questions between the union and outside powers; second, that difficulties between the component parts of the union should be settled by the use of the union *gendarmerie* by the political council; third, that local disturbances, which local authorities cannot quell, arising in the territory of any unit of the union shall be taken care of through the use of the *gendarmerie* of the political council, provided that the council decides to do so on the request of the government of that unit. It seemed to him that it was necessary for the political council to await the request of a member state in order that, at the beginning, it might be possible to get the countries to join the organization.

Mr. Cohen asked what would happen if there arose a question as to the identity of the local government and Mr. Armstrong interjected that that was a problem which had not been settled in other political groupings. Continuing, Mr. Cohen said that in that instance, should the council decide which group should be recognized, or should there be a means of appeal to the international body? Mr. Welles said that he did not think you could deprive an autonomous government, such as Hungary, for example, of the right to appeal to the world organization on a question which is an inherent right of sovereignty.

Mr. Pasvolsky said that the union would begin with a government representative of each state on the political council, so that Mr. Cohen's question would arise only if something should remove that government. Mr. Welles put the question as to what would happen if some *coup d'état* should take place. Mr. Pasvolsky replied that the question of recognition would then come up. Mr. Welles said that then a sovereign government has the right, like any other sovereign government, to appeal to the world organization, but Mr. Pasvolsky wondered whether the union should not decide that question in the first instance. Mr. Welles concurred, but repeated that there should be the ultimate right of appeal. Mr. Pasvolsky thought that the appeal should take place only after the decision by the political council. If then something arises which concerns the peace of the world, then there is the right of appeal. Mr. Welles thought there was more than the peace of the world to consider. There was the right of any sovereign people to appeal. If the government of Hungary should be overthrown and other members of the council desired that the government that had been overthrown should be re-established, it seemed clearly unjust and undesirable that the political council should use the *gendarmerie* of the union to put back a government which the people did not want to be reinstated. In that case there should be the right of appeal. Mr. Cohen remarked that it was a very difficult point and Mr. Welles said he did not think that we could take the right of appeal to the world organization from any sovereign country.

Mr. Berle said that if we recognize a new government in Hungary, for example, we should have to leave the nature of its institutions to later developments and Mr. Welles said that that could be taken care of by any appeals procedure that may be set up.

Mr. Bowman thought that Mr. Berle's point possessed merit because we can struggle with the question and we still have not reached the end of the road concerning the conditions of recognizing a new government. We are not likely to be sure of making a workable system under new conditions in a new union. Underlying these three principles is a condition, not a principle, namely, the will to have a union. One of the conditions of the document here before us is that the representatives shall see that their government is informed and steps are taken in consonance with the dispositions of the political council. That will has to be created before you can make refinements of your political scheme. Mr. Welles said that he thought that was completely true.

Mr. Hackworth wished to raise another question. The *gendarmerie* is spoken of as being regional and is for use by the council in regional undertakings and regional quotas are to be set up. Should there not be something to the effect that these quotas shall constitute the police force of the respective regions, except when they are called into operation by the council for general regional purposes? Mr. Welles wondered if this could be done. Suppose that each unit has its own police force to maintain local order. Suppose a situation arises in one or two units of the union, making it necessary for the council to use all the intra-regional gendarmes to keep that situation quiet. He thought that in time of disturbances other governments could send police forces out of their own country, but in such case they might leave nothing at home to keep things quiet there.

Mr. Hackworth had been referring not to a city police force, but to an over-all police organization. He had in mind an organization like the militia of the American states. Each state can call out the militia for any use which it desires so long as the President of the United States does not call it out. If you have only a regional force without providing that each part should have a separate force, they are left without an overall police force. This puts the local unit in a dangerous situation in case of an uprising which the local police could not handle. Mr. Welles asked whether two separate bodies were not necessary. There are city police here and a state constabulary. That was the thesis which the subcommittee was working on.

Mr. Hackworth agreed, but noted that the states of the United States possessed a militia in addition and there is no comparable organization provided for the units of the East European Union unless the units may use the police force under this plan, except when they are called into action by the council. Then you do give them that overall police force, in effect.

Mr. Welles thought that this overall police force would be recruited from all the countries and would be separate from other forces and would be established in various points of the entire union. They should be moved from time to time to avoid being too closely identified with any given area. Mr. Hackworth added that there would then be a situation as though the President had called them into action. Mr. Pasvolsky thought that the regional *gendarmerie* would be equivalent to our Army. There would thus be three forces – a city police, the national armed force and the federal armed force.

Mr. Welles said he had been operating on the basis that if disarmament takes place as it should, there would not be any standing army. Mr. Pasvolsky said that we would call them by a different name. Mr. Welles thought it would be simpler to divide the forces into two parts – there would be a country or district constabulary and the federal constabulary under the command of the political council.

Mr. Cohen asked if it was the understanding that the control of the *gendarmerie* was to be the sole executive function of the council. It seemed to him that while that is probably primary, that the use of the term "sole" in the draft was too strong. Mr. Welles agreed, saying that it would be better to say the "chief" function of the political council would be the maintenance of intra-regional security. Concerning the administrative functions of the council, he wished to raise the question as to whether the council should have responsibility for the enforcement of the customs regulations. The question is whether the power should be in the economic or the political council.

Mr. Pasvolsky wished to raise a related question, namely, whether each country would have its own diplomatic and consular representatives. Mr. Welles said that that was stated in the draft and Mr. Notter said that it was listed under rights and duties of the states and he read the relevant sentence.

Continuing, Mr. Pasvolsky said that the council would have a single international policy and the action of the individual states' representatives would have to be consonant with that policy. Mr. Welles said that that would be the task of the political council – to obviate difficulties and obtain unity in the policies chosen. Mrs. McCormick agreed with this view.

Mr. Welles said that Mr. Notter had called his attention to certain specific questions remaining unanswered, such as that of the method of procedure by which the council can take cognizance of problems of foreign policy. Mr. Welles thought that these questions were too detailed to go into at this time. Such matters would go into the constitution of the union as worked out later. What we want here are the main principles underlying the project and questions of details should be left until later. He wondered if the committee would wish to go into such detail even in the second round of discussion. What was wanted now was to lay down general principles and leave the shaping of the details to the individuals charged with the drafting of the constitution.

Mr. Armstrong asked whether it was decided how the political council should vote, although that might be only a detail.

Mr. Notter said that there was only one respect in which that problem had been determined and that was with regard to the election of the President.

Mr. Welles thought that it would be difficult to secure the participation of the states in a union if they felt they were going to be overridden in their own policies by a majority vote. It would be best to leave this open – then the states will understand that they are coming in as sovereign powers. Mrs. McCormick thought that it was best for this reason to leave as many points open as possible and Mr. Welles said that in principle he would agree.

Mr. Welles said that he did not see why any country should have diplomatic representatives if its policy could be overridden by a vote of the majority.

Mr. Pasvolsky replied that this question would arise because of the problem of protection of citizens. If there were a separate citizenship in the union then each country would have to have representatives. If not, that function would be given to the political council. Mr. Welles had not conceived of the possibility of getting a new nation in Eastern Europe. The most he had hoped for was the beginning of the start toward what might become a close union.

Mr. Pasvolsky said then there would be several citizenships. This should be provided for then by separate diplomatic representatives.

Mr. Armstrong was in favor of not trying to do anything by majority vote. The question might be left open but we could hardly expect that these states would enter a real federal union in which anything like a majority vote would settle vital rights. The best which could be hoped for would be a body where things are discussed and where the minority will come around through the application of all sorts of pressures, economic and otherwise, which its neighbors may be able to exert.

Mr. Hackworth thought that you would say that the action by the council should be taken by such a vote as is agreed on by the members of the union and leave it to them to decide how the council is to take action. This will show that we are not trying to lay down rules for them. Mr. Shotwell suggested that that kind of question could be referred to a special commission and then the commission could report to the council for decision, whether unanimous or not. Mr. Welles agreed, but asked if this would not all come much later and Mr. Shotwell concurred.

Mr. Welles said that the question of the customs duties did, however, bring up a matter of principle. It seemed to him that it was properly a function for the political and not the economic council. If it has charge of a *gendarmerie*, it should control also the customs services and should have power for that reason. This is not, of course, the determination of what the duties should be, but merely their collection and apportionment.

Mr. Hackworth thought that the collection might be left to the states, while the council might be given some supervision. However, thought Mr. Berle, if the council is going to get any money from the customs, it had better get it the first place.

Mr. Hackworth said that the states would not like the idea of an overall organization coming in to collect customs. You would save their face for them by giving the council some supervision over the matter. A similar situation had occurred in China where foreigners collected the customs. The revenues had been pledged as security for Chinese obligations. Both the British and ourselves have had collectors, but in each case they have been Chinese officials. They collected the customs and turned them over to the powers.

Mr. Cohen thought that this was a different case since, in China, there was no question of a customs union. In this union a portion of the imports might come in over one boundary and then pass through the union into another state. Thus, in this fashion, one state would be collecting customs for another state. Mr. Hackworth thought that the goods would pay another duty, but Mr. Cohen did not agree because he was assuming a customs union; that is, that there would be free trade within the area. This seemed to him to differentiate the case from that of China or other states where customs had been pledged.

Mr. Hackworth said that he was thinking more of the sensitiveness of the states. The more you cut in on sovereign rights, the more they will hold out.

Mr. Cohen said that if we cut in on the tariffs, he thought it was almost a corollary that we must cut into their powers of administration.

Mr. Hackworth agreed that if the states would accept this, then his objection would not hold.

Mr. Welles said that what is suggested is that there would be a single customs service rather than twelve different ones.

Mr. Cohen said that Mr. Hackworth did bring up a point; it would be important that they use the citizens of the respective states as the customs officials in their own state. This would have the double advantage, not only in making each state feel that it was really part of the union, but also of giving a number of individuals an interest in the preservation of the union. The providing of jobs may serve a good, as well as a bad, purpose. Mrs. McCormick agreed with this point, saving that the more people the union can employ, the stronger the union will be.

Mr. Welles stated that that of course would mean that the customs service would be used to collect duties on goods coming from without the union and not on those passing between component members of the union. This gives another incentive towards the union.

Mr. Pasvolsky thought that the situation might be described as follows: that the political council be responsible for the unification of the customs duties, and, on the advice of the economic council, for their apportionment.

Mr. Welles asked what he meant by "unification" and Mr. Pasvolsky said that the customs receipts would go to a union treasury. This would solve another question – the funds for the maintenance of the union. They would be deducted from the customs receipts. In the apportionment a part could be set aside for the budget of the union and the rest be apportioned among the states on the basis worked out by the economic council. Collection is just a police function and this should be done by the political council, but the apportionment is a task which might be given to the economic council, if the latter were not considered purely advisory.

Mr. Welles thought that the proper division of functions would be that the political council should have responsibility for maintaining and administering the unified customs service and, on the recommendation of the economic council, for the apportionment of the revenues. Then, it should be added, the expenses of the union's overall machinery shall be met from the customs revenues as so collected. Mr. Shotwell wished to add a proviso that the customs union be maintained, for we want to lower the customs barriers to the outside world.

Mr. Pasvolsky suggested that it might be said "insofar as the customs receipts would suffice for the union's expenses". He thought that free trade was not being envisaged here. Mr. Shotwell agreed, but he wished to reiterate his remark as a caveat. Mr. Welles thought that Mr. Shotwell's point was well taken and Mr. Shotwell said that he was afraid that the matter of a tariff for revenue might become a slogan. Mr. Welles agreed and suggested that the *proviso* that the expenses of the union should be taken from the customs should be omitted.

The chairman asked if there were any further suggestions and Mr. Bowman wished to raise a question concerning the last paragraph, namely, that "the members of the council would be responsible for the action by their individual governments to secure national approval and enforcement of decisions". He said that this was not what was meant there. It means that the members of the council would be "responsible for *initiating* action with a view to securing national approval". Mr. Welles agreed and said that that paragraph should be changed accordingly. Mr. Bowman said that the two representatives of Poland, let us say, would be "responsible for seeing to it", etc. All that they can do is to go back and initiate action and Mr. Welles said that what was meant was that the council members should act as liaison officers between their governments and the council.

The chairman then suggested that discussion pass to the economic council and he read the appropriate section of the draft memorandum.

Concerning the second sentence, he asked whether there were any contingencies where the economic council should not be advisory. He personally could not think of any things which should be entrusted to it.

Mr. Shotwell wondered whether there was going to be anything comparable to an Interstate Commerce Commission. If so, it would have a certain amount of administrative autonomy.

Mr. Welles said that what we have here, is a body of experts which would determine, purely from an expert view, the economic activities of the union.

Mr. Shotwell said that there was a difference between the ICC and the Tariff Commission. One has been effective and the other has not. He wondered if the economic council should be allowed to be effective. Mr. Cohen was of the opinion that there might be a development and evolution of the union and a desire on the part of the political council to set up certain administrative bodies like the ICC to handle things. It was possible that members of the economic council might serve on such agencies, but he thought that that work should be separate from the general work of the council. The two functions should not be confused.

Mr. Shotwell said that he was trying to clarify his mind on this. If the economic council was advisory only, he feared that it might be unimportant. Where discussion has to have responsibility for action, you get a different atmosphere. It should be understood that there is some place where you could count on that effective action. It might be better to have it concentrated in the political council.

Mr. Berle wished to raise a question. If you have an ICC, should the power of appointments to it rest in the economic or the political council? He would like to see the economic council have the right. Even though it was an unusual function for such an organization, he thought it might be useful to have it act as a board of regional directors.

Mr. Shotwell thought that there was an advantage in this proposal if one could get up enough optimism to think that the leaders in the union would rise sufficiently above political intrigue. Mr. Armstrong thought that the more one went in that direction, the better, but he was afraid that such a development might mean that there would be fewer experts than political appointees on the council.

It was Mr. Cohen's view that the international organizations, when they plan to aid the union, might use their influence to have such appointment made by the political council on the advice of the economic council. A balanced judgment by the economic council is desirable, but states should have the feeling that the power of political officers is behind any given decisions. Otherwise there is a danger of the growth of a feeling of separation between political and economic power.

Mr. Berle said that the experiment had never been tried. In the United States we have not had any cases of appointment by economic bodies – they have always been political. Here was a weak political organization; to give it the power to make those choices would strengthen it considerably. Do you want to give strength to the economic or the political council?

Would it not be both expedient and sound, suggested Mr. Welles, to leave the power of appointment in the hands of a political council? Could it not be provided, in special categories where expert qualities are required, that appointment should be made from a list provided by the economic council? Mr. Berle agreed, adding that perhaps some form of confirmation might be adopted.

Mr. Pasvolsky noted that the economic council would be separate. The political council would include prime ministers. All economic decisions within countries would be made by parliaments and their executives. These are represented by their highest officers in the political council and final decisions will be in their hands. He thought that the economic council should be advisory to the political council rather than to national governments, as provided in this draft plan. Since we have the political council without which no decisions of union concern could be made independently by the states, it seemed to him that the economic council should be advisory to the political council and the latter should undertake, under the last sentence of the draft, paragraph 5, to secure the enforcement of the agreements reached. Otherwise there would be political bickering within the countries – a result which we are trying to avoid. If responsible heads of the governments meet in the political council, they will be in a better position than anyone else to carry its decisions through the national governments and secure their approval.

Mr. Bowman thought that there was one merit in this proposal in that it increases the confidence which he would have in the possibilities of the union. That is, those political men – the prime ministers and their associates – would be in a more secure position at home in trying to resist the political council, if the latter's decisions did not run counter to decisions of the economic council, but rather ran counter to advice of an economic council. If the prime minister could say that the economic council consisted of people who were not working in the interest of his state, he could oppose its wishes. If, however, he goes back and says that this is the program of the political council and he resists it because the advice received was of such and such a character, he would be in a far more secure position – he is resisting advice and not resisting an organization. Mr. Welles agreed that this was a strong point.

On the other hand, said Mrs. McCormick, the original idea was that we wanted to put emphasis on the economic problem.

Mr. Bowman said that previously the subcommittee had started from the assumption that there were political forces at hand at the close of the war – now we are at a different stage. Here we try to figure out how to make the system work in the individual country and in trying to do that we have to take account of the individual countries. The center of gravity is shifted somewhat in looking at it now.

Mr. Shotwell thought that the question was which plan would give more kudos to the economic setup and Mr. Welles agreed that the practical question was how to make the economic council most effective.

Mr. Bowman said that previously we had thought of this by having real experts and we had sought to make their work real by separating them from the political side of the question. Mrs. McCormick said that what ought to be avoided was a weakness like that of the Little Entente, which was purely a political setup, by uniting these states economically.

Mr. Pasvolsky thought that the decision would still have to be made by the political bodies within the states. The council makes recommendations which then go to national parliaments and at that stage the prime ministers could say that they disagreed with the policy. A different situation would develop if the prime minister could say that on the recommendation of our advisers this or that seemed to be the best policy.

Mr. Welles thought that this would work both ways. If the plan remains as in the draft, any prime minister can say the same thing. He could use the advice of the economic council to oppose national action also. He feared both the caliber and the character of the prime ministers in this union. If a council is made subordinate to them, in a short time they will have honeycombed it to suit their own purposes. In recognizing the fact that the council's advice is sound and impartial, its position will be strongest. Only from the standpoint of administration did it seem to Mr. Welles that Mr. Pasvolsky's suggestion possessed merit. It was better to canalize recommendations to the councils rather than have them go to the twelve several powers.

Mr. Pasvolsky said he feared that government officials would appear to act as experts, but would in reality remain government officials. In the past they had come together at the League on financial and economic committees which were advisory and they would agree on very high principles and then go back to their countries and reassume their functions as officials and sabotage those principles. When the recommendations were made to the Council of the League, the official went back home and acted differently. His suggestion would put a stop to this kind of action – by making the economic council advisory to the heads of the governments we do not eliminate risks, but he was afraid the risks would exist even if the council were set up on an independent basis. If, for example, the governors of the central banks were members of the council, they would come to be political appointees. Their position would become of added importance and therefore the prime minister would see to it that the representation on the economic council, while conforming to the rules laid down for experts, would consist of political people, in fact.

It was Mr. Shotwell's feeling that the right persons should be found for the technical job. He thought such a development would be more likely in specific bodies which have a definite program. As we know, the larger determination of policy, whether economic or not, will be in the hands of the political people.

There is the need for having some things done by competent people and that may aid the political education of the region. The more we can parcel out the work to the economic council, the more real work can be devoted to specific fields of international economic life – the more reality there is in the whole thing.

Mr. Welles said that what he wanted to do was to bolster the economic council to make it as important a weight-carrying body as possible. He questioned whether this can be attained by tying that kite to the tail of the political council. Mr. Hackworth noted that a prime minister was to be on the political council and was also the head of his government and he could sabotage the thing as prime minister, as distinct from his membership on the council. In the council there would be a discussion between prime ministers and one might be swayed by the views of the other members. If he does not confer with his colleagues on the council, he may kill the thing as prime minister. Might it not be desirable to say in the third sentence (page 3, paragraph A of the draft) that "Its recommendations would be referred to the governments of the independent states and to the political council". In this way the economic council would have direct communication to the governments as well as to the political council. If the latter should take favorable action, well and good; if it does not take action, the whole project would still be before the governments in their respective capacity.

Mr. Welles thought that this might be a solution to the problem and asked for Mr. Berle's opinion. Mr. Berle thought that to leave it as it is would leave the economic council to depend on the international organization. Otherwise no change is necessary. Implementing of economic decisions is always political, as we know from experience in this country.

It was the view of Mrs. McCormick that putting a recommendation directly to the governments would have some publicity value for it would be a good idea to have people know about the plan. Mr. Welles thought that this was an important point.

Mr. Cohen felt that, on the other hand, one would not want to exclude discussion in a meeting of prime ministers, of an economic problem which might affect the whole union. Mr. Berle pointed out that that could be done under the present plan and Mr. Cohen agreed, saying that he just did not think that it was meant to exclude that or discourage it.

Mr. Armstrong asked if offers of help from an international organization would reach the governments through the economic council and Mr. Welles said that his thought was that they would; in some cases through both councils. Mr. Armstrong thought that in that case the economic council's recommendations should be made both to the governments and to the political council. Concurring, Mr. Welles said that that was why Mr. Hackworth's solution might be a wise one. If an outside organization or country offers to assist the union, a decision has to be made, first of all, by the political heads of the states and it would be appropriate to come through the political and economic councils as well. Mr. Berle added that this would mean that the measure would have to go through two bodies. We might wind up with a kind of bi-cameral system.

Mrs. McCormick wished to reiterate that we ought not to make the economic council subservient to the political and Mr. Welles said that that was why he did not agree with Mr. Pasvolsky's suggestion. The economic council should have its existing rights and also should report to the political council. Mr. Pasvolsky thought that in the end the two proposals would come to the same thing, but Mr. Welles said that he did not think that that was correct. By reporting to the several governments you assure publicity. Otherwise the recommendations would be known only in the councils. Mr. Pasvolsky said that the recommendations would be known only to the heads of the governments in each country under the other proposal. Mr. Welles said that where the draft uses the word "governments" his thought had been that that word referred to "parliaments" of the member states. Mr. Pasvolsky thought that in that case there would have to be a provision that the report of the economic council should be placed before the cabinet and parliament of the member countries. Mr. Bowman thought that such a provision would have to be watched since, on technical grounds, the report might be locked up in a safe by the executive. Mr. Welles said that that could be avoided by providing that the report be made to the executive and legislative branches of each state.

Mr. Bowman thought that it would be necessary to put the recommendation in the hands of sufficient people directly, so as to set up discussion of the recommendations, which would have to be faced by the prime minister. He would then be in the position of explaining why the political council thought it desirable to depart from or accept the recommendation.

Mr. Armstrong pointed out that this could be turned around. The prime minister might find it more difficult to deal with a question discussed in the political council where things will be given attention; rather than when, after he is called back home, he gets a recommendation that he does not like. Discussion in the political council would arouse popular interest more than if it had not been discussed.

However, said Mr. Welles, the political council would probably not hold public sessions. It would consist of a small group acting as a closed corporation. This will not give any assurance of publicity for the recommendations of the economic council. If the recommendations are to be made to the political council – to the executive heads of the governments – and to the several parliaments of the states, then you insure publicity.

Concerning Mr. Hackworth's point, Mr. Shotwell said that a wily politician would be able to tell his government that a project would be decided upon in the other body and to tell the international body that it would be decided upon nationally. This would allow a shifting of responsibility. That was why he thought it might be best to put responsibility in one place. Further, he suggested that the word "approval" at the end of the sentence would have to be looked into – which is the place, the international body or the other where it would be approved? Mr. Welles thought that this problem would be solved only by a process of selection.

He thought that the subcommittee had now provided a means of assuring publicity. He asked if this were satisfactory to the members of the subcommittee. Mrs. McCormick said that the one thing we want to avoid was to make the organization political to begin with. We want emphasis on the economic rather than on the political side, but Mr. Welles said that in order to get action, both the executive and political sides have to act. It might be said that instead of the word "approval" to which Mr. Shotwell had referred, the word "action" might be substituted at the end of the third sentence of paragraph A, page 3. Mr. Shotwell agreed.

In the final sentence of that paragraph, Mr. Welles thought that the word "should" ought to replace the word "might" and Mr. Pasvolsky expressed agreement.

Mr. Welles said that the council has to receive these plans from somewhere – directly from the international organization or from foreign countries. They must be submitted to the economic council by someone. Mr. Berle asked whether it was wished to allow outside offers of aid from one country, or whether you should inhibit the council from receiving aid from other than an international source. Mr. Welles thought that any aid from whatever source ought to be received. The question is whether to give the economic council power to deal directly with states and international organizations, or whether it should deal only through the political council.

Mr. Berle suggested that if the RFC[1] should wish to loan money for an Iron Gates dam, would it go to the economic or to the political council if it wished to deal directly? If it goes to the political council then the economic council is only a debating society. Mr. Welles thought that the economic council should be authorized to receive plans for aid both from states and from international agencies. Mr. Armstrong asked if this would prevent states from getting aid directly and Mr. Welles thought that there was nothing in the plan to prevent that.

Mr. Pasvolsky said that in this regard, individual states might submit projects to the economic council for its opinion. A component state would not use the economic council if it could get what it needs by other means. The principal purpose of the economic council is to make plans and arrangements for efforts by the whole group. An individual state might make agreements outside the economic council, the political council, or the international organization.

Mr. Welles noted that you could not deprive any sovereign state of the right to negotiate for any local improvement and Mr. Pasvolsky suggested that some provision ought to be made for keeping the economic council at least informed of such action. Mr. Berle thought that the economic council might take cognizance of any plans of general significance and Mr. Shotwell thought that the council should have the right to examine plans which might affect the region as a whole.

---

[1] Reconstruction Finance Corporation was founded by Congress in 1932 as an emergency agency to operate during the depression. Although the agency was meant to last no more than 10 years, Congress extended its lifetime to 1957. It had authority to lend money to banks, railroads, schools, business firms, and public agencies. The RFC raised funds by issuing bonds. It played an important part in financing war industries during World War II.

Documents

Mrs. McCormick asked what would happen if an individual company proposed to provide a water supply system in Greece and Mr. Berle thought there was no problem raised in that case.

Mr. Atherton asked whether, if state A should desire an economic agreement outside the union, it would have to go to the economic council before making it and Mr. Welles thought that that provision could not be made if you hoped to get the states into the union. Another hypothetical case was posed by Mr. Pasvolsky. Suppose one state gets financial aid to develop an industry. Looked at in one way, it might be an internal matter, but looked at another way, it might change the whole competitive position of another country. Mr. Welles said that such a case might arise where Greece would enter an arrangement with a development corporation to raise sheep and this might diminish the competitive ability of Poland. He could not conceive of Greece's getting into the union with an understanding that she could not develop her own resources within her own ability.

Mr. Pasvolsky presented another situation. In the 30s when the prices of cereals went down, someone got the idea that it was to the advantage of a country to convert its cereals into meat. Thereupon hogs were raised in quantity and the same situation developed with hogs that had been found with cereals. The countries then formed agricultural conferences to try to determine how they could handle the situation so as not to cut each other's throats. Unless there is machinery by which that contingency can be discussed and prevented, the development of the whole region is going to be bad.

That is the kind of thing, said Mr. Welles, that the economic council should do as an advisory body. He could not agree that the economic council could *veto* a right of any sovereign, independent state when the development is purely national. He believed that this was the classic difference of view between the Articles of Confederation and the Constitution.

Mr. Shotwell said that in the above case the countries almost got an economic common action out of common interest and Mr. Pasvolsky said that was why provision should be made that the council should be informed of developments. Mr. Welles agreed that this was proper, but reiterated that the economic council must not possess any *veto* power.

Mrs. McCormick thought that the economic council might draw up a plan for the balanced economic development of the region, in which the countries might be presumed to cooperate. Let us then make an amendment to the draft, said Mr. Welles: (1) that the economic council can receive projects directly from the international organization to the states or to the national corporations; (2) that it will be informed of any arrangements of that character into which component states enter. He then read the paragraph on the functions of the economic council and said that on point B of the paragraph the answer clearly should be "yes", the term "functions" remaining in the advisory sense.

Mr. Bowman thought that until we know what the administration consists of, it was difficult to express an opinion on the question raised in point A of paragraph B. There is an inconsistency between that and other things earlier in the draft. Union administration of economic arrangements calls for another type of mind and another kind of organization and he wondered whether the point could not be made without much discussion here. The economic council, continued Mr. Bowman, is not responsible for union administration, but for a *critique* and an advisory or supervisory relation to that administration. The administration itself is set up by agreement among the states. Mr. Welles said that that was clear to him and what was required was a critique of economic arrangements but not administration as such.

Mr. Shotwell thought that this suggestion might be covered by the directive – the "council should be kept informed..." and Mr. Welles agreed that this should cover the matter. Continuing, Mr. Welles read the section on the composition of the economic council. This represented the considered opinion of the subcommittee and it seemed to him that this was about as detailed as we could get at this time. He said that he must admit that the question of voting puzzled and worried him a good deal. He realized the value of the argument that in order that a small minority cannot block matters of great importance, other states... (Mr. Welles was called from the room).

Mr. Berle said that he thought it made a difference, depending on what was to be voted on. According to the draft, the only votes are (a) voting on recommendations and (b) a possible vote on recommendations for assistance. Do you leave the double vote as it is?

Mr. Pasvolsky thought that it was impossible to exclude a minority opinion on advisory opinions and Mr. Berle thought that the necessary action would be the approval by X number of states of a specific measure implementing the plan. Suppose there was a plan on transport and a recommendation is made that such and such a measure be taken by certain states; we advise that this be done. Having set up machinery, then it goes to the states and if they all say yes, then someone can get the work done. The advisory opinion could be cast in that form, but usually they do not give that kind of opinion. Might an advisory opinion in effect be a revenue measure?

Mr. Pasvolsky thought that the question of when the voting was important was when the ratification becomes effective.

Mrs. McCormick thought that this was a question for the constitution makers and Mr. Berle said that this aggregate of ideas would be the raw material from which a constitution could be drafted.

Mr. Hackworth noted that there were two plans in the minority vote – one is in the council and the other is for the states. Since the council's vote is a recommendation only, a majority would be sufficient. Mrs. McCormick agreed that it was a vote of submission to the governments and Mr. Hackworth, continuing, said that as for the action of the states, that is a difficult problem. Taking our own system here, we have a two-thirds majority in the Senate for treaties and a majority of two houses for legislation and three-fourths of the states are required for constitutional amendments. He presumed that either two-thirds or three-fourths should be required for the adoption of a recommendation of the council.

Mr. Cohen said that if the economic council should make a recommendation for joint economic action and only two states agree with it, those two could carry out the recommendation by themselves if they wished. In view of the size of the union, there would be many recommendations that would not affect all the states. So you might have the problem that where the plan required the consent of all member states it would be difficult unless you changed the political council to have a less number than the whole. Other proposals could be put into effect with three or four states.

Mr. Berle agreed with this view, suggesting that if the Holland tunnel[1] had been considered an international project, that it would have been impossible to build it if the permission of all the states East of the Mississippi had been previously required. He thought that you could not go into this underlying state voting problem without reference to the thing that is being voted on. Mr. Pasvolsky said that when a recommendation is placed before the governments, it will also be transmitted to the political council. If it is approved there by a majority, it will then depend upon the approval by the states for its application. The time of its going into effect would have to be determined in each case. There are twelve votes in the economic council, he noted and suggested that when seven of those are in favor of a recommendation, that recommendation should go through. Then it would be referred to the states.

Mr. Berle felt that it could be referred to the whole union or to any interested state or states. This would leave out the question of secondary voting. That is a matter for the political council to get action on, if there is general interest in the case. Mr. Armstrong asked if the political council would decide which states should receive the plan and Mr. Berle thought that the economic council should decide in each case on this question.

Mr. Bowman wished to ask what was the idea in the drafters' minds in the last sentence of the second paragraph under paragraph E, page 4: "Provided not contrary to the Articles of Union". He thought that was shooting off to one side of the mark. What we are talking about here is things of importance to the union economy – not contrary to the Articles of the Union. Also, suppose the economic council comes to an agreement and two states decide they are going to take action contrary to the advice. That would not be against the Articles of Union. It is a switch from the interests of the union to the constitutional question of the "Articles of Union". Mr. Pasvolsky said that such action might be contrary to both. The question would depend on who made the decision. Mr. Bowman noted that the economic council is discussing questions that are in the field of unspecified powers.

Mr. Welles returned, saying that he was sure that the committee had settled everything in his absence. He was immediately called out again.

Mr. Berle suggested that the discussion be summarized as follows: (a) the vote should be by the majority of states in the economic council when recommendations are made. The recommendation thus adopted shall be referred; (b) the reference of the recommendation should be to the political council and also to the states deemed interested. The number of states may be all or a portion of the total.

---

[1] One of the tunnels linking New York City's Manhattan Island and New Jersey. The tunnel, named after its constructor, Clifford Milburn Holland, was opened to traffic in 1927.

Mr. Hackworth said that this paragraph of the draft talked about two different things – it is talking about the action by the economic council concerning recommendations of the economic council. What about recommendations of the political council, he asked. The economic council's action should be finished and there should be a separate paragraph with respect to the action by the states concerning the action of both councils.

Mrs. McCormick said that it was not her impression that the political council should make recommendations on economic affairs.

At this point, Mr. Welles re-entered and he agreed with the repetition of the above summary by Mr. Berle. He thought that it was satisfactory to avoid taking up the question of what the states would do on recommendations.

Mr. Hackworth said there was overlapping in paragraph A. The recommendations of the economic council can be referred to the political council and the states. This is also under paragraph E. You have covered the same proposition but in a smaller degree. There should be an amendment in A; saying that recommendations will be referred to such governments of the states as may be interested. Then you would not need the same provision in E. Paragraph E might be taken out altogether.

Mr. Welles said that paragraph E would then be limited to the point of voting.

Continuing, the chairman said that he had nothing to suggest on the problem of foreign advisers.

Mr. Bowman thought that the provisions of that section could be changed easily later as shown necessary by experience.

Mr. Welles said that the recommendations in the draft on this point are good enough to start out with. He thought that the draft was now in such shape that it would serve as a good basis for the research staff and also to serve the subcommittee in taking it up in the last lap of its race.

At the next meeting the subcommittee will start in again on the Germanic problem; the least crystallized and the least settled of any question before the subcommittee.

The meeting adjourned at 12:55 p.m.

Bryce Wood, Secretary

10

STATE DEPARTMENT
Division of Special Research
Secret
P Document 24-c
October 19, 1942

Typescript, original
NA Notter File, box 54

AN EAST EUROPEAN UNION
(AS CONSIDERED TO OCTOBER 10, 1942)

Basic Assumptions

The regional organization should have the form not of a federation but of a union of independent and sovereign states, cooperating for limited objectives through common non-legislative institutions, loosely rather than tightly organized. Provisionally the union is considered as including all states of Central and Eastern Europe between Russia and Germany from and including Estonia on the north to Austria on the west and Greece on the south.

The union should be imposed, if necessary and should be guided for an indeterminate time, by the United Nations. Its main object should be security, but economic incentives and advantages should be developed. Overall international security would be guaranteed by the United Nations and the world organization and the security organization of the union should be integrated with the world security organization within which it should function.

The United Nations should promote the formation and stability of the union by making all necessary boundary adjustments in the region as rapidly as possible after the war.

Summary of Functions of Regional Organization

1) Security relations with the outside world and with international organization;
2) Intra-regional security and order by means of a regional constabulary of *gendarmerie*;
3) Foreign relations of the union as such and cognizance of external relations of component states;
4) Intra-regional economic relations; and
5) Economic relations with the outside world.

Constitution

The regional constitution, in the form of articles of union, would include written guaranties of certain individual and group rights – certain civil rights such as freedom of speech and religion, free elections and rights of ethnic minorities. The union organization would have clearly defined and limited powers at the beginning, with the possibility of growth provided.

Executive

An executive would be chosen by majority vote of the political council (or presidium) and empowered to carry out delegated duties in regard to security. He would be subject to removal by and special instructions from the political council.

Political Council

(a) *Composition*. The political council should consist of two members from each component state. One of the representatives from each state should be the Prime Minister or his plenipotentiary; the other should be a representative of the national parliament or his alternate.

(b) *Functions*. At the outset, at least, the functions of the political council would be deliberately limited.

Its chief executive function would be the maintenance of intra-regional security, effected through control of the regional *gendarmerie*. It would establish and exact the regional quota of forces required of the component states for the maintenance of the *gendarmerie* of the union and appoint the chiefs of staff of the *gendarmerie*. The regional *gendarmerie* would be established at various points throughout the union and would be moved from time to time to avoid too close identification with any given area. The political council would be responsible for filling the regional quota required for the police force of the international security organization. Discharge of the security function would be lodged in the executive described above.

The council's political functions would include the foreign policy of the union in its relations with the rest of the world and the taking of cognizance of any national relations of component states with outside nations or groups which were in violation of the undertakings of the union. Controversies arising between the union and outside powers would fall within the jurisdiction of the world organization. The council would seek to prevent disputes between component states and undertake the settlement of such disputes. The regional *gendarmerie* would be available to the council in maintaining peace between the component parts of the union and, at the council's discretion, in settling local disturbances which the local authorities are unable to handle when the government of the unit concerned requests the council to act. In case there is a question as to the identity of the local government, calling for a decision on the part of the council as to which rival group should be recognized, the council's decision should in all cases be subject to appeal to the world organization. The council would decide the contribution of the component states for the necessary expenses of the union.

Its administrative functions would be the maintenance of a regional administration including a central secretariat. The political council would be responsible for maintenance and administration of the unified regional customs service and, on the recommendation of the economic council, for the apportionment of the revenues. The power of appointment would be vested in the political council, with the proviso that where expert qualifications are required, appointment might be from a list provided by the economic council.

The members of the council would be responsible for initiating action in their states to secure national approval and enforcement of council decisions, thereby serving as liaison officers between their governments and the council.

Economic Council

(a) *General Nature* – The economic council would be separate from the political council. It would be an advisory body. Its recommendations would be referred to the political council and to the executive and legislature of the interested states – either all of the component states or a portion of the total number – for action. It would represent the region as a whole and not merely the interests of individual states; accordingly the council might be called "Council for the Economic Development of the East European Union". This council should be the medium through which international plans for economic development of the region were handled.

(b) *Functions* – This council would be charged with making recommendations to the governments of the component states on economic interests of concern to the region and it would have powers as broad as possible to initiate recommendations on general economic policies. The economic council could receive directly from the international organization on from individual states projects for aid to the component states or to the national corporations and should be kept informed of any arrangements of such character entered into by the component states. However, the economic council will possess no *veto* power. The Council should be informed of economic arrangements approved by the component states and it should be charged with enumerated functions relating to such matters as freedom of transit, communications, tariff, etc., in the union as a whole.

(c) *Composition* – Each state should be represented in the economic council by not more than five experts. Each state would select any number of experts up to the maximum. Such experts would be selected by the government in each state, from the Central Bank, industry, labor, agriculture and the professional classes. The terms of reference to the governments regarding the selection of representatives should stress that the delegates should know what they were to consider and should be competent as experts in those subjects. The experts would be assisted by staffs.

The Chairman of regional corporations and authorities (Power, Transport, Central Bank and Development Corporation) which may be established should be *ex officio* members of the economic council with a voice but no vote.

(d) *Tenure of office of the members* – The length of terms of the members would not be fixed.

(e) *Voting* – The delegation from each state in the economic council would vote as a unit. When recommendations are made, the vote should be by a majority of the states represented on the economic council. The question of approval by the states of the council's recommendations was left open.

Any number of states could voluntarily undertake common measures they might desire provided not contrary to the articles of union.

(f) *Foreign advisers* – Three economic advisers would be appointed by the United Nations to represent them in the economic council. These advisers would serve for three-year terms but initially so scaled that one might come up for appointment or re-appointment after one year, the second after two years and the third after three years. No one of the three should come from Europe (including Russia).

These advisers would have a voice in the council but have no vote or *veto* power. Their practical power would reside in the denial or grant of economic benefits by the United Nations. They should advise the whole council, not the component delegations. They should not represent individual economic interests. They should be competent on economic problems in general. They would be assisted by staffs. They should have the widest possible power of initiative with respect to recommendations on economic problems of the region.

The advisers should be closely linked to appropriate world organization committees which would be established, (possibly similar to the Economic and Financial Committees of the League of Nations); these committees might appoint the advisers or they might be selected by some type of United Nations' body, perhaps set up for the purpose, representing the United Nations' authority. These matters were deferred for discussion in connection with problems of world organization.

Judicial Organization

A regional judicial system would be created, to include a regional court with provision for appeals to a court of international justice in cases important to the union or its members. Appeals are envisaged in the following:

1) disputes or differences between component states;
2) any cases arising from an allegation that any state had not performed its duties under the Articles of Union;
3) any allegation by an individual that the Bill of Rights had not been carried out in respect of him and that he had no redress.

The Component States of the Union: Rights and Duties

Each state of the union could maintain the diplomatic relations customary to independent and sovereign states. Each state would be responsible for contributing to the international security force such quota as the political council agreed each state should provide. Contributions of men from each state would be in accordance with the population. The state quotas of men in the regional *gendarmerie* are neither envisaged to be situated in the states from whence they came, nor in the event of need to use union security forces to maintain peace in the union would the state quotas be used in their own states if avoidable. No state would have national military forces; local police forces only to maintain order would be permitted in the states.

States would retain the power to approve or disapprove the recommendations from the economic council and they would be free voluntarily to make economic arrangements among each other that were not in violation of the articles of union.

In the event of a regional approach to international organization, the delegates of each state to the international political organization might be its two representatives in the political council of the union, voting by states rather than together as a region, but this remains to be considered in connection with world organization.

Relations with the United Nations and International Organization: Summary of Tentative Views

(a) *Gendarmerie* – The United Nations would vest control of the regional *gendarmerie* in the political council after making the essential decisions concerning military forces in the region. The commanding officers would at the outset be selected by the United Nations, which would also determine the size of the force for a stated period.

(b) *Security* – The general security organization would require of the union the regional quota or contribution necessary for the international police force. Regional security arrangements would be integrated with the general security system.

(c) *Political Relations* – The union as such might not be represented in the international political organization; this remains for later consideration.

(d) *Economic Relations* – The United Nations would give advice to the union on economic questions through three advisers.

(e) *Judicial Relations* – Provision for appeal from the judicial organization or tribunal of the union to an international judicial organization would be made.

11

Council on Foreign Relations
Studies of American Interests
in the War and the Peace
Territorial Series
Secret
October 26, 1942

Print, original
Notter File, box 61

MEMORANDUM ON RUSSIA
AND EAST EUROPEAN FEDERATION

Rapporteur: Isaiah Bowman

I

In the discussion of possible means for stabilizing the postwar development of East Central Europe, much attention has been given to proposals for a federation, or for a series of federations. These suggestions have been presented from the point of view of the peoples of the East Central Europe, as a means of overcoming their divisive tendencies and of safeguarding their future security against Germany and Russia. The proposals have also been examined from the view point of the Atlantic powers, as a means of pacifying the area from the Baltic to the Aegean without unduly extending their own permanent commitments in a region relatively inaccessible to the influence of sea powers. The potential importance of a federation in protecting the people of East Central Europe against a resurgence of German expansionism has been assumed.

Little thought, however, has been given to the prospects of Russian acquiescence in or opposition to such projects of federation. For that reason, even a preliminary and skeletonized statement of the Soviet interests involved may serve to focus attention on this side of the problem. Russia's direct motives for opposing the creation of any sort of non-Soviet federation in East Central Europe appear to be far stronger than the factors which would induce it to accept or to support such an attempt at a new organization of the area. However, it may be useful also to list the lines of reasoning, which might be stated in an effort to induce the Soviet government to accept a federal solution of the problem of East European stability. For the purposes of such a statement, it is assumed:

1) That at the close of hostilities of Soviet Russia will be a power and will have army in being;

2) that Russia will have a strong but presumably not a paramount concern in the future status of the hundred million Europeans living between the Soviet boundary of 1938 and that of Germany.

II

The motives of a presumptive Soviet opposition to the establishment of an East European federation are numerous and strong.

1. If a federation were established, Russia would lose the advantage of dealing separately with many small states and of playing on their rivalries for its own advantage in accordance with the principle that "my neighbor's neighbor is my friend". The possibilities of supporting Czechoslovakia against Poland, Hungary against Rumania, Yugoslavia against Hungary and so forth, present an almost limitless field for maneuver by Russia to make its influence strong and even preponderant among the disunited states of East Central Europe. After 1920, Russia was practically precluded from exerting decisive military or diplomatic pressure on this area; the collapse of Communist movements in Hungary[1] and in other parts of the region[2] and the defeat of the Red Army on the Vistula,[3] meant that direct Soviet influence was checked at its new western boundary, while the post-1918 policies of the states of East Central Europe were dominated by a western orientation. After this war East Central Europe will presumably offer a profitable arena for Russia's intrigue and influence unless it and the other victorious powers agree to limit the scope and to define the nature of their influence by some sort of "self-denying ordinance[4]" such as would be embodied in their joint resolve to promote the formation of an East European federation.

2. A federation would presumably be better than a number of separate and rival states to assert the claim of its members to disputed regions to which Russia also may lay claim. In order to earn the loyalty of its member-nationalities and to prove that it offered tangible advantages, a federation might be driven to serve as the organ of national ambition or revenge, to Russia's detriment. Russia's direct interests, then, might lead her to extend her boundaries as far as possible to the west, at the expense of the Baltic states. Poland and Rumania and at the same time, by supporting the ambitions of Czechoslovakia and Yugoslavia and perhaps of Hungary and Bulgaria, to render its aggrieved neighbors impotent to reassert their claims to the newly-created *irredenta*. Such

---

[1] A reference to the Soviet Republic of Hungary, founded by the Communist Party headed by Bela Kun in March 1919. It was crushed on 1 August of the same year by a joint offensive of Rumanian, Czech, and government troops.

[2] A reference mainly to the revolution in Germany of 1918, a series of strikes organized by the Spartakus Group and the emergence of workers' and peasants' soviets.

[3] A reference to the victorious Polish offensive of August 1920. The repulse of the Red Army from the very outskirts of Warsaw was seen, at the time, as saving Western Europe from Communism. Lenin himself described the war against Poland as "the Revolution's glorious progress towards the West".

[4] A instance of wishful thinking, previously associated with the UN.

a policy, if pursued by Russia, would disrupt any plan of federation even before it could be brought into the realm of practical formulation.

3. A federation would presumably rest on or tend toward a certain internal conformity of social and political structure, which, whatever it might be, would not be Soviet. On the other hand, in the absence of a federation, individual states, under social and national stress, might be Sovietized[1] from within or without and be brought into membership in the Soviet Union. The extremes of social exasperation, now further intensified by Nazi invasion and oppression, might fuse with pan-Slavism[2] to support a wave of Soviet expansion. On the other hand, a federation would tend to strengthen the resistance of its members both to pan-Sovietism and to pan-Slavism and would again look mainly to the West as its model.

4. A federation would represent a potentially large if heterogeneous military force and would be stronger in defense than each of its members acting separately. In its absence, the various national forces might tend to balance each other, or might even cancel each other out, in their effect on Russia's strategic and military calculations. The latter situation would enhance Russia's military position.

5. The exports of such a federation would compete on world markets with certain Russian exports, particularly cereals, lumber and oil and a federation would presumably compete more effectively that could a number of several rival states. In its trade with the area contained in the federation Russia might find it difficult to bargain as advantageously as it could with the individual states.

6. A federation would be resistant to the newly revived pan-Slav feeling, as it could be neither pan-Slav nor anti-Slav if it were to exist at all. Any advantage which might accrue to Russia through its championing of the Slav cause in the present war would thus to be lost. In addition, a federation would have to make suitable provision to include several peoples, Slav and non-Slav, which have displayed a chronic fear of Russian encroachment and which have entered the war against Soviet Russia with fatalistic if not enthusiastic conviction. Within a federation, the interests and traditions of these traditionally antagonis-

---

[1] A remarkable lucidity of vision, though one based not so much on premises derived from the aims and practices of imperial Soviet policy as on the internal situation in affected countries.

[2] Pan-Slavism – a nineteenth century idea named by Slovak writer Jan Herkel. "This is the new wall erected between Russia and the rest of Europe, between East and West" – wrote Ivan Sergeyevitch Aksakov in 1868. Previously attacked by Communists as a reactionary movement, it was used during the Second World War to present the national war of the U.S.S.R. as a war conducted in defense of 300 million Slavs. The first two pan-Slavic Congresses took place in Moscow in August 1941 and April 1942, the third in Sofia in March 1945, the fourth in July the same year in Bratislava. After the war, with the name "Neopanslavism", it found a home in Belgrade (another congress took place there in December 1946). Panslavism went into decline after the Yugoslav schism (the last congress was held in Prague in March 1948). See Kohn, H., *Pan-Slavism, Its History and Ideology*, Notre Dame, Indiana 1953.

tic states would nullify, from a Soviet nationalist viewpoint, the pro-Soviet orientations of certain other members of the federation.

III

The motives of a presumptive Soviet acquiescence in, or support for, the creation of an Eastern European federation can only be stated less directly and certainly appear far weaker than those suggested by a rapid appraisal of the traditional Realpolitik to which the Soviets have increasingly professed their allegiance. However, even these motives might, in the circumstances created at the close of the war, be not without force in the long run.

1. A federation would give to each of its member states greater sense of security than any of them could achieve by its own efforts. The resulting feeling of regional consolidation might allow the federation to be less intransigent toward Russia in the disposition of some of the disputed borderlands. For example, Poland which played a leading role in a close-knit federation would find in this association greater strategic security than in again extending its eastern frontier beyond the Pinsk marshes; Rumania, assured of protection for its intra-regional frontiers, might be reconciled the sooner to the probable loss of Bessarabia. In dealing with a federation, Russia might thus secure more advanced frontiers in the west, without thereby incurring the permanent hostility of the federation as a whole. In fact, members of the federation not directly affected by such territorial changes would probably exert themselves to restrain the irredentist ardors of the member states directly affected.

2. If Russia's paramount interest in East Central Europe is to be that of strengthening its own security, it might find it more profitable to join with Great Britain and the United States in exerting a stabilizing influence over the federation as a whole, as a permanent safeguard against a new German push to the east. The experience of 1939-41 has shown that Russia has a profound interest in containing any German aggression at Germany's own borders and that, generally speaking, Germany can play the game of building a political clientele in East Central Europe more effectively than Russia. For Russia the alternative to supporting the consolidation of this "interstatial Europe" is to acquire enough client-states within the area to maintain the disunity of the region. Russia's client-states would be at odds with their neighbors and with any great powers antagonistic to Russia. Particular alliances with the separate states of East Central Europe would create many dangers of unnecessary and unprofitable Russian involvement in the quarrels of this region. These dangers might be lessened if the entire region were subjected to Soviet control. It is not likely, however, that Russia's partners in victory could afford to see[1] one hundred million Europeans added to the Soviet power.

3. A federation, strong in defense, would share with Russia the responsibility of checking a renewal of German expansion to the east. The alternative for Russian alternative which has been discredited since June 22 1941 is to favor a militarily strong Germany as a partner in dividing out East Central Europe.

---

[1] Strange yet true.

Because of its already vast area, Russia's aim should be to have as many friends as possible rather than to have as much additional territory as it might be able to take by force the moment of Germany's collapse. For Russia to extend its military and political control beyond adjoining areas which have a certain cultural and social affinity for it, is to postpone the pacification of the East Central Europe and to hasten the revival of German power. Self-control in the moment of triumph should lead Russia to work for overall controls with a long-range protective value for Russia rather than for indecisive and costly territorial accretions.

4. A Soviet Russia friendly to an East European Federation, would exert a strong pull within that structure. Such influence, based on cultural and social factors, would be more fruitful for Russia in the long run than to assemble an uneasy following of client-states which in turn would exploit Russia's strength for their own parochial interests and quarrels (*sic*). The stronger this peaceful influence became the less Russia would have to fear that the federation might eventually prove hostile to Soviet territorial and other interests.

5. In the economic sphere, both Soviet Russia and a federation would probably find their exports and agriculture goods and raw materials playing a diminishing role in their respective economies, as their industrialization advances and standards of consumption rise. Exports of foodstuffs and raw materials have played a relatively small role in Soviet foreign trade of recent yeas and they may become even more insignificant as Soviet requirements in machine-tools are supplied increasingly within the country or if they should be provided in part through economic planning or an interstate plane. Similarly, the more hopeful prognostications for the economic future of East Central Europe agree in pointing to moderate industrialization and to intensification of agriculture as its chief needs. In the case of continuing competition for outside markets for their lumber, oil and cereals, both Russia and an East European federation might find their interests better served by entering into worldwide producer-consumer arrangements than by playing a lone game in which each would succumb to the competition of the overseas producers. The federation might in time find in Russia a market for certain machine-tools and for high-class consumer goods, while Russia could furnish to it some non-ferrous metals and furs.

6. With a defensively strong federation to the west, guided in its early steps by the combined influence of Great Britain, the United States and Russia, the Soviet Union would be able to relax the strain of its armaments and to turn its efforts toward realizing the long-deferred promises of a higher standard of living for its own peoples. By controlling German armaments in cooperation with Britain and the United States, and by promoting the pacification and consolidation of East Central Europe through a similar policy of tripartite cooperation, Russia would be able to devote a far larger share of its industrial effort to the production of goods for consumption. A "peace" which compelled the Soviet people to continue the 1929-41 pace of armament and sacrifice would be a profound disappointment and might in the long run have serious consequences for the internal stability of the country.

IV

Presumably no federation can arise in East Central Europe if it is opposed by Russia, which will possess many means for disrupting it, especially in its formative stages. Nevertheless, a multiethnic, hence defensive, federation, with its effort of self-assertion turned against Germany, might offer greater security to Russia for the long run than its alternative, a congery (*sic*) of quarreling satellites and their rivals. Since no genuine federation can be created in East Central Europe by Russia alone or against Russia, it can be established, if at all, only by the Western democracies in cooperation with Russia or at least with Russian acquiescence. What a federation would need from Russia is toleration; from Britain and the United States it would need active and detailed supervision, and perhaps even dictation (*sic*), in creating the first bases of its existence, and then careful nursing and constant attention to its economic needs and potentialities. While Russia's immediate interests seem to be in direct opposition to the establishment of such a federation, a long-range view of Russia's place in the world suggests that a common ground might be found on which Russian aims and Central European aspirations for stable and autonomous self-development could, under favorable circumstances, be reconciled.[1]

---

[1] For a discussion of this document in the context of an analysis of American policy towards the U.S.S.R., see Mania, A., *op. cit.*, pp. 21-23.

12

DEPARTMENT OF STATE
R 38 T 224
Confidential
January 28, 1943.

Typescript, copy
AN Notter File, box 55

BRITISH OPINION ON POSTWAR ARRANGEMENTS IN EASTERN EUROPE
(Preliminary)

I. The Anglo-Soviet Treaty of Alliance

Although the presumptive basis of British postwar policy toward Eastern Europe has assumed concrete form in the Anglo-Soviet Treaty of 1942, there is no disposition by British opinion to consider the agreement as in any sense an exclusive arrangement apart from the Atlantic Charter and the interests of the other members of the United Nations. After signing the Pact, Mr. Eden declared that "there is nothing exclusive in our agreement. (...) But understanding between us is one of the foundations of peace, not for us alone, but for the world".

The framework of United Nations consultations, in which the Treaty negotiations were set, is emphasized as fundamental to the Pact's interpretation. The text of this Pact shows the marks of the long deliberation which commenced on July 12, 1941, with the entrance by the British and Soviet governments into formal treaty relations to effect full mutual assistance during the war. This initial Alliance was the first step toward a broader approach to the war. It was followed a month later by the Atlantic Charter, to principles of which Russia subsequently adhered and the terms of which became the basis for the agreement of September 24, 1941[1] to establish an Allied bureau for research and for the coordination of postwar reconstruction plans. Mr. Eden's secret visit to Moscow in December,[2] out of which emerged the joint *communiqué* of December 29 announcing an Anglo-Russian exchange of views on questions related to the prosecution of the war and the postwar reconstruction, was succeeded by

---

[1] The date of the access of the U.S.S.R. to the Atlantic Charter at the Allied conference in London, also attended by representatives of Belgium, Czechoslovakia, Greece, Holland, Luxembourg, Norway, Poland, Britain and Yugoslavia. A total of forty-seven countries, signatories of the UN Declaration of 1 January 1942, acceded to the Charter.

[2] For a description of the talks, see Rzhewski, O. A., "Visit Edena w Moskvu w dekabre 1941 g. Peregovori z J. V. Stalinom i V. M. Molotowom", *Nova i Noveyyshaya Istoriya*, February 1994.

further conversations in London into which the United States was brought, along with the Dominions and the European Allied Governments.

This concept of the Anglo-Soviet Pact as a document representative of the collective interest and opinion of the United Nations is the aspect of the Treaty which is most stressed by British opinion. "At every turn the widest range of advice and support was solicited; and it can be said that the Treaty which has emerged, though it is the concern of only two of the United Nations spring in a sense from the collaboration of all of them".[1] Thus interpreted, the signing of the Anglo-Russian Pact may be regarded as an implementation of the Atlantic Charter, "In it the broad outlines and general principles of the Atlantic Charter begin to take positive shape. Here they applied to the special problems of a particular area, The area is Europe, the cauldron out of which the first two world wars have boiled up."[2]

The military aspects of the Treaty, including an unprecedented twenty-year British military commitment in Eastern Europe, is generally viewed as "essentially an *ad hoc* arrangement – an instrument first for defeating and then for restraining Germany and her satellites: so much indeed, is suggested by its very selection of the term of twenty years. Victory and the police work which will tame and muzzle the German wolf during these crucial first twenty years – it is easy to see how Britain and Russian must bear a dominant responsibility here."[3]

Such a war and postwar police partnership, however, is not in itself according to most British comment, an adequate basis either for European or foe world government. Article 5 of the alliance, which pledges the contracting parties to cooperate for the prosperity of Europe and to act in accordance with the two principles of "no territorial aggrandizement" and "non-interference the internal affairs of other States" operates to place "the pivots of the new system" on "collective defense against aggression and economic collaboration in raising the standards of living".[4] The terms of the military alliance specifically provide that it shall eventually be superseded by the establishment of a system of "common action" among themselves and "other like-minded States ... to preserve peace and resist aggression in the postwar period". Upon the successful creation of such a collective system, "this alliance between two countries will be merged in some larger combination. Only if action to establish such a system does not in fact take place will the Anglo-Russian military alliance run for its period of twenty years – with further continuance unless terminated by one or other of the parties."[5]

---

[1] *The Economist*, 13 June 1942, p. 815 (this and the following notes to this document are by the authors of the memo and reveal the nature of their information).
[2] *Ibid.*
[3] *The Round Table*, September 1942, p. 449.
[4] *The Economist*, 13 June 1942, p. 816.
[5] Samuel, V., "Britain, Russia and the World", *Contemporary Review*, London, August 1942.

II. Eastern Europe and the Collective System

British opinion is acutely aware of the fact that, if the Anglo-Soviet Alliance rests in fact upon a reconstructed collective system, the actual determination of the pattern of such a system, at least as far as Eastern Europe is concerned, must rest largely with the U.S.S.R. There seems to be no inclination. to repeat the experiment of the interwar period of setting up "a sort of cardboard structure of small powers, incapable of defending themselves", which Britain "proved unable to protect". It is clearly recognized that for the smaller powers, even more than for the larger, there is no permanent pledge of peace otherwise than in a permanent guarantee of Britain, America and Russia. If so, Russian views as to how this is to be achieved will have to be taken into as much account as "our own".[1] There is widespread agreement that the "Middle Zone cannot exist, no matter how great its cohesion, in a state of conflict with Germany and Russia. It must choose between the two – and there can be no doubt what the choice ought to be. It must, while avoiding conflict with Germany as far as possible, remain on good terms or perhaps even in a condition, of semi-alliance, with Russia."[2]

Assuming the paramountcy of Russian influence in the reconstruction of Eastern Europe, British thought has recently turned in the direction of removing the grounds for a Russian westward expansionist policy by reaffirming in unmistakable terms Britain's determination to make a peace which will "make the Germans, no matter what form of government they adopt, forever unable to go to war again".[3] This point of view is in direct contradiction to the balance-of-power implications of trends of opinion current in the summer of 1941, which foresaw "that the leadership in Western Europe should fall to Germany and in Eastern Europe to Russia".[4] It was this notion of Britain's return to a balance-of-power policy which Viscount Samuel, apparently with a view to allaying Russian suspicions, recently discussed at some length in the House of Lords.

In a recent debate in the House of Lords (Viscount Samuel writes), I drew attention to the suspicion, which may still linger in the minds of Russian leaders, that political groups in this country, who had been the most hostile to the Soviets and may now have accepted the alliance only with reservations, might be unwilling, when it came to the point, to see Germany weakened too much for fear of Russia growing too strong. They might wish to see some settlement aimed at in Eastern Europe in the nature of a Balance of Power between Germany and Russia – a balance in which Britain might play the part of makeweight. I summarized the arguments against the principle of the Balance of Power: that my balance that might be established has always proved precarious, easily upset by shifting alliances; that, the period in European history when the

---

[1] Sir Bernard Pares, "The Russian Alliance", *Contemporary Review*, London, August 1942.
[2] Editor's note, "The Baltic States", *Nineteenth Century and After*, May 1942.
[3] Editor's note, "Great Britain, France and the Balance of Power", *Nineteenth Century and After*, June 1942.
[4] Ibid. See also a leading article in *The Times*, London, August 1941.

doctrine was dominant was one of constantly recurring wars – this country being at war for as many years as it was at peace; that the consistent policy of England had really aimed, not at some clever equipoise, but at the defeat of any attempt that might be made by a single Power to establish a domination in Europe; and that the only method by which stability could be reached was to organize a system of collective security. I asked whether the Government could make a statement that would show that such suspicions, if they still existed, were wholly without foundation.

To this, Lord Selborne, answering on behalf of the Government, gave a considered reply, which it may be useful to quote. He was not aware, he said, that there were any people in this country who might seek to preserve a strong Germany to act as a counterpoise to Russia. In any case he gave the assurance that that formed no part of the policy of His Majesty's Government. The Atlantic Charter, in its Eighth Article, postulated as a fundamental condition the complete disarmament of Germany; and a Germany completely disarmed could not be described as an effective counterpoise to anyone.[1]

Although the concrete outlines of a collective system for Eastern Europe have not yet emerged, British opinion appears to emphasize the necessity of providing the maximum of national freedom which is compatible with the principle of a strong Middle Zone and full Russian cooperation. This line of reasoning is developed even as far as to attempt to provide reasonable grounds upon which the Soviet might conceivably favor the inclusion of independent Baltic States in such a Middle Zone.[2] However general support for the commonly supposed Russian determination to re-annex the Baltic territories may be, it "is implicit in the foreign policy that is developed in leading articles that have appeared in *The Times*. *The Tribune* recently demanded that the British Government give *de jure* recognition in advance to the Russian re-conquest of these territories."[3] This view appears on the whole to have found few critics.

The clearest indication of British opinion to date on the most feasible approach to the problem of freedom for Eastern European States within the orbit of such a collective system as the British public hopes will supersede the Anglo-Russian alliance, is given in Mr. Eden's speech of September 26, 1942:

> Smaller states, I am glad to say, declared Mr. Eden, are also alive to the need of collaboration among themselves. There are Polish-Czech and Greek-Yugoslav agreement, both of which call for and express a sense of unity. We shall continue to foster such agreement and encourage smaller states to weld themselves into larger, though not exclusive, groupings. Thus they will be better able in collaboration with the great powers to play a part in maintaining peace.[4]

It is generally recognized that only solid Anglo-American guarantees against future German aggression "can fairly claim from Russia a liberal joint settlement" of the specific territorial and other questions involved in the suc-

---

[1] Samuel, V., "Britain, Russia and the World", *op. cit.*
[2] Editor's note, "The Baltic States", *Nineteenth Century and After*, May 1942.
[3] *Ibid.*
[4] British Information Services, Press Service, 28 September 1942.

cessful reconstruction of Eastern European states. British opinion is approaching the problem of the postwar status of East European states by accepting as a basic Anglo-Russian assumption the necessity of a strong and friendly Poland and Czechoslovakia as a barrier against future German aggression eastward.[1] This appears to suggest something in the nature of the old *cordon sanitaire* turned against Germany, rather than against Russia!

PS: Ridgeway: ZMB: JRB: VVP: MHP

---

[1] Sir Bernard Pares, "The Russian Alliance", *Contemporary Review*, London, September 1942.

13

DEPARTMENT OF STATE
Secret
P document 204
February 10, 1943

Typescript, copy
Notter File Box 57

THE FEASIBILITY OF AN EAST EUROPEAN UNION[*]

I. Introductory

The region of Eastern Europe for which union has been envisaged embraces an area of approximately 445,000 square miles and includes a population of 119 million persons. An investigation of the feasibility of unity within so extensive and populous a territory requires assessment of the influences which have made for division and those contributing toward unity and a consideration of what steps might be taken to reduce the former and to develop the latter.

II. Divisive forces within the Region

A. The Absence of Common Roots

In a very real sense the Eastern Europe under consideration, stretching from the Gulf of Finland to the Greek islands, is only a geographic expression. The one political experience common to the whole region is the present German exploitation.

Various parts of the area took their character from differing compounds of Greek, Latin, German, Slav and Asiatic influences. The scene of numerous invasions of peoples and of cultural influences, Eastern Europe was condemned by this diversity of competing forces to deep-seated divergencies that hampered the development both of the region as a whole and of the constituent ethnic groups.

B. Cultural Diversity

There are represented among the more than one hundred million people some nineteen different ethnic groups speaking as many languages and dialects

---

[*] Document by Notter, Mosely Harris, Rothwell, of the Political Section and Stinnebower, Knight, Wadleigh, Elridge from the Economic Section.

and owing allegiance to five religions and to even more religious organizations. (East European series, maps 2 and 5).[1]

Running through the area is not only the religious watershed of Europe but also the social line which divided the region of city-dominated culture and village-dominated culture. Roughly corresponding to this line is that separating the areas of industrial importance from those of a backward peasant economy with their marked differences in standard of living and educational attainment. The social structure is further complicated by the fact that not infrequently the towns are occupied by people of one ethnic group and the countryside by less advanced members of another group.

C. Nationalism

Included in the area are twelve independent states, of which five are kingdoms. The spirit of nationalism, present in varying degrees among the several peoples for over a century, became virulent after 1914. This spirit received expression in movements for national unity, in high protective tariffs, in the oppression of minorities and in the cultivation of resentments against neighbors (East European series, map 13). Since the present war began, the animus between several of the states, *e.g.*, between Bulgaria and Greece, between Hungary and Rumania, has been greatly increased and the conflicts between ethnic groups within one state, *e.g.*, between Czechs and Slovaks, between Serbs and Croats, has (*sic*) become more bitter.

D. External Political Influences

Likewise making for division in Eastern Europe has been the time-honored habit of the Great Powers of exerting special influences in certain states. Before 1914 it had been the professed hope of the Great Powers to regulate the problems of the Balkans through the concert of Europe, but separate and conflicting interests frequently led to failure. For a decade after 1919 the old form of competition was no longer so apparent but French, Italian, German and Russian activities have pulled various areas into diverse foreign orbits. These foreign interventions have not so far caused the East European states to band themselves together into a united front of resistance, but have frequently had the opposite effect of increasing friction and hostility. The chief political collaboration between East European states, the Little Entente, was an alliance of three of these states directed originally against one of their neighbors.

E. Economic Developments

The economy prevailing in East Europe has not been conducive to intraregional unification, but has worked rather in the direction of expanding relations between the individual states and those of other areas. In 1925 about one-third of the foreign trade of the East European states was with each other, but the world depression reduced that trade to approximately one quarter in the years 1935–1937. Only Hungary had more intra-regional than extra-regional

---

[1] Missing in Notter Files

Documents

trade in 1929. The industrialized states of Austria and Czechoslovakia were next in the order of magnitude (East European series, map 1).[1]

Except for Hungary and for the industrial areas in Austria, Czechoslovakia and Southwest Poland, East Europe is predominantly a thickly populated agricultural region in which very poor peasants produce low yields of grain crops in small holdings. Their lack of purchasing power and the generally similar character of their products provided no strong common economic bonds.

Transportation facilities, developed largely by western capital, primarily connect East Europe with the outside and particularly with Central and Western Europe and there has resulted a relative scarcity of intra-regional railway connections, particularly between North and South. There are more adequate facilities in the northern states than in the Balkans where there is an almost complete lack of routes suitable for strategic purposes. The existing lines, however, do provide exploitable contacts between the industrialized districts and the agricultural areas to the East and South.

The more significant economic relations of the individual state with Western Europe have been increased by the fact that capital has come from the West and that the chief markets for agricultural products and raw materials have been found there and notably in Germany.

III. Movements Tending Toward Unity

The principal integrative force of a political import within the region has emanated from the peasantry and has assumed three forms: the emergence of peasant parties with common aims and a disposition to co-operate across state lines, the development of the so-called Green International and the growth of the cooperative movement.[2]

A. Peasant Parties

Organized peasant parties reached the high point of their influence in the countries of Eastern Europe during the late twenties. They attained significant political force in Poland, Czechoslovakia, Rumania, Yugoslavia and Bulgaria. These individual parties were strongly motivated by the desire to effect a more equitable distribution of land and to secure wider measures of social and economic welfare. For a time there were close relations between the leaders of the several peasant parties and some effort was made to coordinate the policies of the governments in which they were represented.

---

[1] Missing.

[2] This emphasis on peasant parties and their role in Central European countries is of some interest. It won the support of the State Department, and then of the National Committee for Free Europe, for peasant politicians who escaped from Communist countries, such as Stanisław Mikołajczyk, Ferenc Nogy, Georgi Dimitrov, as well as for the reborn "Green International". This came as a shock to many *émigrés*. See J. Laptos, *'Komitet Narodowy na rzecz Wolnej Europy a komitety narodowe emigracji środkowoeuropejskiej'. Księga pamiątkowa ku czci prof. Józefa Buszki*, Cracow 1999.

These successes, however, were short-lived. The international view point and effort of the peasant parties declined during the depression years under the impact of nationalist sentiment and activity.

B. *The Green International*

The so-called Green International,[1] which existed for a brief period after 1919, included representatives of the peasantry in the Ukraine, Croatia, Macedonia, Serbia and Bulgaria and had the sympathy of Polish and Rumanian peasant leaders. The peasant international operated on the theory that territorial, minority and security problems in Eastern Europe could more readily be solved in the spirit of peasant pacifism and tolerance than by the methods of nationalist and capitalist governments. The somewhat romantic conception of the solidarity of the peasantry of Eastern Europe gradually disappeared because the Green International lacked an effective organization and because of the consolidation of nationalist governments, of the growth of nationalism among the peasants themselves and of the economic fluctuations of the 1920s.

C. *Cooperatives*

The cooperative movements which developed considerable strength in most of the states of the East European region afforded an important field for collaboration among the peasant leaders. Numerous congresses and exchange visits among representatives of the cooperatives took place until the outbreak of the present war. In general the leaders of the cooperative movements tended to emphasize the need for peaceful reconstruction and to minimize the territorial and other purely national aims of their respective states. A serious weakness of the cooperative movements, from the standpoint of an international community of interest, was their emphasis on finance rather than production and marketing.

These various peasant movements may be regarded as indicating a community of interest among the important and numerous agrarian elements of Eastern Europe. Their positive contribution to the development of either a sense of unity or a will to unity has not been great. Agrarian internationalism has been outweighed by peasant nationalism. Only the cooperative movements had sufficient vitality to maintain an international point of view. Until they were crushed by the war, the movements had a solid achievement to their credit.

D. *Communism*

Prior to 1939 the communist movement, although it was strong in many East European states, did not exert great unifying effect among the peasantry or working classes in the region or to bind them to the Soviet Union. While the pan-Slav motive, exploited in some places by local communist groups, exercised some influence in the direction of loyalty broader than the nation-state, in most countries the communist movement fed upon local issues and national rivalries and was colored by the provincialism and political ignorance of its peasant constituents.

---

[1] See Doc. 1, footnote 2, p. 75..

Communist tendencies have strengthened in parts of the East European region during the present war. There is reason to suppose that they will acquire even greater strength and influence in the period of readjustment following the war. Should this occur, it is not improbable that a much more coordinated communist movement may develop across state lines throughout the region.[1]

E. Effects of German Control

German control over the East European region during the present war has led to substantial economic development, which has included a moderate diversification of agriculture, a considerable improvement in the transportation system and an expansion of industry. The German-fostered industrial development, instituted primarily for war purposes, has been in two directions: 1) an increase in the production of coal, iron and steel and petroleum, principally in formerly industrialized areas such as Silesia and 2) the transplanting from Germany for reasons of safety of finishing industries, notably those for the manufacture of machinery, textiles and military equipment. In many instances the latter industries have been moved to formerly rural areas in the Balkans, as well as in the Danubian states.[2]

Permanent advantages will accrue to the East European states from these developments because they will retain some, at least, of the imported German industrial equipment and because they are acquiring a corps of skilled native workmen, trained by the Germans in essential industrial techniques.[3] German control has only incidentally contributed, however, to laying a foundation for economic unity throughout Eastern Europe, largely because the German practice has been to integrate the new economic developments in this region directly with German war economy or to envisage them as part of a European economy centering upon Germany. In some instances, German control has even increased the disunity of the region by breaking up larger political units such as Yugoslavia and linking the individual parts separately with the German economic system.

IV. Steps Necessary to make Union Effective

In view of the fact that Eastern Europe has felt the impact of virtually none of those dynamic forces that would aid in creating a unity out of this diversity of peoples, *the creation of a union and its maintenance for an indefinite period,*

---

[1] An interesting remark, possibly based on OSS reports for the State Department. It shows that ignorance of the Communist threat in those countries cannot explain, as often maintained in British and American historical literature, the U.S. position on Central Europe at the Teheran and Yalta conferences.

[2] Assumptions based solely on assumed logic, with no support in facts apart from Czechoslovakia, due to its developed industry, its proximity to the main front line and its feeble resistance movement. The exploitative character of the German economy there was totally disregarded.

[3] This stereotype, akin to German propaganda, is even more surprising when stated by members of the Committee.

would have to be in large measure the work of the great victor powers or of the international organization. [our italics – JŁ & MM]

A. Guaranties of Security

Of prime importance would be guaranties of security that would protect not only the constituent states against the attacks of each other but also the union and its members against external aggression.

1. *Intra-regional Security* – Since there exist deeply rooted hostilities between several of the states within the region, there is some doubt that the regional organization, even with a *gendarmerie* at its command, could keep the peace for some considerable time to come. In the past the smaller states of Europe have composed their difficulties peacefully when they were under the firm and concerted pressure of the Great Powers; when unanimity among the latter was lacking, dangers frequently arose. The apparent key to tranquility in Eastern Europe would seem to be, therefore, a resolute insistence on the part of the principal United Nations that the member states of the union work harmoniously together. The problem of securing a common purpose among the Great Powers with respect to this area is one part of the larger problem of maintaining the unanimity of the chief victors through an effective international organization.

2. *Security Against Outside Interference* – Security of Eastern Europe from external attack depends on whether the United States, Great Britain and Russia, either as allies or through the international organization, agree to enforce the peace.

B. Territorial and Political Adjustments

While a *veto* on trouble-making in Eastern Europe would afford an opportunity for the healing processes of time to work – as they did with considerable success in the interwar period – the turn toward peaceful living would be hastened by a determined insistence upon and help in, making adjustments of those political issues which have been the causes and the symptoms of bad relations within certain of the states, between states of the region and between these states and foreign powers. Guaranties of security, with their assurances of safety from outside attack and their prohibition of aggressive adventures, would, if effectively carried out, make a real contribution toward reducing the importance of several of the old conflicts. There are, further, several inequities that could be materially rectified by frontier changes, by respect for individual rights and by a devolution of political control through federal arrangements or autonomy in composite states.

C. Positive Measures

Guaranties of security and territorial and political adjustments, however, would be essentially negative measures – steps to restrain or abate the influences that have made for trouble. Because of the absence of integrative forces in the region as a whole, negative provisions on the part of the sponsors would not suffice for the task of creating a union. Over and above them there would need to be measures calculated to give these diverse peoples some sense of unity and some very definite benefits from and some vested interests in, the development of an organic unity in Eastern Europe.

1. *Political* – The sponsoring powers could profitably encourage activities designed to foster a sense of community and a willingness to undertake progressively closer political collaboration. Regional conferences on common problems and institutes for mutual understanding would be essential means for making these peoples acquainted with each other.

In the long run, the experiment will be successful only if the millions of people of Eastern Europe are induced to think in terms of the union as a useful political and economic agency and to give it a basic loyalty. As a further means to that end it might be wise to dramatize the union by giving it as important part in the representation of the region in the international organization. It can be anticipated, however, that most of the constituent states and particularly Poland and Czechoslovakia which played important roles on the European diplomatic stage, would resist a curtailment of their individual activities in the councils of the new international order.

There would unquestionably be an advantage in a regional system of security as a court of first instance if such a system could be created. The responsibility for maintaining order might be more immediately felt by the peoples of Eastern Europe provided these states had a collective accountability and a machinery of their own. A few instances of successful self-discipline highly commended in the world press might, in turn, create a wholesome *esprit de corps* and increase the popular support of the union. On the other hand, *a regional system of security could hardly be instituted and could hardly exist for an indeterminate future without a continuing unanimity of the victor powers sufficiently strong to keep the peace* [our italics – JL & MM] whether or not there was an Eastern European system of security.

2. *Economic* – Among the major steps to be taken with a view to an improvement of economic conditions in the area as a whole are:

a) Modernization of agricultural production, processing and marketing, with a view to: increased production per acre; a better diversification of output; grading, canning, packing, freezing and other processing by local labor and plants; scientific farming with selected seeds, proper fertilizers, mechanization, etc.; joint marketing agencies for all markets in order to eliminate competitive sales; rapid education of the peasants in better production methods; creation of warehousing and related facilities;

b) The promotion of public works projects for the improvement of transportation, flood control, drainage and hydro-electrification;

c) Expansion of the basic industries;

d) The expansion of finishing industries where they can be made efficient;

e) The coordination of export policies;

f) Appropriate financial facilities to make possible the carrying out of the foregoing.

The carrying out of these functions would require well-developed political as well as economic collaboration among the East European states and would necessitate regional arrangements and agencies. Among them, the following might be considered:

a) *A customs union* – For the time being, this might be merely a tariff union, maintaining lower rates between members than toward outside countries, with a view to safeguarding against great or sudden pressures upon established enterprises and occupations and as a transitional measure toward a full customs union. This might not be sufficient in itself in order effectively to promote trade across political boundaries; some regional control of cartels and other private groups operating in more than one state might be necessary, otherwise private arrangements might effectively substitute their own controls for the customary tariffs and quotas. Furthermore, a customs union would not be enough in itself. The arrangement would have to be broadened to restrain the numerous types of indirect protectionism and also to provide the necessary financial and monetary coordination.

b) *Regional collaboration in control of international payments* – To make the tariff or customs union effective, cooperation at least in the field of payments arising directly from trade would probably be necessary.

c) *Regional monetary cooperation* – Cooperation in the monetary and foreign-exchange field (*i.e.*, a broader field than encompassed in (b) above) would undoubtedly promote unity and might even be indispensable to bring about currency and exchange stability and sufficient compatibility in the fiscal policies of the various constituent governments to render the area essentially a unit for trade purposes. Cooperation in this field would be less important if currencies in general were placed on a fairly stable and exchangeable basis.

d) *A regional development authority* – While the feasibility of a regional organization for borrowing and for servicing most loans, may be open to doubt, a regional agency for the construction and administration of public works affecting two or more states would clearly be useful an constructive. Subsidiary operating agencies might be necessary in some cases and advisable in others.

e) *A regional agricultural administration* – This might be necessary, to carry out agreed divisions of production and marketing, to coordinate a common program of modernization and to prevent sources of friction from reaching the customs organization suggested above.

f) *A regional transport authority* – Evidently transport would need reorientation to fit the new common policies and activities. Since new construction and maintenance of rail, road and other routes would be involved, there would have to be some regional organization. Perhaps the regional development authority would also handle this activity.

Assistance from outside the area, both in the form of credits and technical aid, would be of great importance for the attainment of the foregoing economic objectives. Furthermore, the creation of inter-regional facilities such as those outlined above might serve as an inducement for bringing the countries of the region together into some form of union.

V. Summary

A union, even one loosely constituted, would be fundamentally a synthetic creation. The motive force for establishing and maintaining it would have to come in large measure from the outside. The essential means to this end would be (1) protection against internal disorders and external attack, (2) economic aid in the form of credits, commercial arrangements and a system of advice tantamount for some time to indirect control and (3) the support and recognition necessary for cultivating a community of interest and of responsibility.

An organization strong enough to embark on a program of union-wide economic activities and able to maintain the peace among its constituent parts would inescapably mean a limitation on independent national action. Acquiescence in such a radical reform and the perpetuation of the union would require, therefore, not only a willingness on the part of the constituent states to accept it, but also a common and enduring purpose among the victor powers acting either informally together or through the medium of an international organization.

14

DEPARTMENT OF STATE
Division of Special Research
Document P 206
Secret
February 18, 1943.

Typescript, original
NA Notter File box 57

SOVIET AND BRITISH ATTITUDES TOWARDS EAST EUROPEAN UNION

A. The Soviet attitude toward an East European union or unions

1. Present Attitudes

On the basis of information at present available in P[olitical] S[ection], the Soviet Government is apparently hostile to the idea of the creation of an all-embracing East European Union, unless, perhaps, such a Union were established under the preponderant influence of the Soviet Union. An examination of the Soviet press and periodicals has disclosed no discussions of such projects for an Eastern European Union as have been put forward from time to time in Britain and the United States. Soviet attitudes as publicly expressed place strong emphasis upon the satisfaction of Soviet territorial claims, as, for example, in the article by Zaslavsky in *Pravda* of February 8, 1943.[1] In conversations with individual representatives of Eastern European governments-in-exile, Soviet spokesmen have from time to time indicated, in a personal and non-binding form, their strong belief that the separate national states within the East European area can become strong and prosperous only in close cooperation with a powerful Soviet Union.

In recent conversations in the Department Mr. Van Zeeland indicated, on the basis of conversations with leaders of governments-in-exile in London, that the Soviet Government seemed "very suspicious and distrustful of any project for Eastern European union or federation which would involve a political union". He had gathered the impression, however, that "if a project for Eastern European union were to be limited solely to economic and financial ties, the Soviet Government would approve such a project because of its belief that the creation of such an economic and financial federation in Eastern Europe would redound to the, economic advantage of Russia".

---

[1] This paper has not been found.

Some more recent information suggests that Soviet suspicion of any attempt to plan jointly for the postwar reorganization of the "Middle Zone" lying between Russia and Germany goes rather deeper than was assumed by Mr. Van Zeeland. A recent dispatch from Ambassador Biddle[1] reported that Soviet representatives were discouraging any discussion of postwar federation or alliance among the governments-in-exile.[2] Whether a prior recognition of Russia's so-called "security frontiers", approximating to those of June 22, 1941,[3] would relieve the apparent Soviet fears that any form of Eastern European union would be a barrier to the extension of Soviet territory and influence remains uncertain. In any case it appears to be generally held by the governments concerned that projects for an Eastern European union can be elaborated only with the knowledge and, if possible, with the approval, of the Soviet Government.

With regard to partial unions, such as the Czechoslovak-Polish and Greek-Yugoslav federations, the Soviet attitude appears, in general, also to be unfavorable. From recent public statements of Czechoslovak spokesmen abroad, it seems clear that the Soviet Government has lately discouraged M. Beneš from pursuing the further elaboration of plans for a Czechoslovak-Polish federation or confederation.[4] Whether this attitude represents an unveiling hostility towards the idea of a Czechoslovak-Polish Confederation, or whether it is based on a Soviet desire first to deal separately with Poland concerning the problems which affect the territorial interests of both states, it is impossible to say. The Czechoslovak Government, which has no direct territorial conflicts with the Soviet Union, except possibly and remotely in Ruthenia, and which looks to close cooperation or alliance with the Soviet Union as an essential element in its postwar security, is understandably reluctant to take part in Polish-Soviet territorial controversies, the more so as the Polish Government has so far not settled its own territorial dispute with the Czechoslovak Government over Teschen.[5]

---

[1] Anthony D. Biddle (1896-1961), American diplomat, ambassador to Warsaw (1937-39) and to the government-in-exile in Angers and London. An official or unofficial U.S. envoy at all Central European meetings.

[2] Not included in American diplomatic documents. But they do contain a similar dispatch, dated 20 February 1942. See FRUS 1942, Vol. I, p. 109, Biddle to the Secretary of State. He sent an identical letter to Welles, the Under-Secretary.

[3] *I.e.* a frontier including the Baltic states, eastern Polish territories after the 17 September 1939 aggression and Besarabia.

[4] For Beneš' shift of position, see P. S. Wandycz, Czechoslovak-Polish Confederation and the Great Powers 1940-43, Indiana University Publications 1956, p. 76 and *passim*. The Division of Special Research Studies' presentation of Beneš' policy to the Subcommittee can be seen in document R. 2 (NA Notter File, box 55) of 2 June 1943: "This growing coolness to the idea of Polish-Czechoslovak federation is attributed by Minister of State Dr. Hubert Ripka to 'the present Soviet policy of great reserve toward these efforts'. He went on to say that his government has from the first insisted that friendly relations between countries and the Soviet Union must be a prime condition of any Polish-Czechoslovak agreement". Based on a New York Times report from a meeting of the Czechoslovak State Council, 1 March 1943.

[5] This issue re-emerged as a pretext for a less enthusiastic approach to confederacy.

There had been some indication that the Soviet leaders might look with more favor on a Polish-Czechoslovak confederation limited to economic cooperation. However, even this measure of Polish-Czechoslovak cooperation has apparently been frowned upon of late by Soviet representatives abroad. In any case, the question of whether effective economic cooperation between these two states would be possible without definite political and security arrangements requires exploration.

With regard to the proposed Greek-Yugoslav Confederation, the Soviet attitude has also been cold. There have been indications that some Soviet spokesmen feel that this project, if carried into effect, would tend to weaken the influence of pro-Soviet elements within Yugoslavia; presumably its adoption might eventually stand in the way of carrying through some more drastic regrouping of the Balkan peoples under Soviet influence.

2. *Presumptive disadvantages of an Eastern European Union or Unions, from the Soviet Point of View*

Any attempt to analyze the presumptive grounds for Soviet opposition to the creation of an Eastern European union must rest in part on observation of past Soviet policies, in part on conjecture concerning the Soviet interpretation of what constitutes its own best interest. The considerations which follow have been elaborated by the research staff as an attempt at analysis through conjecture.

a) Ever since the November Revolution[1] the Soviet regime has feared a new coalition of the so-called capitalist world against itself. This psychosis of encirclement has been one of the constants of Soviet policy. The idea of creating a union of 100 to 120 million people along Russia's western frontier may well remind Soviet leaders of the post-1918 attempts, in part successful, to create a "*cordon sanitaire*"[2] from the Baltic to the Black Sea. While such a union might appear to the United States and Britain to be directed mainly against a resurgence of German power, the fact is that several important members of the union fear Russia at least as much as Germany; once Germany is defeated and disarmed, they might well fear Russia more than Germany. Aware of this factor, Soviet leaders may fear that any such union would eventually become a barrier to the westward expansion of Soviet rule and influence.

b) The Soviet regime has frequently seemed to pursue two policies simultaneously, a "limited" policy and an "unlimited" policy. A "limited" policy looks to the achievement of specific territorial and security objectives consonant with

---

[1] Although the term "October Revolution" has been common usage for 70 years, present-day literature often refers to it as "the Bolshevist coup".

[2] "*Cordon sanitaire*" – a French term first used at the Congress of Vienna, 1815, to denote a policy that was to protect France from the return of Bonapartism or of revolution. It became popular after World War I as a reference to the Entente's policy to create a barrier against Bolshevism, of which Poland felt itself a major element. Soviet propaganda employed it during World War II in its campaign against the confederacy in an analogy to the "Curzon line" with respect to Poland's eastern frontier.

maintenance of the national independence of other states; and "unlimited" policy strives for complete domination of a people and its absorption into the Union of Soviet Socialist Republics. This ambivalence of purpose was illustrated by Soviet policy during the war of 1939–1940[1] with Finland. The Soviet Government first put forward specific claims to Finnish territory on grounds of strategic security. When some of these demands were rejected by the Finnish Republic, the Soviet Government withdrew recognition from the Finnish Republic and extended recognition to and signed an alliance with, a newly created "government" of a Finnish Peoples Republic, headed by Otto Kuusinen,[2] a Finnish Communist long employed in Moscow by the *Comintern*. Later, the Soviet authorities signed a treaty of peace with the established Finnish Republic and the Kuusinen "government" disappeared from view. The most plausible interpretation of these events is that the Soviet Government was pursuing alternative policies of "limited" and "unlimited" objectives. When its "unlimited" objective failed of achievement, it returned to its original policy of "limited" objectives.

In respect to the postwar status of the countries of Eastern Europe, it is possible that one purpose of the Soviet leaders in discouraging the formation of a union and of federations or alliances is to keep the situation in that region fluid; in order to hold open as long as possible the choice between "limited" and "unlimited" objectives. Whether postwar plans for the federation of the peoples of Eastern Europe within the framework of the Soviet Union have been elaborated by Soviet or *Comintern* authorities remains unknown. In any case, the acceptance now of definite international arrangements for the postwar settlement in Eastern Europe would, in the light of past experience, imply a Soviet commitment to follow a policy of "limited" objectives in this area and to abandon an "unlimited" policy.

c) An Eastern European union would tend to rest on a certain internal conformity of social and political structure and aspirations, which would not be Soviet in character, but would rather look to Western Europe and the United States for inspiration and support. For Russia to lend its direct support to a social order quite different from its own, except on a limited basis of security and other international arrangements, would require a difficult psychological adjustment in Stalinist thinking.

---

[1] The Soviet-Finnish war, also known as the "winter war", began with the Soviet aggression of 30 November 1939. Despite its heroic resistance and significant success, Finland had to make a number of concessions in the peace treaty of 12 March 1940. See: V. Tanner, *The Winter War: Finland against Russia 1939-1940*, Stanford University Press 1957; A. Kastory, *Finlandia w polityce mocarstw 1939-1940*, Cracow 1993.

[2] Otto Vilhelm Kuusinen (1881-1964) Finnish politician, founder of the Communist Party of Finland (1921), and secretary of the Executive Committee of the Third International (1921-1939). On the second day of the Soviet aggression, he joined the puppet government of the Democratic Republic of Finland in the frontier town of Terijoki, which signed a treaty of mutual assistance and friendship on 3 December 1939.

d) In the absence of an Eastern European union or of partial federations, Russia would be able to deal separately with nine or twelve small states and to play on their fears and rivalries. A disunited Eastern Europe would present an almost unbounded field for the maneuvers of power-politics. After 1917 Russia was precluded from exerting decisive military and political pressure in this part of the world. After this war Eastern Europe will be open to Soviet influence and even predominance unless Russia should join with the other victorious powers in some kind of "self-denying ordinance"[1] designed to tranquilize this region and to assure the peaceful development of its peoples.

3. Possible Arguments in Favor of an East European Union or Unions, from the Soviet Point of View

The following considerations are necessarily conjectural in character, as there is no evidence of their having been taken into account so far in the recent trend of Soviet policy. Since it would be essential at some stage to outline certain arguments in favor of Soviet support for any such regional arrangements, these reflections may, however, be worth committing to paper.

a) Since a union would greatly enhance the feeling of security among its member states, it might be more easily reconciled to the transfer to Russia of some of the disputed border-regions now claimed by the Soviet Government. For example, a Poland strengthened by playing an important role within a regional grouping might the sooner abandon irredentist claims to any eastern provinces ceded to the Soviet Union as part of an overall settlement.

b) Russia's long-run security might be better served by the consolidation and pacification of Eastern Europe through exerting its necessarily strong influence[2] in favor of regional union rather than by building up a clientele of small states. Particular alliances of Russia with small states within the region would leave the area disunited, would promote competition in armaments and might lead to the building up of counter-alliances directed against Soviet preponderance.

c) A Soviet Union friendly to an Eastern European federation would exert a strong pull within its structure. Such influence, based on cultural and social factors and strengthened by trust in the non-aggressive aims of Russia, would in turn lessen any Soviet fear that such a union would be hostile to Russia's territorial and other interests. Such a federation could also share with the Soviet Government the responsibility for checking any possible renewal of German aggression towards the east.

d) With a defensively strong federation to its west, guided in its early stages by the joint influence of Russia, Britain and the United States, the Soviet Union would be able to relax the tremendous strain of its armaments and to turn its efforts toward promoting a higher standard of living at home. A "peace"

---

[1] A good example of wishful thinking dominating American policy at the end of the war.

[2] This suggestion reflects the growing conviction of many politicians that the territory should become part of the Soviet sphere of influence, in contrast to plans of 1942, which assumed no influence of European powers in the union.

which compelled the Soviet Union to continue the 1929-1941 pace of armament would be a profound disappointment to the Soviet people. A constructive approach to the problems of the "Middle Zone" would thus represent a useful supplement to any program for the control of Germany and Japan, for an international security system and for the continued cooperation of the principle United Nations in assuring a durable peace and opportunity for economic advancement.

e) With the consolidation of the security and the stability, social and political, within Eastern Europe, this area should develop a higher standard of production and livelihood. This in turn would favor the development of mutually advantageous exchanges between it and the Soviet Union.[1]

B. British Policy Toward Federation in Eastern Europe

The British Government has indicated that it will welcome and encourage the federation of smaller European states, particularly within the East European region. It regards such collaboration as a means toward strengthening the ability of the smaller states to participate in the maintenance of peace and the promotion of economic welfare within the terms contemplated in the Atlantic Charter[2] and the Anglo-Soviet Treaty of Alliance.[3] In the opinion of British spokesmen, such groupings should not be exclusive, but should be open to the collaboration of other states. The British Government seems to desire that such federation should be defensive in character and should offer no obstacle to the revival of international trade on the widest possible basis. On this view, it has specifically approved the Polish-Czech and Greek-Yugoslav agreements. It has welcomed the former as a possible nucleus for a Central European federation and the latter as a basis for a Balkan confederation.

---

[1] A striking similarity to a fragment of W. Sikorski's statement from a OSS report of 30 January 1943 : "The realization of this ideal, of which I am a fervent advocate, will safeguard not only the security of nations situated between Germany and Russia, who will thus form a kind of international family, but it will likewise be a natural rampart of protection for Soviet Russia, always so concerned about her Western security. Such a peaceful family of nations would not only be a factor of security, but also one of permanent European stability and economic development through the creation, over a vast area, of possibilities of large scale exchange" (NA Int. 33 Po 5, p. 8. "Memorandum by the Foreign Nationalities Branch to the Director of Strategic Services - The visit of General Sikorski in retrospect").

[2] Atlantic Charter – a declaration signed by U.S. President F. D. Roosevelt and U.K. Prime Minister W. Churchill on board the 'Prince of Wales' cruiser on 14 August 1941. Section 4 proclaimed an equal access of small and great states to trade and world resources as a condition of their prosperity. The adherence to the Atlantic Charter by the Soviet Union happened at a resolution adopted at the second meeting of the Inter-Allied Council in London on 24 September 1941.

[3] The treaty was signed in London on 26 May 1942. It adopted the rules of the Atlantic Charter. Its final form ignored the issue of Central European federation, though early drafts included a reference to it. See O. A. Rżewski, "Vizit Edena v Moskvu w dekabre 1941 g. Peregovori z J. V. Stalinom i V.M. Molotovom", *op. cit.*

The British Government has predicated the success of postwar British policy in Eastern Europe upon the maintenance of Anglo-Russian cooperation. It early secured, through the Anglo-Soviet Treaty of Alliance, the pledge of the Soviet Government to act in accordance with the principles of policy laid down in the Atlantic Charter – the principles of no territorial aggrandizement and of no interference in the internal affairs of other states. In encouraging the development of confederations composed of weaker European states, the British Government has made clear its recognition of a strong Russian interest in the East European region.

Recently the British Government has taken occasion to allay possible Russian suspicions regarding any intention on the part of Great Britain to foster a balance of power in Eastern Europe between Russia and a revived Germany. A Government spokesman in the House of Lords has disavowed any such intention and has pointed to the Eighth Article of the Atlantic Charter which postulates a completely disarmed Germany, as making impossible the return to a balance of power policy in Eastern Europe.

15

DEPARTMENT OF STATE
Advisory Committee
for Postwar Foreign Policy
Division of Special Research Studies
Document R 205
Secret
February 19, 1943

Typescript, copy
NA, Notter File, box 57

INTERLOCKING CONFEDERATIONS IN EAST-CENTRAL EUROPE

I. The Problem

In view of the difficulties involved in establishing a union of all the twelve states of Eastern Europe, it might be useful to consider the possibility of making security arrangements through a series of confederations within the region. The Danubian area and the Balkan states, and to a lesser degree the Baltic states, constitute more coherent entities than the area as a whole and these separate groups have had certain experiences in collaboration which might be capitalized in the attempts to organize a security system.

II. Possible Subregional Unions

A. The Polish-Czechoslovak Federation

1. *Steps taken thus far* – Relations between the two new states of Poland and Czechoslovakia were embroiled in 1919 when the latter took possession of Teschen. From that time until Poland took part in the destruction of Czechoslovakia the two countries were on unfriendly terms except during those times when their common interests were threatened by the Great Powers.

Common sufferings at the hands of the Germans and common fears for the future, however, have contributed in the last two years to bringing the two exiled governments together. By January 1942 they had agreed on several principles of a confederation between them. Their announced common purpose was "to assure common policy with regard to foreign affairs, defense, economic and financial matters, social questions, transport, posts and telegraphs". While there has been no announcement of the details of the confederation, the agreement envisages a customs union and close collaboration in economic, social and cultural activities. The agreement further stipulates that the constitutions of the two states should guarantee civil and political liberties. The accord also provides for a common general staff in time of peace and a single supreme command in time of war. For the purpose of insuring common policy with respect to these activities the establishment of common organs for the confederation is envisaged.

The two governments expressed the desire that the confederation include other Eastern European states with which their vital interests were linked but no negotiations to this end have as yet been initiated.

2. *Obstacles to Final Agreement* – While negotiations apparently are still in progress, the discussions between the two governments have encountered the following obstacles: a) the Teschen dispute, b) the opposition of the Soviet Union to the proposal of confederation,[1] c) the hesitation of the Czechoslovak government to act without the approval of the Soviet Union, Great Britain and the United States and without the consent of the people of Czechoslovakia, d) Polish fears of a too intimate Soviet-Czechoslovak association, e) a Polish desire to include Hungary in a confederation with Poland and Czechoslovakia; and f) unofficial Polish aspirations to have a quadruple confederation with Czechia (*sic*), Slovakia, Poland and Hungary.

Despite the absence of any historical basis for a Polish-Czech federation, and despite the serious nature of the obstacles, to such federation, many prominent Czechs and Poles are genuinely convinced that neither country can exist independent of some form of collaboration.[2]

B. *Greco-Yugoslav Federation: Towards A Balkan Union*

1. *Composition* – A federated Greece and Yugoslavia would include an area of 145,000 square miles and embrace a population of approximately 23,300,000 inhabitants. A Balkan Union embracing all the states except Turkey would have an area of 293, 000 square miles and a population of approximately 43,000,000 inhabitants.

2. *Steps thus far* – The Greco-Yugoslav pact of January 1942 was intended by the two signatory governments not only to establish a confederation between themselves but also to lay the general foundations for the organization of a Balkan Union. The agreement provides for three types of cooperation: a) economic and financial collaboration in working out a customs and monetary union, b) development of common foreign policy, and c) common plans for defense. To carry out these purposes there are to be established a Political Organ, a Permanent Military Organ, an Economic and Financial Organ and Permanent Bureau or Secretariat.

---

[1] A 12 January 1943 memo sent by Col. Donovan, OSS director, to Secretary of State Hule mentioned that "a basic difference persisted [between Poles and Czechoslovaks *émigrés*] regarding the Soviet Russia. It was the Czechoslovak view that Poland should reach an agreement now with Russia on the question of the Eastern boundaries". NA OSS INT - 9 Cz-308.

[2] See the Introduction for instructions on literature on the federation.

Documents

3. *Obstacles to Balkan Union* – Greco-Yugoslav collaboration might not meet with great difficulties since the two countries have not been unfriendly in the last twenty years. In the past, however, efforts for union of all the Balkan states, as represented by the Balkan Entente and the Balkan Conferences, have met obstacles, many of which still exist. Among them are excessive nationalism, boundary disputes, minority problems, limited opportunities for intraregional trade, and outside pressures.

4. *Movements favoring a Balkan Union* – Although these obstacles have hitherto proved insurmountable, there has been a genuine movement toward some form of Balkan unity. Popular trends in that direction were apparent in the agrarian, socialist and communist movements. Supplementing them was a long-established intellectual movement. Beginning in 1930, the Balkan Conferences developed a series of projects for political, social, economic and intellectual cooperation. The Balkan Pact of 1934, a treaty of mutual guaranty of the frontiers of Greece, Rumania, Yugoslavia and Turkey, was a limited projection of the work of the Conferences. Although primarily political in form, the pact looked to the development of collaboration along the lines laid down by the Conferences.[1]

C. A Danubian Confederation

1. *Composition* – Unofficial proposals[2] for a Danubian Confederation have involved varying combinations of the states of Eastern Europe, most of them involving Austria, Hungary,, Czechoslovakia, Yugoslavia and Rumania. These states have a total area of 325,000 square miles and a population approximately 66,000,000 persons. These proposal encounter difficulties similar to those involved in the Czechoslovak-Polish and Greco-Yugoslav understandings. Between the states along the Danube there are sharp differences in political, cultural and economic attainment and serious conflicts over territorial and other interests.

2. *Considerations favoring confederation* – A large portion of the Danubian peoples have had an experience in living together under the Habsburg monarchy. Politically this experience tended to drive the succession states apart because of inherent inequities, but economically it laid some basis for collaboration. Between 1919 an 1938 in conditions prevailing in that area suggested to many persons the desirability of reconstituting some form of collaboration on a more equitable basis.

---

[1] See, for instance, a study co-authored by two members of the Advisory Committee, J. R. Kerner, and H. N. Howard, *The Balkan Conferences and the Balkan Entente. A Study in the Recent History of the Balkan and Near Eastern Peoples*, Berkeley 1936. Valuable Polish language publications include Beata Łyczko-Grodzicka, *Dyplomacja polska a Ententa Bałkańska 1933-1936*, Cracow 1981.

[2] An allusion to the plans of Tibor Eckhardt and John Pelényi, and of Otto von Habsburg. Documents of the Committee proceedings also include plans by two Austrian *émigrés*; Julius Deutsch, economist and Socialist, former minister in Ludwig von Mises' government; and Ernest Karl Winter, former vice mayor of Vienna. These were plans not so much about the Danubian Confederation itself as Austria's adherence to it. (AN Notter File, box 55 P - document 46).

The Little Entente, formed by Czechoslovakia, Rumania and Yugoslavia, was the one regional organization that materialized. It originated in a common opposition to Hungarian revisionism and Habsburg restoration but went on to lay some basis for social, economic and cultural cooperation.[1]

D. Baltic Union

1. *Composition* – A Baltic Union might be composed of Poland, Estonia, Latvia and Lithuania. The region has an area of 217,000 square miles and a population of approximately 43,000,000 inhabitants. Without Poland the area is approximately 66,000 square miles and the population of 5,000,000 persons.

2. *Difficulties* – There have been unofficial proposals, inspired by the Baltic Entente of 1934, for the federation of Estonia, Latvia and Lithuania. Some of these proposals have included Finland and Poland but they have not gone beyond preliminary outlines.

Since 1940 Estonia, Latvia and Lithuania have been formally a part of the Soviet Union, according to the official Soviet view.[2] Practical experience in collaboration took the form of the Baltic Entente modelled on the Little Entente and the Balkan Entente (*sic*). The hope in 1922 for a larger group including Poland[3] was not realized because of the fear of Polish preponderance and because of the Polish-Lithuanian dispute over Vilna.

III. Interlocking Groups

In two or three groups were to be established in Eastern Europe, some kind of interconnection between them might be desirable in order to promote a greater degree of cooperation, Rumania and Yugoslavia, for example, might become members of a Danubian and a Balkan Group, as they were of the Little

---

[1] For the integrative aspects of the treaties, see A. Essen, "Mała Entanta, Entanta Bałkańska, Entanta Batycka – pakty regionalne czy zamierzenia integracyjne", in M Pułaski (ed.) *Z dziejów integracji europejskiej. Od śreniowiecza do współczesności, Studia Polono-Balcanica*, Vol. VII, Cracow 1995, pp. 67-81; *Aut. Cit.*, *Polska a Mała Entanta 1920-1934*, Cracow 1992.

[2] The Soviet aggression was preceded by ultimatums to Lithuania on 14 June 1940 and to Estonia and Latvia on 16 June 1940. All included a series of accusations, one of which is worth mentioning here. The three Baltic states were accused of participating in treaties against the Soviet Union, with the Baltic Entente seen as one such. Spurious elections held in July the same year were followed by the countries 'access' to the Soviet Union on 3-6 August. See A. N. Tarulis, *Soviet Policy toward the Baltic States 191-1940*, Notre Dame, Indiana 1959. P. Lossowski, *Tragedia państw bałtyckich 1939-1941*, Warsaw 1990.

[3] The treaty of entente between the Baltic states, the so-called Baltic Union, was signed by Estonia, Latvia, Poland and Finland on 17 March 1922. It was not ratified by Finland and thus became void. For more, see A. Skrzypek, *Związek Bałtycki. Litwa, Łotwa, Estonia i Finlandia w polityce Polski i ZSRR w latach 1919-1925*. Warsaw 1972; J. Łaptos, "Od bezpieczeństwa zbiorowego do aktywnej neutralności. Szkic z dziejów Ententy Bałtyckiej (1934-1940)", in A. Kastory, A. Essen (ed.) *Bałtowie. Przeszłość i teraniejszość*, Cracow 1993.

Entente and of the Balkan Entente. Poland might be in close association with Czechoslovakia on the one hand and with the Baltic Entente on the other.

A responsible Czech statesman had suggested close collaboration between the Czechoslovak-Polish and Greco-Yugoslav federations. A resolution of the delegations of the Czechoslovakia, Greece, Yugoslavia and Poland at the 1941 meeting of the International Labor Organization expressed hope for the extensive social and economic collaboration after the war in Central and Eastern Europe.[1] A Planning Board was set up in New York as a result of this resolution.[2]

There has also been a suggestion of establishing an East-Central European Reconstruction Board and a Balkan Board, with one delegate each from the member states, and with interconnections between these boards.

H. Howard, Harris, V. V., E. L.

---

[1] For the text of "Joint Declaration by the Government and Employers' Delegations of Czechoslovakia, Greece, Poland and Yugoslavia to the International Labour Conference", see Gross, F., *Crossroads of two Continents. A Democratic Federation of East-Central Europe*, *op. cit.*, pp. 107-109.

[2] For his program, see *Ibid*. pp. 109-111. The organization was headed by Sava N. Kosanović, Jan Masaryk, Aristides Dimitratos and Jan Stańczyk. The Secretary General was Dr. Felks Gross. In an Advisory Committee evaluation: "This group consists, in general, of moderate liberal and socialist elements which are not altogether identified with the exile governments of their countries even though officials of those governments are members" – A. N. Notter File, box 57, P Document 46, 19 August, 1942 pp. 7-8.

16

DEPARTMENT OF STATE
Advisory Committee
for Postwar Foreign Policy
Political Subcommittee
Secret
P – Minutes 58
June 5, 1943

Typescript, copy
AN Notter File, box 55

BRITISH POLICY CONCERNING REGIONALISM

Present:
Secretary Hull, presiding
Mr. Hamilton Fish Armstrong
Senator Warren R. Austin
Mr. Adolf A. Berle
Representative Sol Bloom
Senator Tom Connally
Representative Charles A. Eaton
Senator Walter F. George
Mr. Green H. Hackworth
Representative Luther A. Johnson
Mrs. Anne O'Hare McCormick
Mr. Leo Pasvolsky
Mr. James T. Shotwell
Mr. Myron C. Taylor
Senator Wallace H. White, Jr.
Mr. Laurence Duggan
Mr. James C. Dunn
Mr. Stanley K. Hornbeck
Mr. Paul Daniels
Mr. Harley Notter
Mr. Durward V. Sandifer
Mr. C. Easton Rothwell
Mr. James Frederick Green

After an opening statement was read and two memoranda were paraphrased for the subcommittee, the following views and comments were expressed on the problem of regional organization:

British Policy concerning Regionalism

Prime Minister Churchill's recent speech about a Council of Europe[1] and a Council of Asia is entirely consistent with British Foreign policy as expressed by Sir Austen Chamberlain. The latter made clear that Britain could not accept unlimited and universal commitments and warned the small states to look to their own neighborhoods for salvation. At that very time, however, the League Council and the World Court were dealing with issues that affected the whole world rather than restricted regions only. The Chamberlain policy was almost disastrous, because it permitted Germany to test Britain's local obligations one by one at their weakest point and to force Britain into war under adverse strategic conditions.

Mr. Churchill, in proposing regional organizations, might have had in mind the likelihood that the European war may end before the war in Asia, in which case a regional organization in Europe might be needed.

Problem of a Pacific Council

The most comprehensive statement concerning the proposed Pacific Council is that of Lord Hailey. This statement, which did not indicate precisely the membership, responsibilities and enforcement procedures of such a council, gives rise to the following questions:

1) Should council membership be restricted to sovereign and quasi-sovereign countries in the region, together with Britain and Canada, or should it also include Mexico and other pacific states in Latin America and all states that were parties to the Nine-Power Treaty?[2]

2) How would China, the Soviet Union and Japan react to British-American preponderance in the council since four of the most likely ten members would belong to the British Empire and a fifth, the Netherlands would be British *Protégé*?

3) Would the Unites States and other countries enjoy more consideration than in an universal one?

4) Is there any real analogy between the Pacific region and the Western Hemisphere? Have the Pacific countries a common interest in any field except security? In the security field, while the member states might cooperate in com-

---

[1] Churchill said in BBC broadcast on 22 March 1943 that he envisaged, ultimately, the creation of a Council of Europe and a Council of Asia which would initially embrace members of the United Nations and eventually all nations. He has declared that the Council of Europe must have a high court to settle disputes among members and armed forces to enforce common decisions and prevent aggression in the future. In this Council, he believed, small nations should be grouped into confederations. These larger units would in turn participate on a basis of equality with the great powers.

[2] Possibly a reference to the Washington Treaties of 1922, signed by China, Belgium, France, Holland, Japan, Portugal, the U.S., the U.K. and Italy, and including a treaty on chemical warfare prohibiting the use of poison gas, and a treaty of the nine powers on Chinese sovereignty, independence and the creation of indivisibility, condemning spheres of influence but upholding an "open door" policy for Chinese ports.

pelling Japan to keep the peace terms, could they solve difficulties among themselves?

Although a South Pacific grouping may be feasible, it is difficult to envisage any workable Pacific arrangement that would include the Soviet Union, China and Japan, with their divergent and conflicting interests and it is impossible to contemplate inclusion of Japan at the outset.

Changes in the Concept of Regionalism

Geography no longer serves as an adequate basis for regionalism. Since most important activities are now carried out along functional lines, the term "regions" connotes separatism that does not exist. In fact, there is no more a true region than there is a country absolutely independent of other countries in the modern world community of nations.

Relations between Regional and World Organization

Although the first goal should be the establishment of a universal authority with substantial flexibility, there is necessity of regional authority and responsibility. The character of the regional arrangements probably cannot be written into the instrument for an international organization because of wide variation in the nature and international implications of local issues.

The problem is where to draw the line between local disputes that can be settled regionally and those of general interest and to make sure that if regional efforts at settlement fail, the dispute will be carried to some higher authority. In drawing such a line, universal settlement should be favored.

Although regional organizations are needed, they must be dependent upon the world organization and the latter must have appellate jurisdiction. If regional organizations were empowered to deal only with local questions, with appeal to the world agency, a double check on all questions and a necessary "cooling off" period would be provided.

The subcommittee appeared to agree that the primary need is for a strong world organization capable of maintaining peace. Regional organizations were thought necessary to deal with purely local problems, but they should be subordinate to the universal body. The general organization should have original jurisdiction over broad international disputes and should have appellate jurisdiction over all regional matters involving a threat to peace. The universal organization should not be constructed on regional organizations as its basis.

Role of the United States

If the United States is to participate in handling European regional problems, how can it answer the demand of other powers or participation in Western Hemisphere arrangements?

The United States should be represented at one or more stages of all political discussions, so that it can precipitate or retard action as the situation and its conception of morals and interests might dictate. The American people must realize, however, that if they do participate in such decisions, they must also assume obligations for the enforcement of those decisions.

Documents

17

DEPARTMENT OF STATE
Advisory Committee
Document -T 405 R 72
Secret
November 9, 1943

Typescript, original
AN Notter File, box 61

THE SOUTH SLAV PEOPLES: POLITICAL REORGANIZATION

I. Introduction

At the end of the war the South Slav peoples, from the Slovenes in the West to the Bulgarians in the East, will face the problem of reconstructing their political systems in such a way as to provide the greatest possible freedom for each of the national groups without sacrificing their economic prosperity and strategic security. Consideration should be given to the means by which this might be accomplished, with special regard both to the unusual conditions obtaining in Yugoslavia and to the role of Bulgaria in the present war. While the political reorganization of Yugoslavia is the most pressing problem, the possibility of including Bulgaria in a South Slav federation should also be explored.

The role of Yugoslavia in a postwar political reorganization of the South Slav peoples depends to a great extent on the loyalty of the national groups in Yugoslavia to their government. The Yugoslav government-in-exile has continued to function under the imposed[1] constitution of 1931, which received the support of some of the major political parties after 1939 and has expressed no desire to see the establishment of a constitutional regime based on the consent of the governed.

A major factor in the re-establishment of Yugoslavia is the role of the monarch. The dynasty is Serbian in origin, with a tradition of leadership dating back to the early nineteenth century and has held the active responsibilities of government since 1903. While the prestige of the dynasty reached a low ebb under the regency, there is reason to believe that its position within the country could be restored after the war by the conscientious exercise of its responsibilities. (...)[2] From the point of view of the political reorganization of the South Slav

---

[1] An allusion to the royal dictatorship of Alexander, who, in 1929, suspended the constitution of 1921 and imposed one of his own.

[2] The discussion of the dynastic problems in Yugoslavia and in Bulgaria has been omitted.

peoples, the retention of the monarchy in Bulgaria would tend to limit the extent of its cooperation with the neighboring states, whereas a republican regime might facilitate the inclusion of Bulgaria in a closely-knit federation.

In addition to the constitutional issues facing the South Slav peoples, a discussion of their political reorganization should take into account two further sets of problems: those raised by the relations of the South Slav peoples with each other and those involving their relations with foreign states. The former category includes in particular the acceptability of a political reorganization by the peoples concerned and the question of the boundaries between the various units, while the latter includes the probable attitude of the neighboring Balkan states to a South Slav federation and the position of such a federation in the system of the Great Powers.

II. Alternative Solutions

A. Complete Unification

This form of organization would bring together the territories included in the Yugoslavia of 1940, with such frontier changes as may be agreed to by the principal United Nations, Yugoslavia would be restored as a unified state with few concessions to the peoples of which it is composed. The government would presumably be based on the consent of a majority of the entire population regardless of linguistic or religious preferences. The new government would be required to furnish to the United Nations guarantees against the domination of the whole country by one or two of the component peoples and to prevent discrimination in military as well as in civil institutions on grounds of religion or national origin. The inclusion of Bulgaria in such a Yugoslav state could take place only under conditions of forcible annexation combined with continued military occupation.

B. Restricted Local Autonomy or Federation

In case the Yugoslav peoples should desire to obtain greater control over their local affairs, a restricted measure of autonomy could be granted to one or more of these groups. The Serb-Croat Compromise of 1939[1] has been recognized in principle by the government-in-exile and might well serve as a basis for such a system, although the means of its implementation has continued as a subject of acute disagreement. Under it all those powers relating to purely local affairs would be transferred to the provincial government, whereas those matters concerning the welfare of the country as a whole would remain in the hands of the central government.

A plan providing for the further decentralization of Yugoslavia would take the form of a federation. The component parts of a Yugoslav federation would include at least Serbia, Croatia and Slovenia. Under this system the central

---

[1] The so-called "Sporazum" Serbian-Croatian compromise of 26 August 1939 was signed by Prime Minister Dragiš Cvetković and Vlatko Maček, leader of the Croatian Peasant Party. It provided for Croatia's autonomy in internal affairs, education, the economy, finance and social matters.

government in Belgrade would remain supreme in finance, national defense and foreign affairs and would retain all other powers not specifically assigned to the component states. Such a plan would give the non-Serb peoples of Yugoslavia a greater part of the freedom which they have frequently claimed without depriving them of the benefits of living within a larger political framework.

A federation might be based either on the provincial or the ethnic principle. If a provincial basis were regarded as preferable, autonomy could be extended not only to Croatia, Slovenia and Montenegro, which have certain traditions of self-government, but also to Bosnia, Herzegovina and Macedonia, which, while they are less accustomed to autonomous rights, have frequently expressed the desire for local privileges. Such subdivision of Yugoslavia would greatly weaken the unity of the state, however and would doubtless be opposed by the three major peoples. A federation composed only of Serbia, Croatia and Slovenia, on the other hand, would represent a more efficient and viable form of organization. At the same time, the danger exists that under such a system the Serbs and the Croats would band to gather all political power into their own hands at the expense of the lesser peoples. A federation of this type might offer considerable benefits to Bulgaria if it were given equal rights with the three major Yugoslav groups.

C. Confederation of Sovereign States

If it should prove to be impossible for the component national groups in Yugoslavia to agree on some form of closer association, a confederation might prove to be feasible. Slovenia, Croatia and Serbia could be established as substantially independent states, maintaining close collaboration only in questions of economic and foreign relations. While such a system might involve some sacrifice of security for the South Slav peoples, it would tend to appease the conflicts among them by granting them a greater degree of sovereignty than would be possible under a federation while still maintaining vestiges of the larger unit. Under these conditions the frontiers of a Yugoslav confederation might be extended to include Bulgaria. While the obstacles presented by the dynasty and the frontiers would still have to be overcome, the prospects for Bulgarian participation in a confederation would be very favorable. At the same time the position of the minorities, which would still be numerous unless exchanges of population were organized, might well be rendered more precarious than under a unified state unless their rights were adequately guaranteed.[1]

---

[1] It is worth remembering a certain gap in the proceedings of the Advisory Committee on the region about what the members could learn from an OSS report on the position of the *émigrés* in the U.S.: "(...) A federal union of South Slavs has also been proposed, apparently in a wholly independent manner, by certain Yugoslav officials in this country and by sections of the American-Yugoslav Community. Both Ivan Subasich (Subasić), Ban of Croatia, and Sava Kosanovitch (Kosanović), ex-Minister of State, have lent support to the conception of a Greater Yugoslavia, stretching from the Adriatic to the Aegean. Bulgaria would be included in the federal Yugoslavia envisioned in a resolution adopted by the American Croatian Congress in February 1943, and in private conversation. Ban Subasich has suggested that an autonomous Macedonia might also be member of such a state". From Memorandum

J. Laptos & M. Misztal

D. Confederation of Soviet Republics

Another possible form of confederation would be one composed of Soviet republics under the *aegis* of the U.S.S.R. This form of organization is one which a republican Bulgaria would be able to join without serious difficulty and which might draw the South Slav peoples into closer relations with their Balkan neighbors. Their political and economic policies could be more or less completely merged with those of the Soviet Union. The losses in local autonomy under this system, however, might well be compensated for by the benefits of greater strategic security and of a larger economic structure. Considerable difficulties may be foreseen, however, in fitting the economy of the South Slav peoples into that of the Soviet system.

E. Dissolution of the Yugoslav State

A final possibility would be the complete dissolution of the Yugoslav state. Among the pro-Allied groups the Croat Peasant Party, while favoring a federal system, has tended to prefer autonomy to the centralist state created in 1921. Certain of the Serb extremists likewise favor a separation of the Serbs from the Croats. Since such a solution would be the outcome of extreme antagonism among the various national groups concerned, any intimate cooperation between the independent units would be unlikely. Independent states of Serbia, Croatia and Slovenia would thus exists side by side but would have no closer relations than those obtaining between the various Balkan states before the present war. Under this solution, however, the deterioration of the position of the minorities might be even greater[1] than under a confederation. (...)[2]

No. 122 of Foreign Nationalities Branch to the Director of OSS: A Trend Towards Ethnic Federations, January 30 1943, NA Micr. Int 33 Po 5.

[1] A noteworthy perspicacity, apparently diminished in later decades.

[2] The positions of the individual Yugoslav factions have been omitted.

18

DEPARTMENT OF STATE
Advisory Committee
Political Subcommittee
R. Minutes 7
Confidential
November 12, 1943

Typescript, copy
AN Notter File, box 84

[SOME IMPLICATIONS OF THE SOUTH SLAV CONFEDERATION]

Present:
Mr. Isaiah Bowman, presiding
Mr. Adolf A. Berle, Jr.
Mr. C. E. Black
Mr. Percy Bidwell
Mr. John C. Campbell
Mr. Waldo Chamberlin
Mr. Leo Pasvolsky
Mr. Vernon L. Phelps
Mr. Jacob Viner
Mr. Benjamin Gerig
Mr. Harry N. Howard
Mr. Harley A. Notter
Mr. David Harris
Mr. Melvin M. Knight
Mr. Philip E. Mosely
Mr. Ralph H. Bowen

Mr. Bowman announced that, in the absence of Mr. Armstrong, he had undertaken to preside. He understood that Mr. Black was prepared to give the subcommittee a résumé of T Document 405[1] which considered some of the implications of a South Slav Confederation.

Mr. Black noted that a South Slav Confederation might take any one of several alternative forms ranging all the way from a complete union, presumably under the leadership of Yugoslavia, to a dissolution of Yugoslavia into its constituent parts. In the latter case there would be four separate states, Serbia,

---

[1] See previous document.

Croatia, Slovenia and Bulgaria. Factors bearing upon the feasibility of any alternative form of organization might be considered under two main headings: first, the internal organization of the union; and second, the attitude of adjacent states and of the great powers. Mr. Black considered that a complete union between Yugoslavia (as of 1939)[1] and Bulgaria would be opposed by Bulgaria and could only come about as the result of military domination by Yugoslavia. He believed that the Croats would also be cool toward such a combination. The latter had succeeded in obtaining a large measure of autonomy in 1939 and the trend under German rule had been toward a nominal extension of this autonomy. He thought it possible that a close federation might be organized which would give a large degree of autonomy to each group along the lines of the Serb-Croat Compromise of 1939, whereby Croatia was given its own assembly and a governor appointed by the King. This arrangement might be extended to Slovenia. If a solution to the dynastic question could be found, it might be possible to include Bulgaria on a similar basis. If the constituent nations should adopt republican regimes the dynastic problem would disappear.

Mr. Black believed that the neighboring states might be reluctant to see the formation of a South Slav Confederation which would have 22 or 23 million inhabitants and 138,400 square miles of territory. Greece, Albania and Italy, especially, would fear the economic and military pressure which such a combination could exert. The Turks might see it as a potential base for Russian aggression.

Mr. Black thought that, so far as the great powers were concerned, the establishment of one dominant power in the Balkans might likewise be regarded as undesirable. A loose confederation among all the countries of South Eastern Europe might have considerably better prospects of success than an exclusively South Slav grouping. Bulgaria might be more willing to become a member of such federation and friction among the other members would be minimized. Such a confederation might be constructed out of the constituent parts of Yugoslavia plus Bulgaria as well as Rumania, Greece and Albania. The extreme nationalists in both Serbia and Bulgaria would probably disapprove of such a combination. Mr. Black though (*sic*) it probable that both the adjacent states and the great powers would prefer such a loose confederation to one in which one single state was dominant, since the former would neutralize aggressive forces and permit the great powers to guide the Balkan countries as one unit.

Mr. Bowman inquired whether Mr. Black could document this last point with respect to the attitude of Russia. Mr. Black replied that his conclusion was not based on any tangible evidence of Russian views but that there was some reason to think that Russia might not be altogether hostile to a confederation of this type. Mr. Bowman remarked that Mr. Black's summary had been a model one. He proposed that the subcommittee should begin by discussing the acceptability of a Balkan confederation to the great powers and particularly to Russia.

---

[1] Black is wrong as to the date and the character of the "Eternal Friendship Pact" signed by the Kingdom of Yugoslavia and Bulgaria in Belgrade on 24 January 1937. It was a bilateral act, by which the two sides agreed to respect their borders and to peaceful resolutions of conflicts, with no further obligations.

Mr. Howard remarked that Russia had appeared to favor the Balkan Entente in the period prior to World War II, apparently regarding it as the nucleus of a possible Balkan confederation. Foreign Commissar Litvinov[1] in 1934 had endorsed the principle of regional agreements. Some Turkish observers have recently expressed the view that the Soviet Government, while opposing a large East European federation or a Polish-Czechoslovak union, might not have the same objections to a Balkan union. Such a union would be smaller and, unlike an East European union would not include Poland. Mr. Berle remarked that when the Polish-Czech confederation was agreed upon, both parties had believed that the Russians were not opposed to the idea. The worsening of relations between Russia and the Polish government-in-exile, however, has since resulted in a change in the Russian position. The Czechs have withdrawn from their discussions with the Poles ostensibly because the Poles were unwilling to abandon their claim to the Teschen area, but in reality because of Russian opposition to the combination. However, the Russians offered the Czechs a military alliance[2] with an adherence clause leaving the agreement open to Poland,[3] Hungary, Rumania and possibly to Yugoslavia and Austria with Russian approval. Mr. Pasvolsky remarked that a military alliance of this kind was quite a different thing from a regional federation. Mr. Berle said that although the declared aim of the proposed alliance pact was limited to mutual assistance against attack, the moral implications would be much broader. Mr. Pasvolsky pointed out that the members of such an alliance would still be completely sovereign units. He suggested also that the Russian attitude six months hence might well be different from what it is today. The subcommittee should therefore, he suggested, attempt to discuss the question of East European unification quite apart from the Russian attitude. Mr. Berle wondered what reason Mr. Pasvolsky had for thinking that the Russian attitude might shift. Mr. Pasvolsky replied that the establishment of a reliable world organization might result in giving the Russians a greater sense of security. He wondered

---

[1] Maxim Litvinov (1876-1951), Soviet diplomat and Foreign Commissar in 1930-1939; in 1941-43, and Deputy Foreign Minister and Ambassador to the U.S. in 1941-43.

[2] The treaty, not a military one, but one of friendship, mutual assistance and help, was signed in London on 12 December 1943. For its text, see Štovièek, I., Valenta, J., *È Èeskoslovensko-polská jednáni, op. cit.*, pp. 532-537.

[3] The issue boiled down to a proposal for a trilateral Czechoslovak-Soviet-Polish treaty, supported by the U.S. and the U.K., and aimed at constraining Germany. Talks between Beneš and Mikołajczyk, and between Eden and Mikołajczyk of 12 November 1943 came to nothing. *Ibid.* pp. 362-365. In more detail: Anita J. Prażmowska, *Britain and Poland 1939-1943. The Betrayed Ally*, Cambridge University Press 1997 (2nd ed.); Marek K. Kaminski, "Dyplomacja polska i brytyjska wobec projektowanego paktu czechosłowacko-sowieckiego" (June-October 1943) (in) I. Stawowy-Kawka, W. Rojek, *Ku zjednoczonej Europe. Studia nad Europą środkową i poludniowo-wschodnią w XIX i XX wieku*, Cracow 1997, pp. 65-81.

whether Mr. Mosely, who had just returned from the Moscow Conference,[1] might be able to throw some light on this question.

Mr. Mosely thought that Mr. Pasvolsky's point was well taken. At present, he believed the Russians were extremely skeptical toward any scheme of Eastern or Southern European confederation. The Russians based their objections to such projects on two arguments which seem to have considerable strength. In the first place they argue that any agreement made among the governments-in-exile before the end of the war must necessarily be made without the consent of the peoples involved. In the second place they point out that the formation of an East European confederation would, if these countries were included on an equal footing with Allied nations, prejudge the issue of how enemy powers like Hungary and Rumania are to be treated.

Mr. Berle remarked that these were short-term considerations and he wondered what the long-range Russian attitude might be. Mr. Mosely replied that the Russians appeared to regard projects of Eastern European federation as a form of *cordon sanitaire*. Arguments that such a bloc would be directed not against them but against Germany failed to carry complete conviction with the Russians. Mr. Pasvolsky emphasized that any future *cordon sanitaire* would be directed against Germany and would be established as insurance against the failure of a world organization. He felt that the question of Russian agreement to such a plan was a question of the future. The subcommittee should concern itself with the problem of whether viable entities could be created, leaving aside the question of what the attitude of outside powers towards such combination might be. Mr. Mosely agreed. He pointed out that the Russian arguments against making plans on the basis of agreements with governments-in-exile would also, presumably, exclude the possibility of a Russo-Czech alliance. For this reason he expected that the Russians would not completely accept the implications of their own argument. He agreed with Mr. Pasvolsky that the subcommittee should by all means go ahead with its study of possible regional groupings, taking into account the probable interests and views of Russia at the same time.

Mr. Pasvolsky observed that the problem of South European unification has always been one of dynasties. He considered that a republican regime was an impossibility. He thought it possible that Yugoslavia and Bulgaria might be brought together in a crown union. The prospects for such a union had become much more favorable as a result of the weakened position of the Bulgarian dynasty. He believed that a quadruple state (Serbia, Croatia, Bulgaria and Slovenia) might be the most practical solution. The Serbs would, on balance, be inclined to accept such an arrangement provided that the Karageorgevich[2] dynasty was retained. This solution would involve the disappearance of the Bulgarian dynasty. Mr. Pasvolsky believed that the main probable alternative to such a state would be the dissolution of Yugoslavia into three states resulting in

---

[1] The conference of the U.S., the U.K. and the U.S.S.R. on 19-30 October 1943.
[2] Karageorgevich; a dynasty of princes and, since 1908, kings of Serbia, of the United Kingdom of Serbs, Croats and Slovenians and of Yugoslavia, founded by George the Black. The last of the dynasty, Peter I, was dethroned in 1945.

the failure of all plans for unification. He was convinced that a federation of Bulgaria, Rumania and Greece would not be possible.

Mr. Bowman wondered what the advantages of a quadruple state might be, as opposed, for example, to a single unified government. Mr. Pasvolsky expressed the belief that the only choice was between a larger unit and a series of smaller ones. In answer to Mr. Bowman's question, he believed that a crown union of the Southern Slavs would combine the advantages of both alternatives. Mr. Bowman suggested and Mr. Pasvolsky agreed, that such a union would probably be less objectionable to Russia than some other type. Mr. Pasvolsky believed, however, that strong opposition would come from the Czechs and probably from the Greeks. Italy would probably object, but her position would not be strong. The Turks might have serious reservations as well. The Czechs would oppose the project because they have long regarded themselves as Russia's foremost outpost in Europe and might not like the idea of sharing this role with a South Slav confederation. Russia, on the other hand, would probably not be averse to having two satellites. It was plain, he thought, that the kind of union which the Russians least desired was one in which Poland would be the largest member. Mr. Pasvolsky believed, therefore, that the Poles faced an extremely disagreeable decision. They would probably have to abandon their pretension to be regarded as first-rate power.[1]

Summing up the possible obstacles to an exclusion of a South Slav union, Mr. Black believed that the main opposition would come from the Serbs, who would probably not welcome the proposition of belonging to a union which would include some 12 million Croats and Bulgarians and only six or seven million Serbs. Serbia might well prefer independence to such an arrangement. Among the adjacent states and great powers it was probable that Greece, Turkey, Rumania, Czechoslovakia and possibly Great Britain would oppose the establishment of a union and might possibly induce Russian to reconsider its support for the project. Many internal forces would also operate as obstacles to union, for example, the autonomy movements in Macedonia and Montenegro. Mr. Black believed that the establishment of republican regimes throughout the area might result in strengthening the internal forces favoring union and it was probable that Russian influence would help the republican cause. The extension of autonomy to small minority groups would even further undermine the position of Serbia within the combination. Mr. Pasvolsky was of the opinion that the achievement of union would be, by itself, a defeat of Serbia, but that the Serbs must in any case face the prospect of defeat. Mr. Viner inquired whether Albania should be treated as a separate case. Mr. Pasvolsky replied in the affirmative. Mr. Black pointed out that the conflict between Greece and Albania would operate to prevent closer relations between those two countries and that

---

[1] This pejorative description of territorial concessions was forced upon Poland by the U.S.S.R. with the support of U.S. and the U.K.: "pretention (...) of first-rate power", is an allusion to Sikorski's image in the State Department fostered by Ambassador Biddle: "He pictures himself as the leader of postwar Poland, on the other hand, now that France has disappeared as a dominant influence on the continent, the leader of the continental *Europe*" – Biddle to the Secretary of State, London, 20 February 1942, FRUS 1942, Vol. I, p. 108.

Italy would probably attempt, in addition, to retain Albania as a foothold in South Eastern Europe. Mr. Pasvolsky wondered what means would be available to these countries in case they should wish to oppose the establishment of a Southern Slav confederation. Mr. Black suggested that they might use tactics similar to those employed by Hungary after World War I.

Mr. Bowman confessed that it was difficult for him to imagine what starting point could possibly be found for the creation of stability in South Eastern Europe at the close of the present war. Presumably peace would be restored only by degrees and political forces would take form in the meantime. He wondered where the initiative was going to come from. Even assuming that plans for a confederation should fail and that Yugoslavia should split into its constituent parts, there would still remain the necessity for a reconstruction of trade and economic life and a great many old problems would arise in an aggravated form.

Mr. Bidwell observed that the discussion thus far had taken little account of economic factors. He wondered if Mr. Pasvolsky believed that a Southern Slav union would offer any important economic advantages. Mr. Pasvolsky expressed the opinion that the peoples concerned would regard economic considerations as being relatively unimportant in comparison with other problems. Mr. Viner expressed agreement with that point of view. Mr. Pasvolsky added that considerations other than those of economics had always played a for greater role and that economics would continue to be treated mainly as a scapegoat.

Mr. Bidwell inquired whether enough economic advantages might result from union to assist in smoothing out some of those political difficulties. Mr. Pasvolsky replied that some small economic advantages might result but that the political decision must come first. Economic improvement would come only as a result of political collaboration. Mr. Viner suggested that possibly the main economic advantage of union would be to increase the relative weight of the area in bargaining with outside countries.

Mr. Bowman observed that in the case of the unification of the Czechs and the Slovaks the main emphasis had been on the achievement of political and cultural unity from the very beginning. Economic considerations had played a decidedly minor part. Mr. Pasvolsky agreed. He recalled that the attitude taken by Masaryk and Beneš had been that they would accept any economic disadvantages in order to achieve political unity. Mr. Viner remarked that it had been largely a piece of accidental good fortune for the Czech-Slovak combination that the two halves of Czechoslovakia proved to be complementary from an economic point of view. Mr. Pasvolsky added that the most advantageous combination in South Eastern Europe from an economic point of view would be a union between Greece and Bulgaria provided that problems of population movements could be solved. He emphasized that, aside from an increase in bargaining power, the economic advantages of a Yugoslav-Bulgarian combination would be small. The problems, he emphasized, were mainly political. Economic benefits might flow from the establishment of peace and stability, but in the formation of a union economic issues would be unimportant.

Documents

Mr. Bowman wondered what positive forces would operate in favor of a union after the present war and what attitude this country ought to take if it should be determined that a union would be desirable. Mr. Pasvolsky was of the opinion that peoples involved would neither need nor desire guidance or assistance from outside sources. He suggested that in the event that an agreement could be reached between the Partisans under General Tito[1] and the Serbian guerrillas under General Mihailovich[2] it might be possible for the Yugoslavs to come to an agreement with Bulgaria. The death of King Boris,[3] he believed, had enhanced the possibility of solving the dynastic problem.

Mr. Bowman wondered what the situation might possibly be like at the end of the war. In the event that a chaotic situation should develop in Bulgaria under a weak regency and in the event that Allied forces should occupy the region he wondered whether it should be the policy of the Allies to encourage the formation of a federation. Mr. Pasvolsky thought that this question might be answered in the affirmative provided that Generals Tito and Mihailovich could reach an agreement on the question of a dynasty. Mr. Berle thought there was little hope that such an agreement would be reached. The indications were, in fact, quite the reverse. Mr. Bowman suggested that the period of military government might be extended until the political situation should have crystallized and until a measure of stability was established. Mr. Pasvolsky agreed that this solution might be possible provided that King Peter[4] could be prevented from entering the country immediately after the close of hostilities. Mr. Bowman thought it might be difficult to prevent the King from returning at once, especially in view of his impetuous nature. Mr. Knight suggested that the King might be inclined to wait for some clearing of the military situation, but Mr. Bowman and Mr. Pasvolsky discounted this possibility. Mr. Knight said that was his understanding that Tito was not in favor of maintaining the dynasty. Mr. Pasvolsky replied that it is very difficult to know just what it is that Tito does want.

In reply to a question from the chairman, Mr. Black remarked that the subcommittee had discussed most of the main points involved. If members desired to go further into detail, there was the question of the religious distribution within the proposed confederation. Mr. Pasvolsky observed that the majority would be of the Greek Orthodox faith but that the Orthodox Church itself would

---

[1] Josip Broz Tito (1892-1980), Yugoslav politician, Communist activist, member of the Communist Party of Yugoslavia, and participant in the Spanish Civil War. He organized the Communist resistance after the German attack. Supported by Churchill and Stalin, he was recognized as the sole representative of the new Yugoslavia. In 1948, banned from Comintern, he remained independent of the U.S.S.R..

[2] Draža Mihailovich or Mihajlović (1893-1946), Yugoslav general, leader of the chetnik resistance movement fighting both Germans and Tito's Communists. Named Minister of War by the government-in-exile, lost the support of the Allies. He was condemned for treason and shot in 1946.

[3] Boris III (1894-1943), Czar of Bulgaria, son and successor of Ferdinand I. After Bulgaria's adherence to the Axis, he agreed to station German troops in his country. He was succeeded by his son, Simeon.

[4] Peter II (1923-1970), King of Yugoslavia (1934-1941). An *émigré* to the U.S. after the war.

be divided into two branches, the Serbian and the Bulgarian. Mr. Black added that the religious lines would not, however, coincide with political divisions.

Mr. Viner suggested that a long period of Russian occupation was perhaps not out of the question. He wondered whether such an occupation might not be the best solution of a large number of problems. Mr. Black was of the opinion that this solution would certainly be attractive to pro-Russian groups within the region. It was possible, however, that Russia might hesitate to take sole responsibility in the matter. Mr. Berle remarked that Russia had a very lively interest in the future of South Eastern Europe and Mr. Viner noted the possibility that Russian intervention might be demanded by powerful groups, particularly in Bulgaria. Mr. Black believed that the Russians would be strongly influenced by the Anglo-American attitude. He pointed out that Russian occupation of Bulgaria had been welcomed by large groups in 1878 but that the Russians had become more and more unwelcome as order was restored. He thought that the possibility should also be envisaged that the other great powers might succeed in clearing up the internal political situation before the end of the war.

Mr. Pasvolsky remarked that this possibility raised the question of what policy this country ought to adopt. For example, he wondered what instructions ought to be given to the American delegate on the Mediterranean commission in order to cover the situation in South Eastern Europe. Mr. Bowman suggested that the American attitude ought not to be one of exerting pressure toward any kind of combination. This country should exert its influence only to encourage political forces which would arise spontaneously in each country. In Yugoslavia, especially, we should try to see what peaceful collaboration can be promoted among the pre-war groups. If this effort should fail Serbia should be allowed to withdraw, leaving the Croats and Slovenes together. Then we should seek to promote arrangements between these separate areas which would preserve the advantages of the pre-war union. Bulgaria should be limited to its 1939 boundaries. An effort might be made to solve economic problems through a world organization. The difficulties of smoothing over political and cultural differences in the conditions of hunger, civil strife and terror which will prevail after the war, were, Mr. Bowman thought, impossible to overcome. He believed that it would be an impossibility to force any solutions, however well designed, upon helpless peoples in such circumstances. Mr. Berle inquired how far Mr. Bowman would be willing to go in encouraging the re-establishment of a strong Yugoslav state, Mr. Bowman replied that he would make no attempt whatsoever to achieve such an objective, but that, on the other hand, he would refrain from taking any steps which would promote the disunifying forces.

Mr. Viner wondered whether, in case Yugoslavia were to be divided into two parts, the boundary between these parts would be easy to define. Mr. Bowman believed that the principle suggested in the political committee, whereby a boundary line would be imposed and guaranteed by outside great powers, was the only possible solution. Mr. Pasvolsky requested Mr. Black to indicate on the map what territory would be disputed in such a case. Mr. Knight noted if the port of Kotor should be ceded to an autonomous Montenegro, Serbia would become virtually a landlocked state.

19

Advisory Committee
Political Subcommittee
R Minutes 8
Secret
November 26, 1943

Typescript, copy
AN Notter File, box 84

EFFECTS OF A EUROPEAN UNION
UPON AMERICAN POLITICAL INTERESTS

Present:
Mr. Hamilton Fish Armstrong, Chairman
Mr. Percy Bidwell
Mr. Benjamin V. Cohen
Mr. Leo Pasvolsky
Mr. Homer P. Balabanis
Mr. C. E. Black
Mr. Waldo Chamberlin
Mr. Merrill C. Gay
Mr. Benjamin Gerig
Mr. David Harris
Mr. Harry N. Howard
Mr. Melvin M. Knight
Mr. Philip E. Mosely
Mr. Smith Simpson
Mr. Ralph H. Bowen, Secretary

Mr. Gerig presented a revised summary of the effects of a unification of Europe upon American political interests (R-63b)[1]. The subcommittee had felt that the conclusions of his earlier draft had been too sharply negative. He had endeavored to meet these objections and had added a new section which dealt with some implications of the Four-Power Declaration recently agreed upon at Moscow.[2]

---

[1] Not found.
[2] The Moscow Declaration of 1943 on World Security following the Conference of Moscow (19-30 October 1943), issued in the name of China, the U.S., Britain and the Soviet Union, heralded the creation of the United Nations.

One member of the subcommittee suggested that, in his effort to moderate the negative tone of his conclusions, Mr. Gerig had perhaps gone too far in the opposite direction and had perhaps envisaged a more positive measure of encouragement of the unification movement in Europe than this country could appropriately render. It was pointed out, also, that Mr. Gerig had apparently assumed that a Four-Power Pact and a strong world organization would not be compatible one with the other; whereas the Declaration of Moscow clearly indicates that the signatories expect the latter to grow out of the former.

It was suggested that a line of approach somewhat different from that adopted by Mr. Gerig might result in further clarification of the problem. Instead of attempting to determine the varying world conditions in which a European union might be established, it might be preferable to examine the probable character of the union itself. The attitude of the United States would then hinge, not so much upon whether or not an effective world organization existed, as upon its being satisfied of the democratic, non-aggressive and economically liberalizing character of the proposed combination itself. Instead of considering the circumstances under which the United States could afford to take certain risks, the investigation would be directed toward the possibility of eliminating the risks themselves.

Possible Contribution of Certain International Movements to European Unification

Mr. Simpson summarized a study which he had prepared at the subcommittee's request. It had been suggested at an earlier meeting that certain movements in Europe, such as trade unionism and socialism, might figure after the present war as forces promoting unification.

Mr. Simpson briefly adduced the factors which, in his opinion, would influence the strength of the international trade union movement in Europe. He considered that owing, among other reasons, to the role which that movement was playing in underground movements in the occupied countries, it might emerge from the war in a strong position. The policies of Allied Military Government[1] authorities and of UNRRA,[2] Mr. Simpson pointed out, will have an important effect upon the rapidity with which the trade union movement will reconstitute itself at the close of hostilities.

Although European socialist movements are, to a degree, linked with organized labor and although in some occupied countries the socialist groups have been active in the resistance movement, the postwar prospects for political socialism are somewhat unclear, Mr. Simpson continued. Ideological issues may conceivably have less importance as among the sections of the socialist

---

[1] Future occupation authorities in defeated Germany.

[2] United Nations Relief and Rehabilitation Administration, an inter-government organization of 44 countries founded in Washington on 9 November 1943. Its aim was to bring food, clothing, medical and shelter relief to United Nations members freed from occupation. It worked in Europe until 31 December 1946, and in the Far East until 30 June 1947.

movement than was the case after World War I, but unless national antagonisms are moderated, the effectiveness of international socialist action will be questionable.

In some European countries, particularly those with a predominantly agricultural economy, the cooperative movement has more national significance than has the trade union movement.

(...)

With regard to the total significance of these movements in furthering international collaboration after the war, Mr. Simpson did not believe that it is possible to generalize, in view of the extremely limited amount of information now available. It was felt by the subcommittee that further examination of the subject would be desirable and Mr. Simpson was requested to continue his study.

Problems of Yugoslavia

The chairman remarked that among the most difficult as well as the most urgent policy decisions confronting the United States were those which relate to the future of Yugoslavia. He believed that our general aims should be: (1) to prevent, if possible, the outbreak of civil war inside Yugoslavia or war with neighboring states; (2) to preserve, if possible, the political unity of the peoples of pre-1939 Yugoslavia, preferably in some form of federal state;[1] and (3) to regulate our relations with King Peter's government in such a way as not to prejudice our other aims. After the displacement of millions of persons and the death of hundreds of thousands, it will not be easy to organize elections and plebiscites immediately, even with Allied forces in occupation of the country. The chairman considered that the attitude of neighboring states would figure only as a secondary consideration, since all of them (except Greece), being Axis states, would hardly be in a strong position to object to whatever arrangement the Yugoslav peoples decided to adopt.

An urgent group of problems face this country, the chairman emphasized, in connection with our Government's relations with the Yugoslav exile government in Cairo. Should Peter be permitted to return with the Allied armies? Or be prevented from returning? Should the Allied governments undertake to protect him if he does return? The United States appears to be committed to recognition of King Peter's government and to permitting its eventual return. A change in this policy might be taken amiss by the other governments-in-exile. The chairman was of the opinion that the Allies are committed to allowing all the exiled governments to return, but not necessarily to supporting them once they have returned.

The chairman indicated that several types of practical solution ought to be explored. For example, Peter, as a constitutional monarch, can presumably

---

[1] As proclaimed by the Communist Party of Yugoslavia and its leader, Tito, head of the partisans and made public at the 2nd session of AVNOJ (the Anti-Fascist Council of National Liberation), 29-30 November 1943. It was one of the reasons for British support for Tito's government.

appoint a ministry which will be more acceptable to the peoples of the homeland than his present government appears to be. He has shown his willingness to make concessions even to the extreme Croats, a policy, however, which might be carried too far and result in alienating the Serbs. The chairman thought that the summary prepared by Mr. Black for the subcommittee's last meeting furnished an excellent background for a more particularized discussion of specific practical problems such as those he had indicated. Whether or not it is feasible or desirable to include Bulgaria with Yugoslavia in a South Slav confederation should be treated as a secondary question the solution of which would be contingent upon overcoming the specific practical difficulties which will arise in the liberation period.

Some members considered that the earlier discussion of a possible Southern Slav confederation had exaggerated the importance of dynastic considerations and had dealt inadequately with the economic bases and potentialities of such a combination. Mr. Knight objected particularly to the assumption that economic forces and motives would play a negligible part in the political decisions taken in the initial period after the end of the war. Mr. Balabanis was also of the opinion that the peoples of southeastern Europe are much less preoccupied with dynastic and constitutional questions than with the problem of finding enough to eat. Another member emphasized that the United States must concern itself with the long-run viability of any proposed political arrangement in South Eastern Europe, even though other considerations may have more influence upon the decisions made by the peoples themselves during the initial postwar period.

20

DEPARTMENT OF STATE
Advisory Committee
Political Subcommittee
Secret
R Minutes 13
February 18, 1944

Typescript, copy
NA Notter File, box 84

[LEGITIMACY OF THE SOVIET DESIRE FOR CONTROL OVER THE EAST EUROPEAN REGION]

Present:
Mr. Hamilton Fish Armstrong, Chairman
Mr. Percy Bidwell
Mr. Isaiah Bowman
Mr. Benjamin C. Cohen
Mr. Leo Pasvolsky
Miss Elizabeth Armstrong
Mr. Homer P. Balabanis
Mr. C. E. Black
Mr. Charles E. Bohlen
Mr. Cavendish W. Cannon
Mr. Eugene P. Chase
Mr. Norris B. Chipman
Mr. Harry N. Howard
Mr. Vernon L. Phelps
Mr. Howard Trivers
Mr. Arthur P. Whitaker
Mr. Philip E. Mosely
Mr. Melvin M. Knight
Mr. Ralph H. Bowen, Secretary

Provisional Government of Yugoslavia

The subcommittee discussed a revised draft of its views regarding the establishment of a provisional government in Yugoslavia (R-84)[1]. Several verbal changes were suggested and accepted by the subcommittee. Mr. Black was

---

[1] Not printed.

requested to add an additional paragraph to indicate that the subcommittee had discussed the possibilities of a coalition government made up of representatives of the three main national groups. Subject to these changes the statement was approved.

East European Organization

The subcommittee discussed some general implications of a Soviet "security sphere" in Eastern Europe. Mr. Whitaker summarized a memorandum prepared for the subcommittee on "The Monroe Doctrine of the United States" (R-85,[1] Section I), stressing in particular the bearing of his study on Europe and on possible Soviet plans. He pointed out that the American Monroe Doctrine[2] had been primarily a security document, the success of which had been due in considerable measure to its origin in liberal ideas and to its application, for the most part, in a spirit of respect for the rights of other nations.[3] If the experience of the western hemisphere under the Monroe Doctrine had any relevancy to the plans which the Soviet Union might have for Eastern Europe, Mr. Whitaker believed, the essential question about a Soviet security sphere would be whether or not the spirit of its application were similar to that of the American Monroe Doctrine. Mr. Whitaker suggested, in reply to a query, that the liberal spirit of the American system might be attributed to the existence of frontier conditions and to the fact that no major outside power had constituted an immediate threat to western hemisphere security.

Members of the subcommittee noted that the Monroe Doctrine had been established, not only as a security measure, but also as a defense of democratic ideas against reactionary European intervention. One member asked whether greater emphasis might not be placed upon the role of Great Britain in upholding the Monroe Doctrine during the first decades of its existence. Mr. Whitaker pointed out that serious question attached to this interpretation of the British policy, at least before the time of Salisbury, and that the British had either ignored or flouted the Monroe Doctrine during the first seventy years after its promulgation. One member noted that the "American system", as developed over the past ten years, rested upon the inter-American system and he questioned the relevancy of the Monroe Doctrine to the discussion.

One member suggested that a general set of criteria applicable to all forms of regional organization should be formulated. Another member thought that a more fruitful approach would be to attempt to assess the interests of the United States in connection with each specific area in which a larger grouping might be proposed. It was pointed out that the general views of the subcommittee regarding the interests of the United States as affected by the realization of closer political and economic collaboration among all continental European countries

---

[1] Not found.
[2] The Monroe Doctrine, a U.S. international policy prohibiting the intervention of European powers in internal matters of the American continent, was formulated by U.S. President J. Monroe on 2 December 1823.
[3] This *a contrario* reasoning is an attempt at a justification of the Soviet sphere of influence.

had already been formulated (R-63ᵉ)[1] and that the principles outlined in that document might be taken as the basic criteria of American interests.

In connection with a possible East European grouping under a Soviet "Monroe Doctrine" it was pointed out that the Russians regarded that region as part of their security zone. One member believed that the United States might well concede the special character of Russian interests in Eastern Europe and might even concede that the situation demanded that the Russians exercise a strong influence in the region, but that the method of implementing the Soviet Union's security aims remained a matter of close concern to this country. There was a difference, he believed, between a system based on treaties similar to the Soviet-Czechoslovak Alliance and a system based upon a far-reaching social, political, and administrative reorganization in the area. In the latter case the effects of Soviet plans upon American aims and interests would demand careful study.

Members of the subcommittee suggested that the American attitude toward Soviet plans for East Europe might be defined on the basis of the following general principles: 1) the United States should not take the initiative in proposing or opposing any specific solution; 2) the United States should accept no solution not motivated by democratic forces and not resulting in the establishment of a democratic system; 3) the grouping established should not be hostile toward any major power; and 4) the solution should not be prejudicial to the success of a wider system of security predicated upon a strong world organization.

Some members objected that a more general and a more positive statement of long-term American objectives was desirable and it was suggested that some of these might be defined as: 1) the winning of the present war; 2) the establishment of a stable and just peace; and 3) preservation of the unity of the four great powers in order to achieve these ends, so long as their ideals do not diverge too broadly.

Mr. Phelps suggested that, in the economic field, the United States might be concerned directly if the Soviet plans for East European organization involved an extension of the area of state trading.[2] The Chairman noted that Mr. Phelps had prepared a list of relevant considerations regarding the economic interests of the United States as affected by a possible extension of Soviet influence in East Europe and it was suggested that the political division might collaborate with the Office of Economic Affairs in preparing a combined list of "dominant considerations", both political and economic, for the subcommittee's next meeting.

Mr. Howard briefly summarized a document prepared by himself and Mr. Chimpan on "The Regional Policy of the Soviet Union" (R-85, Section V). He noted that the doctrine of Leninism-Stalinism laid claim to universal applicability, but that the main point of comparison between the American Monroe

---

[1] Not printed.
[2] The naivety of this statement seems to show either a belief in the respect for democracy in the Soviet sphere of influence or an ignorance of the mechanisms of the Soviet economy.

Doctrine and the Soviet position was the application of the concept to "security regions". The main difference between the Soviet position and that of the United States was that there was no other great power within the immediate American security region. Members of the subcommittee observed that the United States also claimed that its democratic doctrine was universally applicable. Other members suggested that *the real problem was not the legitimacy of the Soviet desire for control over the East European region, but rather the method by which such control would be implemented,* [our italics – JŁ & MM] the extent to which American interests were involved and the manner in which the United States might effectively safeguard its interests.

21

DEPARTMENT OF STATE
Advisory Committee
Political Subcommittee
R Minutes 14
Secret
March 3, 1944

Typescript, original
AN Notter File, box 84

REGIONAL POLICY OF THE SOVIET UNION

Present:
Mr. Hamilton Fish Armstrong, Chairman
Mr. Percy Bidwell
Mr. Isaiah Bowman
Mr. Leo Pasvolsky
Mr. Myron C. Taylor
Mr. Jacob Viner
Mr. H. P. Balabanis
Mr. C. E. Black
Mr. Charles E. Bohlen
Mr. Cavendish W. Cannon
Mr. Harry N. Howard
Mr. Vernon L. Phelps
Mr. Philip E. Mosely
Mr. Leroy D. Stinebower
Mr. Melvin M. Knight
Mr. Ralph H. Bowen, Secretary

A joint list of "dominant considerations" affecting United States policy both in the political and in the economic field, prepared by the Office of Economic Affairs and by the Divisions of Territorial Studies and of International Security and Organization, was presented to the subcommittee.

Mr. Phelps noted that, in preparing the outline of questions having economic implications, an effort had been made to indicate the main ways in which American interests might be affected by the implementation of possible Soviet regional policies, particularly in Eastern Europe. He suggested that one of the most immediate questions was whether, if the Soviet policy should be consummated before the end of hostilities in Europe the result would be to facilitate a more effective use of the region's economic resources in the United Nations' war effort. Mr. Mosely added that it had been thought necessary to take note of the possibility that a considerable length of time might intervene between the occupation of substantial parts of the East European region by the Soviet armies and the final surrender of Germany. Members of the subcommittee observed that questions involving Lend Lease[1] and "reverse Lend Lease" policy might arise in such circumstances. It was also noted that the attitude of the East European peoples toward the Soviet Union and their willingness to cooperate during the period of occupation, would also be factors bearing upon this problem.

Mr. Howard called the subcommittee's attention to the distinction observed throughout the document under discussion between a "minimum" Soviet program (involving the establishment of a system of mutual assistance pacts, similar to the Soviet-Czechoslovak alliance with each of the states in the region) and a "maximum" program (involving the incorporation of the Eastern European states in the Soviet Union). The "minimum" pattern would not limit the essential freedom of the East European states to maintain political and economic relations with outside countries. Mr. Howard noted further that the Soviet-Czech treaty provided not only for mutual military and economic assistance but also for non-interference on the part of each state in matters touching the sovereignty or independence of the other.

Mr. Phelps expressed the view that in the economic field the crux of the problem lay in the question of state trading. Would it be possible, in the event of an extension of the state trading system, to devise satisfactory methods for handling trade between countries having a complete state monopoly of foreign trade and those based on private enterprise? One member of the subcommittee did not believe that a study of past experience revealed any pattern which would furnish a useful guide to the solution of this problem. There seemed to be a tendency for every exchange to be made on an *ad hoc* basis. In the political field, however, it had been amply demonstrated, he thought, that trade became a continuing source of international friction under a state trading system, increasingly so as more and more of the total area of trades was made subject to state control. Other members questioned whether the history of American trade with the Soviet Union tended to bear out this thesis. It was pointed out in reply that Soviet purchases from the United States had been on a small scale and that trade relations between the Soviet Union and Canada or Great Britain provided a more instructive example, particularly in those instances where the Soviet Union had figured as a large-scale seller. Soviet trade relations with Iran or with Afghanistan were also thought to be illustrative of the tendency of state trading systems to develop along autarkic or exclusive lines. It was objected that it was an open question whether such policies arose out of the nature of state trading systems themselves or out of special circumstances. It was suggested that

---

[1] The Lend-Lease Act – an act on loans and leases passed by Congress on 10 March 1941. It allowed the U.S. to loan, rent or donate all kinds of military equipment to countries at war against Nazi countries. Initially limited to Britain and China, it was extended to other countries in the following year. A separate "master lend-lease agreement" was signed with the U.S.S.R. on 30 October 1941; it amounted to deliveries worth 11 billion U.S. dollars.

Russian trade policies might lose much of their autarkic character if the Soviet Union should come to feel that its security was no longer threatened.

One member suggested that the general question of how an extension of Soviet influence in Eastern Europe might affect the interests of the United States might be phrased as follows: "Would undesirable consequences be inevitable under the maximum Soviet program and would such consequences be avoidable under the minimum program?"

Mr. Bohlen did not believe that the consummation of the Soviet Union's minimum program (a system of treaties with the East European states, under which the sovereignty and independence of the latter would not be impaired) would constitute a threat to American interests. He pointed out that the Soviet Union would be faced, at the end of the war, with an enormous reconstruction problem, possibly requiring fifteen years for the restoration of even the 1941 level of production. He considered it likely, therefore, that the Soviet Union would not attempt to go beyond its minimum program, at least during the immediate postwar period. It must be borne in mind, however, that the Soviet leaders attached less weight to general principles than did the leaders of the western powers and that there might be a tendency for the former to define terms like "friendly governments" differently than would the latter. Mr. Bohlen considered that the future of Czechoslovakia would be acid test of the ability of the Soviet system to exist side by side with a non-Soviet system without attempting to dominate its internal affairs. In view of past history and feeling, Mr. Bohlen did not believe that the case of Poland could be considered representative in this connection, but he believed that in the case of Czechoslovakia there would be better grounds for judging of the long-run compatibility or incompatibility of the two systems in view of the freely-chosen policy of seeking friendship with the U.S.S.R. at all costs, adopted by Czech leaders.

Members of the subcommittee raised some question as to the real motives which had impelled President Beneš to seek an understanding with the Soviet Union, but Mr. Bohlen's thesis was accepted as generally sound. One member pointed out that in as much as Czechoslovakia was a small country, the future result might not indicate much as to the compatibility or incompatibility of the two systems, but merely that large and powerful countries tended to dominate their smaller and weaker neighbors. Mr. Bohlen replied that the central point was whether or not the Soviet Union was prepared permanently to abandon its missionary spirit so far as its relations with neighboring countries were concerned. One member of the subcommittee remarked that his reading of history had not convinced him that harmony was any more likely to prevail between similar societies than between dissimilar societies. He pointed out that Russian ideological intervention in other countries had been a form of defense mechanism during a period when the Soviet Union had felt itself menaced by the capitalist outside world and that the removal of this fear might change the situation entirely.

Procedure

The Chairman proposed that at its next meeting the subcommittee should consider some of the questions raised in R-90 (Preliminary), "United States: Dominant Considerations for Judging Regional Associations in Europe". If time permitted it would also be desirable to have a further discussion of Soviet regional policy in East Europe (R-88) and he requested the staff to prepare a revised list of "dominant considerations" in the light of the discussion which had just taken place.

22

DEPARTMENT OF STATE
Advisory Committee
Political Subcommittee
Secret
R Minutes 15
March 17, 1944

Typescript, copy
AN Notter File box 84

**[CONSIDERATIONS FOR JUDGING REGIONAL
ASSOCIATIONS IN EUROPE]**

Present
Mr. Leo Pasvolsky, presiding
Mr. Percy Bidwell
Mr. Benjamin C. Cohen
Mr. H. P. Balabanis
Mr. C. E. Black
Mr. Cavendish W. Cannon
Mr. Benjamin Gerig
Mr. Harry N. Howard
Mr. Philip E. Mosely
Mr. Melvin M. Knight
Mr. Ralph H. Bowen, Secretary

In the absence of Mr. Armstrong, Mr. Pasvolsky presided.

Mr. Pasvolsky inquired as to what studies had been prepared in the research division regarding regional associations in Europe. Mr. Mosely replied that among those completed were the following: (1) General European Organization (3) Low Countries Federation, (4) Northern Union, (5) Polish-Czechoslovak Confederation, (6) Greek-Yugoslav Confederation, (7) East European Organization, (8) Danubian Confederation and (9) Yugoslav-Bulgarian Union.

Mr. Pasvolsky remarked that the main item on the subcommittee agenda for the present meeting was Regional Document 90,[1] "United States: Dominant

---

[1] Not found. Issues discussed in this document are reflected in analyses prepared by the Inter-Divisional Committee on the Balkan-Danubian Region for the State Department with C. E. Black as drafting officer. The document on Yugoslavia includes a noteworthy discussion on Foreign Policy and Regional Organization: 1. *Foreign Policy* – (...) the subsequent rise of Nazism and the increased participation of the

Considerations for Judging Regional Associations in Europe" and he noted that the outline of questions presented therein was arranged under five main headings. These were:

I. Would the Regional Association affect the Political Stability of the Region or of Europe as a Whole?
II. Would the Regional Association affect the General International Organization?
III. Would the Regional Association affect the Security Interests of the United States?

Soviet Union in European politics introduced a new set of circumstances. Under these changed conditions, Yugoslavia was neither able to retain its earlier alliances on a secure basis nor to reach an understanding with the reviewed power of its former enemies without serious sacrifices of its national interests. By 1941, Yugoslavia thus found itself at the mercy of its enemies and without any hope of aid from its friends. While the Yugoslav Government-in-exile has drafted tentative plans for an alliance with Greece which is capable as serving as the basis for a wider grouping, it is apparent that Yugoslavia will have to rely for its security on a broader international arrangement. However regional agreements supplementary to an international organization will probably have their place after the war. It is likely that the regional grouping in which Yugoslavia would find it most easy to participate would be a South Slav or Balkan Federation. 2. *South Slav Federation.* In case the four principal South Slav peoples – the Serbs, Croats, Slovenes and Bulgars should be inclined to form a federation, they would expect to enter it as equal members. Such a federation would offer the South Slav peoples greater bargaining power with outside world from an economic point of view and would bring together within one political framework peoples of closely related cultural ties. Within such a framework it might be possible to find the solution to the traditional controversies between the Serbs and Croats on the one hand and the Serbs and Bulgars on the other. At the same time, however, a number of crucial problems would have to be solved before such a federation could be realized. In particular the status of the Serb and Bulgar dynasties, the opposition of Macedonian Slavs and the domination of the Serb-Croat and the Serb-Bulgar boundaries would have to be solved before such a federation would be feasible. (...) The large states (Rumania, Greece, Turkey and Italy) might oppose such a federation not only because it would probably be a source of further unrest but also because it might be used as a springboard for one of a Great Powers in an attempt at the exclusive domination of the whole region. 3. *A Balkan Federation* – In view of these objections to the federation of an exclusive federation, the most feasible form of political organization for the South Slav peoples might be the inclusion of Yugoslavia and Bulgaria as members of a general Balkan federation. Built on the foundations laid in the 1930s, such a federation would presumably serve to protect the security of its members and would offer them the economic advantages of greater bargaining power with other regions. It would also facilitate the integration of the system of transportation and insure greater monetary stability within the region. The national antagonisms which prevented the consummation of a Balkan federation a decade ago are now more sharply defined, however, and since the economies of various Balkan states are not complementary the inducements of such a grouping may not be sufficiently strong to counterbalance the political obstacles. Nevertheless, in case such a federation were formed, the relative size and strength of Yugoslavia would give it a leading role in determining the policies of the group. (A.N.T - 1222 PWC-214, (CAC-216), 7 June 1944.

IV. Would the Regional Association affect the Economic Interests of the United States? and,

V. Would the Regional Association affect the Commitments of the United States?

Mr. Pasvolsky wondered whether the members of the subcommittee believed that this arrangement was a satisfactory one. Mr. Knight remarked that the fourth point really dealt with two different sets of considerations and might well be subdivided into (1) considerations regarding the internal stability and welfare of the region and (2) those affecting the external economic relations of the region, including relations with the United States. Mr. Pasvolsky and other members of the subcommittee expressed agreement with this suggestion and Mr. Pasvolsky noted that the outline would then include six headings in all. He proposed that the subcommittee should proceed to a review of the detailed points raised under each main heading. With reference to question A under point I, Mr. Pasvolsky observed that the significance of this consideration was that the United States should examine the differences which exist, or would be likely to exist, within any given group of countries for which a regional association was proposed with a view to determining whether the establishment of a federation would make it easier or more difficult to maintain harmony among them.[1] Mr. Bidwell remarked that these questions could only be answered on the basis of informed guesswork. He believed that if the answer to the question proposed by Mr. Pasvolsky should be in the negative an attempt should be made to use historical experience as a check upon the accuracy of the answer. One way in which this might be done would be to apply the questions asked in connection with the proposed regional association to the situation prevailing in

---

[1] It is also worth referring to another State Department document on Bulgaria (24 April 1944) from the point of view of the Treatment of Enemy States. Section D: *Regional Organization* has a slightly different wording here: "The United States might well look with favor on the development of such forms of regional association as may contribute to the political security and economic stability of Bulgaria, so long as they do not represent a military threat to the integrity of Greece or Turkey. Such regional associations can play a constructive role in a general international organization whether they are independent members of it or are functionally assimilated to one of its organs.

While important efforts were made to establish a Balkan federation a decade ago, the events of the present war have greatly increased the obstacles to its creation. In case national antagonisms should be too strong to permit the formation of Balkan Union, it is possible that the South Slav peoples of Yugoslavia and Bulgaria might wish to form a confederation. While such a grouping would have numerous advantages, it might be considered by its neighbors as a potential menace to their security. The possibility should also be envisaged that a Soviet regional policy in Eastern Europe might be extended either to include Bulgaria within a Soviet security system on a basis like that laid down in the Soviet-Czechoslovak alliance, or to encourage the formation of South Slav confederation oriented toward the Soviet Union. Either contingency would have to be examined afresh by this Government in the light of its effect on general security and well-being". N A T-1222 PWC-143 CAC-145, 24 April 1944.

the thirteen American colonies prior to 1787.[1] Mr. Pasvolsky agreed that historical experience should certainly be used as one of the tests, but that some objective criteria by which the concrete situation itself could be judged were also necessary. Mr. Cannon pointed out that historical comparisons would enter into the analysis at each stage in any event.

Mr. Pasvolsky believed that point A under I might well be stated more explicitly, instead of asking the question "would frictions arise" it would be more to the point to ask "what frictions would arise".

Mr. Bidwell felt that one question might well have been added in the section under discussion, namely, "What evidence indicates that the peoples involved desire the association in question?". Mr. Pasvolsky agreed that this question was very pertinent. He recalled that he had spoken some time ago with Count Coudenhove-Kalergi,[2] who had asserted that 25 million people in the European underground movement desired a unification of Europe, but who had failed to supply any evidence to back up his assertion.

Mr. Gerig observed that another problem which would not appear to be covered by the outline under discussion was how far the United States should go in attempting to influence a recalcitrant state to join a confederation which was desired by all the other prospective members. Mr. Pasvolsky agreed that this question was an important one and remarked that the Czechoslovak Minister of Finance had asked him on one occasion how far the United States was prepared to go in bringing pressure to bear in favor of an East European confederation.[3]

---

[1] A reference to the Articles of Confederation, a formal agreement that had loosely unified the colonies from 1781 to 17 September 1787, when the Constitution was signed. The character of these ties was described by George Washington as a "rope of sand".

[2] N. Coudenhove-Kalergi (1894-1972), a leading proponent of the idea of European integration. In 1923, he created the basis for the pan-European Movement with its branches in the individual European countries. The First Congress of the pan-European Union took place in Vienna in 1926. At the Fifth Congress of the pan-European Union of March 1943, bringing together *émigré* representatives, he presented a plan for a future United States of Europe. He was head of the postwar European Parliamentary Union.

[3] The changes in the State Department's position are reflected in another document of the 'Policy toward Liberated States' document, prepared by the Interdivisional Committee on Russia and Poland, with J. C. Campbell as drafting officer. Section D is quoted here: *Regional Organization* – "The Polish Government in exile favors the creation of a confederation of states situated between Germany and Russia designed to assure their security and to promote their economic welfare on a regional basis. Negotiations for a Polish-Czechoslovak confederation, as a nucleus of a wider union, were carried on in 1941 and 1942 but were abandoned, principally because of the opposition of the Soviet Union to present plans for federation in Eastern Europe. The United States Government is prepared to examine any specific proposal either for a Polish-Czechoslovak confederation or for a wider Eastern European union in the light of its possible contribution to the long-range interest of the United States. *Since the Soviet Union has a more direct interest than the United States in the area in question, this Government should not use its influence to foster regional grouping in defiance of the wishes of the Soviet Government.*

He did not believe that this point was covered unless question G were interpreted broadly enough to include the considerations raised by Mr. Gerig. He suggested that it might be desirable to add an additional main heading which would become VII, dealing with "affirmative action, if any, required of the United States". (...)[1]

Proceeding to the second main heading, Mr. Pasvolsky inquired whether members of the subcommittee believed that the list of detailed questions was sufficiently inclusive.(...)

Mr. Pasvolsky pointed out that the key to the problem of structure would be the relation of the regional association to the general world organization, while the key to the functional problem would be the effect of the regional association upon a general collective security system. He believed that the other questions might then be arranged as subordinate considerations under these two key questions.

Mr. Bidwell believed that it should not be assumed that regional associations and an effective world organization were necessarily incompatible. If regional problems could be solved at the regional level the effect might well be to strengthen the universal system. Mr. Mosely pointed out that the experience of regional groups under the League of Nations tended to show that as the League became weaker different regional groups reacted in different ways. Whereas the Balkan states of the Little Entente had drawn closer in order to strengthen the League, as an offset to Germany's growing power, the Scandinavian states had developed their regional bloc as a means of withdrawing from their general obligations as members of the League. (...)

The Polish Government-in-exile has shown no enthusiasm over the prospect of adhering to the Soviet-Czechoslovak alliance, which is directed against Germany, or of joining any regional group in which the Soviet Union is a participant, on the grounds that such a group would be under Soviet domination. However, there is nothing in the letter of Soviet-Czechoslovak alliance, which makes express provision for adherence by adjacent states, to warrant Polish fears. In general, it is the American view that an adequate general security organization would make unnecessary special alliances and regional security arrangements such as the Soviet-Czechoslovak treaty, and that a worldwide reduction of trade barriers would be preferable to regional economic arrangements as a method of solving the pressing economic problems of states such as Poland". NA T-1222 PWC-216 CAC-220, 20 June 1944, pp. 10-11. (our italics – J.L. & M.M.)

[1] Omissions marked in the text mainly concern a re-wording of the original document.

So far as point III-D was concerned, Mr. Pasvolsky wondered whether the question as to whether a regional association might develop military strength of its own was not really part of the question as to whether the association would affect the balance of power. Mr. Howard suggested that if the association developed enough military strength it might itself become a great power. Mr. Pasvolsky replied that this contingency was still covered by the general conception of the balance of power. He inquired whether members of the subcommittee agreed that III-D might be omitted. Mr. Cohen agreed. Mr. Mosely pointed out that the question of the balance of power was not completely identical with the question of military strength. It was conceivable that the balance of power might be altered by the mere fact of combination without any change in the aggregate military strength of the area; for example the small states of the Danubian regions formed a single bloc of military power, instead of being divided among themselves by rivalries, the balance of power would thereby be altered. Ideological considerations might also affect the balance of power independently of military strength.(...)

Mr. Pasvolsky inquired whether the members of the subcommittee were satisfied with the formulation of questions under the new main heading IV relating to the internal stability and welfare of the region.

Mr. Pasvolsky believed that the most significant question was that set forth under IV-A, "Would it tend to foster economic nationalism as among the members of the association?". He believed that the question of economic nationalism was much broader than was the question merely of trade barriers. He pointed out that in at least one case in history, that of the Austria-Hungarian Monarchy, a regional association had in fact promoted economic nationalism among its parts enforced not by means of trade barriers, but by means of administrative protectionism.

Mr. Pasvolsky regretted that another appointment made it necessary for him to leave the meeting and he requested Mr. Cohen to preside. Taking the chair, Mr. Cohen remarked that perhaps the main question at issue in connection with IV-B was whether the establishment of a given regional association would result in the creation of new economic barriers as against outside countries. Mr. Balabanis remarked that this interpretation was the one which the research divisions have had in mind in drafting the question under discussion. Mr. Knight observed that if that were true then a change in language would be desirable in order to avoid misunderstanding. Moreover in connection with IV-A Mr. Knight believed that the substitution of "economic policies" for "economies" would be unfortunate. It went without saying, he thought that all countries controlled their own economic policies, but the important thing to control was the economy itself, that was to say, the working out of the economic policy. Mr. Balabanis expressed agreement with Mr. Knight's view, adding that a nation's economy was subject to the influence of many developments which lay beyond the control of its economic policy. Mr. Cohen wondered whether the question might not be phrased as follows: "Would the members of the association surrender enough control of their individual economies to give the region stability, or would they retain too little authority to maintain stability within the member state?".

Mr. Bidwell remarked that this statement seemed to him philosophical. He suggested that it might be desirable to phrase a question in the light of a specific situation. He wondered whether the specific situation which the subcommittee had in mind was not one in which the Soviet Union would attempt to impose its own arrangements upon other countries. Or would the subcommittee have in mind, for example, the case of an agricultural country which, by virtue of association with an industrial country, might itself become industrialized.

Mr. Balabanis noted that the question of size would also be important in any specific situation. The problem was somewhat parallel to that of industrial mergers in which a large unit might well impose its organizational of peculiarities upon a weaker co-member. Mr. Bidwell said he did not see how the interests of the United States were affected unless it were a question of some free enterprise country threatened with Bolshevism. Mr. Balabanis felt that the section under discussion dealt with the stability and welfare of the region itself and not with relations between the region and the United States.

Mr. Bidwell wondered whether some question such as the following might be desirable: "Would membership in the proposed association substantially change the social and economic system of the members?". Mr. Cohen agreed that this question might well be included. Mr. Mosely pointed out that this phrasing of the question overlooked part of the economic problem involved in regional associations; for example, when the Czechs and Poles were discussing the possibility of any federation the Czechs assumed that they would retain their grain monopoly and that their standard of living would continue to be substantially higher than that of Poland. Mr. Bidwell agreed that this aspect of the question undoubtedly required careful study. Mr. Knight observed that the main difficulty in drawing up questions of this kind was that the so-called economic questions were really political questions put in economic terminology. If the economic choices were to be made wholly in terms of economic desiderata the answers would be entirely different. Mr. Black suggested that the question might be phrased, "Would economic controls be so desirable between the regional organization and its members as to permit an effective, functioning economy in the region and in the member states?".

Mr. Mosely suggested that although the subcommittee had not completed discussions of the whole document, it would probably be worth while for the research divisions to revise the sections considered in the light of subcommittee discussion and to present the document again in preliminary form at the subcommittee's next meeting.

Mr. Bidwell emphasized that in the case of any given proposal for a regional association the first step in determining American policy toward the proposal should be to say who was behind the proposal and why. Then an effort could be made to ascertain the amount of popular support for the proposal and at the same time an effort should be made to view the proposal against its historical background and to assemble all the available facts. Then, in his opinion, speculative reasoning might be appropriate, but not before. Mr. Cohen pointed out that the subcommittee also attempted to appraise questions which would elicit the kind of information which Mr. Bidwell had in mind. He observed that in many cases history was a useful guide only if historical factors were really involved in the concrete problem itself. The meeting was adjourned.

23

DEPARTMENT OF STATE
Advisory Committee
Economic Subcommittee
Secret
R Minutes 16
March 31, 1944

Typescript, copy
AN Notter File, box 84

REVIEW OF SUBCOMMITTEE'S WORK

Present
Mr. Hamilton Fish Armstrong, Chairman
Mr. Percy Bidwell
Mr. Benjamin V. Cohen
Mr. Jacob Viner
Mr. Homer P. Balabanis
Mr. C. E. Black
Mr. Cavendish W. Cannon
Mr. Clyde Eagleton
Mr. Harry N. Howard
Mr. Vernon L. Phelps
Mr. Philip E. Mosely
Mr. Ralph H. Bowen, Secretary

Announcing that it had been decided, with Mr. Pasvolsky's approval, to bring the subcommittee's work to an end with the present meeting, the chairman noted that nearly a year had elapsed since the first meeting of the subcommittee in June, 1943. During that time the subcommittee had held sixteen meetings or, making allowance for a recess in the summer of 1943, two meetings per month on the average. The world situation and conditions in Europe especially, had undergone profound changes during the past year and some of the schemes studied by the subcommittee had been rendered academic. The chairman felt, however, that the subcommittee had accomplished several worthwhile tasks and had arrived at some conclusions which might be of more than transient value. He referred in particular to the conclusions which the subcommittee had reached regarding the effects of closer political and economic collaboration among continental European countries upon American political and economic interests.

The chairman thanked the members of the subcommittee for their contribution to the subcommittee's work, expressing the belief that the entire group remained willing to serve again if it should be found that they could be of assistance to the Department at some future time. He also extended the subcommittee's thanks to the staff of the special studies divisions for their help in preparing research memoranda and summary documents.

Reviewing the status of documents recently under consideration, the chairman announced that R-88,[1] "United States: Dominant Considerations in Judging Soviet Regional Policy in Eastern Europe", after having undergone several revisions, was now in a form acceptable to the subcommittee. He noted that R-63^e,[2] relating to a general European organization, had been approved at an earlier meeting, but had not, owing to an oversight, been distributed to the members in final form until the present meeting. (...)[3]

The subcommittee was adjourned *sine die*.

---

[1] Not found.
[2] Not found.
[3] Technicalities irrelevant to the debate have been omitted.

Published Books

EUROCLIO – Published Books

* *L'Europe du Patronat. De la guerre froide aux années soixante.* Textes réunis par Michel DUMOULIN, René GIRAULT, Gilbert TRAUSCH (Etudes et documents. 1993)
* *La Ligue Européenne de Coopération Economique (1946-1981). Un groupe d'étude et de pression dans la construction européenne.* Michel Dumoulin, Anne-Myriam Dutrieue (Etudes et documents. 1993)
* *Naissance et développement de l'information européenne.* Textes réunis par Felice DASSETTO, Michel DUMOULIN (Etudes et documents. 1993)
* *L'énergie nucléaire en Europe. Des origines à Euratom.* Textes réunis par Michel DUMOULIN, Pierre GUILLEN, Maurice VAISSE (Etudes et documents. 1994)
* *Histoire des constructions européennes au XXe siècle. Bibliographie thématique commentée des travaux français.* Gérard BOSSUAT (Références. 1994)
* *Péripéties franco-allemandes. Du milieu du XIXe siècle aux années 1950. Recueil d'articles.* Raymond POIDEVIN (Etudes et documents. 1995)
* *L'Europe en quête de ses symboles.* Carole LAGER (Etudes et documents. 1995)
* *France, Allemagne et «Europe verte».* Gilbert NOËL (Etudes et documents. 1995)
* *La France et l'intégration européenne. Essai d'historiographie.* Pierre GERBET (Références. 1995)
* *Dynamiques et transitions en Europe. Approche pluridisciplinaire.* Sous la direction de Claude TAPIA (Etudes et documents. 1997)
* *Le rôle des guerres dans la mémoire des Européens. Leur effet sur leur conscience d'être européen.* Textes réunis par Antoine FLEURY et Robert FRANK (Etudes et documents. 1997)

* *Jalons pour une histoire du Conseil de l'Europe. Actes du Colloque de Strasbourg (8-10 juin 1995).* Textes réunis par Marie-Thérèse BITSCH (Etudes et documents. 1997)
* *L'agricoltura italiana e l'integrazione europea.* Giuliana LASCHI (Etudes et documents. 1999)
* *Le Conseil de l'Europe et l'agriculture. Idéalisme politique européen et réalisme économique national (1949-1957).* Gilbert NOËL (Etudes et documents. 1999)
* *La Communauté Européenne de Défense, leçons pour demain ? The European Defence Community, Lessons for the Future?* Michel DUMOULIN (ed.) (Etudes et documents. 2000)
* *Naissance des mouvements européens en Belgique (1946-1950).* Nathalie TORDEURS (Etudes et documents. 2000)
* *Le Collège d'Europe à l'ère des pionniers (1950-1960).* Caroline VERMEULEN (Etudes et documents. 2000)
* *The "Unacceptables". American Foundations and Refugee Scholars between the Two Wars and after.* Giuliana GEMELLI (ed.) (Etudes et documents. 2000)
* *1848. Memory and Oblivion in Europe.* Charlotte TACKE (ed.) (Etudes et documents. 2000)
* *États-Unis, Europe et Union européenne. Histoire et avenir d'un partenariat difficile (1945-1999) – The United States, Europe and the European Union. Uneasy Partnership (1945-1999).* Gérard BOSSUAT & Nicolas VAICBOURDT (eds.) (Etudes et documents. 2001)
* *Visions et projets belges pour l'Europe. De la Belle Epoque aux Traités de Rome (1900-1957),* Geneviève DUCHENNE (Etudes et Documents. 2001)
* *L'ouverture des frontières européennes dans les années 50. Fruit d'une concertation avec les industriels?,* Marine MOGUEN-TOURSEL (Etudes et Documents. 2002)
* *American Debates on Central European Union, 1942-1944. Documents of the American State Department,* Józef ŁAPTOS & Mariusz MISZTAL (Etudes et Documents. 2002)

The nine volumes of the HISTORY OF EUROPEAN CONSTRUCTION, the basis for creating this EUROCLIO series, are available from Editions Artel (Namur) or their distributors.

Ouvrages parus – Published Books

* *La construction européenne en Belgique (1945-1957). Aperçu des sources.* Michel DUMOULIN. (1988)
* *Robert Triffin, le C.A.E.U.E. de Jean Monnet et les questions monétaires européennes (1969-1974). Inventaire des Papiers Triffin.* Michel DUMOULIN. (1988)
* *Benelux 1946-1986. Inventaire des archives du Secrétariat Général de Benelux.* Thierry GROSBOIS. (1988)
* *Jean Monnet et les débuts de la fonction publique européenne. La haute autorité de la CECA (1952-1953).* Yves CONRAD. (1989)
* *D'Alger à Rome (1943-1957). Choix de documents.* Gérard BOSSUAT. (1989)
* *La Guerre d'Algérie (1954-1962). Biblio- et filmographie.* Denix LUXEN. (1989)
* *Le patronat belge face au plan Schuman (9 mai 1950 - 5 février 1952).* Elisabeth DEVOS. (1989)
* *Mouvements et politiques migratoires en Europe depuis 1945.* Michel DUMOULIN. (1989)
* *Benelux, «laboratoire» de l'Europe. Témoignage de Jean-Charles Snoy et D'Oppuers.* Thierry GROSBOIS. (1990)

Euroclio European Network

A permanent catalogue of sources and bibliographies on the history of European construction

Coordination:
Collège Erasme, 1, place Blaise-Pascal,
B-1348 Louvain-la-Neuve

Germany:
Prof. Dr. Wilfried Loth
Dr. August Hermann Leugers-Scherzberg

Belgium:
Jocelyne Collonval
Yves Conrad
Pascal Deloge
Etienne Deschamps
Geneviève Duchenne
Prof. Michel Dumoulin
Anne-Myriam Dutrieue
Thierry Grosbois
Béatrice Roeh
Prof. Nathalie Tousignant
Arthe van Laer
Jérôme Wilson

France:
Prof. Marie-Thérèse Bitsch
Prof. Éric Bussière
Marine Moguen
Prof. Gérard Bossuat
Prof. Philippe Mioche
Prof. Sylvain Schirmann

Italy:
Dr. ssa Elena Calandri
Dr. ssa Marinella Neri Gualdesi
Prof. Antonio Varsori

Luxemburg:
Charles Barthel
Jean-Marie Majerus
Martine Nies-Berchem
Prof. Gilbert Trausch
Edmée Schirz

The Netherlands:
Dr. Anjo Harryvan
Dr. Bert Zeemann
Dr. Jan W. Brouwer

Switzerland:
Prof. Antoine Fleury
Lubor Jilek